"A deeply affecting and tenderhearted portrait of Pope Francis . . . What begins as a quest to know this man ends as a sublime love letter to all that matters in life. This book is good company."

—GREGORY BOYLE, S.J., author of *Tattoos on the Heart* and founder of Homeboy Industries

. . .

"A beautifully written, deeply researched, and engagingly personal take on one of the most compelling figures of our time—of any time. Mark K. Shriver takes us on a fascinating journey to the places, people, and times that shaped Jorge Mario Bergoglio. And he convincingly demonstrates how such a humble man could become an archbishop, be named a cardinal, and finally be elected pope."

—JAMES MARTIN, S.J., author of *Jesus: A Pilgrimage* and *The Jesuit Guide to (Almost) Everything*

. . .

"Pope Francis says that people's stories are more important than theories. *Pilgrimage* is a treasure trove of real people's reflections on their relationship with 'Jorge' and the author's journey into his own faith. This book is a challenge to all of us to risk living inclusive love."

—SISTER SIMONE CAMPBELL, SSS, executive director, NETWORK Lobby for Catholic Social Justice, and author of *A Nun on the Bus*

. . .

"Mark K. Shriver's biography captures the pope's little gestures as well as the major movements of his life. Shriver offers an everyman perspective: the person in the pew searching for solace in a Church at times undermined by scandal and deemed irrelevant by many. Shriver invites the reader into his personal journey while recounting the journey of the man who told Jesuit seminarians 'to get into the barrio and walk in it.' We walk with both Pope Francis and Shriver in this masterful and moving work."

—STEVE KATSOUROS, S.J., dean and executive director of Arrupe College, Loyola University Chicago

. . .

"Pope Francis has revitalized the faith of millions of people around the world. Shriver's journey to better understand Francis will fascinate and inspire you, regardless of your own beliefs. He travels to Argentina and Italy and meets some of the people who served alongside the pope. His book shows us that we all, rich or poor, Christian or non-Christian, can make a difference in the world."

—BISHOP T. D. JAKES, pastor, The Potter's House, Dallas, and *New York Times* bestselling author

PILGRIMAGE

RANDOM HOUSE · NEW YORK

PILGRIMAGE

My Search for the Real POPE FRANCIS

MARK K. SHRIVER

Published in the United States by Random House, an imprint and division of Penguin Random House LLC, New York.

RANDOM HOUSE and the HOUSE colophon are registered trademarks of Penguin Random House LLC.

Grateful acknowledgment is made to the following for permission to reprint previously published material:
AMERICA PRESS, INC.: Excerpts from "A Big Heart Open to God" from *America* (September 30, 2013). Reprinted by permission of America Press, Inc. For subscription information, call 1-800-627-9533 or visit www.americamedia.org.
BEACON PRESS AND GEORGES BORCHARDT, INC. FOR ROBERT BLY: Five lines from "City That Does Not Sleep" by Federico Garcia Lorca from *Lorca & Jiménez*, selected and translated by Robert Bly, copyright © 1973, 1997 by Robert Bly. Rights outside of North America are administered by Georges Borchardt, Inc. Reprinted by permission of Beacon Press and Georges Borchardt, Inc. for Robert Bly.
HENRY HOLT AND COMPANY, LLC: Excerpts from *The Great Reformer: Francis and the Making of a Radical Pope* by Austen Ivereigh, copyright © 2014 by Austen Ivereigh. All rights reserved. Reprinted by permission of Henry Holt and Company, LLC.
LIBRERIA EDITRICE VATICANA: Quotes from Pope Francis' *Magisterium* texts, copyright © Libreria Editrice Vaticana. Reprinted by permission.

LIBRARY OF CONGRESS CATALOGING-IN-PUBLICATION DATA
Names: Shriver, Mark K. (Mark Kennedy), author.
Title: Pilgrimage : my search for the real Pope Francis / Mark Shriver.
Description: New York : Random House, 2016.
Identifiers: LCCN 2016022799| ISBN 9780812998023 | ISBN 9780812998030 (ebook)
Subjects: LCSH: Francis, Pope, 1936– | Popes—Biography. | Catholic Church—Clergy—Biography.
Classification: LCC BX1378.7 .S54 2016 | DDC 282.092 [B]—dc23
LC record available at https://lccn.loc.gov/2016022799

Printed in the United States of America on acid-free paper

randomhousebooks.com

987654321

FIRST EDITION

TITLE PAGE PHOTOGRAPH: *Stefano Spaziani*
Book design by *Simon M. Sullivan*

For my mom and dad

Contents

I⊤ IS 2:30 on a Saturday morning, and clusters of students from Córdoba University are shouting and laughing as they straggle home from the bar district nearby. Córdoba, Argentina, is known as La Docta, the Learned City, yet the barhopping students are loud.

His bedroom window overlooks the street. He awakens and hears them as he lies on his hard single bed. At an earlier point in his life, he might have thrived here, given his passion for teaching and for students. When he was a high school teacher in Santa Fe, Argentina, he once brought Argentina's most acclaimed writer, Jorge Luis Borges, to class. His students later produced a book of stories for which Borges wrote the prologue.

His room is bare. It feels like the room not of a priest but of a penitent, even a prisoner. It feels like a room the students outside would stare at in bewilderment were they to peer in through his window. It is roughly twelve feet by twelve feet with a single bed, a wooden chair with no cushion, and a kneeler; there is a small table near the bed with a small lamp on it and a bureau with three drawers and a picture of his mother and him.

He himself is thin—too thin—and starting to slouch, weighed by the knowledge that he will likely never hold a position of power, of influence, again in the Jesuit order. Fellow Jesuits who pass him in the hall notice that he rarely, if ever, smiles.

He has been banished to Córdoba, an industrial city in the

interior of the country. Unlike his beloved cosmopolitan Buenos Aires, known as the Paris of Latin America, Córdoba has had many of its enchanting Spanish colonial buildings demolished in favor of cheap brick structures.

He had been the hotshot of the Society of Jesus, often referred to as the Jesuits; he was made provincial, or boss, of the Jesuit communities of Paraguay and Argentina on July 31, 1973, at the unheard-of age of only thirty-six. But now Jorge Mario Bergoglio—or Bergoglio, as he often calls himself—is merely trying to get back to sleep in a small, dank room. (He does sleep, though some of his former students and friends say he defies many basic human needs, sleep among them.)

Back in Buenos Aires, he had been confidently—some say arrogantly—certain that rooting young Jesuits in traditional theology, philosophy texts, and pedagogy was the only way for them to develop the skills, guts, and intellect they would need to serve the world as both keen thinkers and devoted pastors. He was orthodox in his conviction that a regimented lifestyle and a curriculum free of newfangled, borderline-Marxist theories on liberation and politicized faith were key to pastoral and personal success.

He had a profound sway over the old-line, Europeanized Jesuit order in Argentina, the order itself a socioreligious outlier in Latin America, a continent otherwise roiled with aggressive political and theological protest against injustice. His political philosophy, or rather his philosophy about the politics the Jesuits should embrace, ran counter to the post–Vatican II sweep of social change and political activism among many of his fellow Latin American clergy. Change was good, he thought, but it had to come through faith, not politics. Poverty had to be abolished, yes, but through prayer and devotion and good works, not through political insurrection.

But in June 1990, his reign ended abruptly when he was ordered to Córdoba. Years later, very few people will speak much of the exile of Bergoglio. The Jesuits have closed ranks; like a family, they have conflicts, but like a family, they protect their own.

He was shipped to Córdoba by his Jesuit superiors for a number of reasons, perhaps none more important than his authoritarian style when he was provincial and an excess of discipline when he was rector of Colegio Máximo, the Jesuit formation house in Buenos Aires. His rigorous commitment to a conservative structure of Jesuit training was so unwavering that he caused a deep and painful split among the Jesuit community in Argentina.

Saint Ignatius of Loyola, the man who founded the Society of Jesus in 1540, knew this kind of spiritual exile. Once a sword-bearing, damsel-chasing Basque, he was injured in battle and forced to convalesce at his family castle for six months. Inspired by reading a popular version of the life of Christ and tales of the saints, Ignatius started to imagine a life far different from the courtly life he had so passionately desired. Once healed, he laid down his sword, gave away his splendid robes, and spent ten months in Manresa near Barcelona, where in extended periods of solitude he wrestled with his sins and refined his holy ambition to help souls.

Later, while studying at the University of Paris, Ignatius met other like-minded men attracted to his zeal and his down-to-earth, practical spirituality. They became the first Jesuits. They dubbed themselves "contemplatives in action," for they would go wherever the need was greatest and wherever others were not able to go. Their fame, memorialized by Robert De Niro and Jeremy Irons in the 1986 film *The Mission*, stemmed partly from innovative and courageous missionary work in Asia and Latin America in the sixteenth and seventeenth centuries. But they also went to the intellectual and cultural frontiers of their times, helping the Church do its thinking in the age of the Renaissance and Reformation. They were as comfortable working with the poor and marginalized as with the wealthy and well connected, often earning the jealousy and suspicion of religious and political authorities. They became caught in a nasty web of ecclesiastical and courtly politics, and Pope Clement XIV suppressed the Jesuits as a religious order in 1773, but through perseverance and ingenuity, they managed to reclaim their status a few decades later.

It was this tough-minded, hard-charging intellectual approach, this willingness to go anywhere for the Lord, that attracted Bergoglio to the Jesuits. Now his own interpretation of it had put him here in Córdoba, lying awake in the dark early morning hours.

JORGE MARIO BERGOGLIO's first statement as Pope Francis, delivered from the balcony at St. Peter's Square on March 13, 2013, startled me, as it did so many of my Catholic friends. The humility, the kind, sweet tone—when he made fun of the fact that he was from so far away, I could hear the laughter of the crowd. He asked everyone to pray for Pope Emeritus Benedict, and then, before he blessed the throng in front of him, he asked them to pray for him. He bowed his head to receive their blessing.

Has a pope ever done that? I wondered.

His clothes—a plain white robe and a simple cross around his neck—struck me. And that name, Francis—I didn't realize that a pope had never taken the name Francis before. Francis, the saint known for his care for the poor, his love of creation, and his commitment to peace; "Francis" sounded so much more accessible, so much more modern, than "Benedict XVI." I had the sense that at the least, charisma and vitality had returned to the Church I was born into, had grown frustrated by, and more recently had even been embarrassed about.

The next day, I called one of my oldest friends, a Catholic priest, to get his reaction to this new pope, this—of all things—Jesuit from Latin America.

"I always knew you were naive," my friend replied when I said I hoped change might be in the air. My buddy had grown skeptical of Catholic leadership in Rome in recent years, irate over the Church's social policies, pedophilia scandals, and corruption.

"You really think a seventy-six-year-old guy can change the Curia all by himself, Mark?" he said, his words terse and his tone abrupt. "It's harder than changing things in Washington. Way harder."

We finished our chat with our customary sarcastic ribbing, and my momentary interest in Pope Francis had diminished by nightfall. Or so I thought.

But then, two weeks later, my email in-box started overflowing with stories about Pope Francis's visit to a juvenile detention center where he washed and kissed the feet of two girls, including a Muslim Serbian immigrant, and ten other inmates.

Almost thirty years ago, I had created a program for juvenile delinquents in Baltimore. I had a soft spot for troubled kids, seeing in them something I surely would have become if faced with the same poor education and limited opportunities. Full of faith and hope, I longed to apply my Catholic notions about social justice through politics and activism. When I saw the photograph of the pope kneeling on the hard ground of a juvenile facility—a child prison, really—washing and kissing the feet of those young criminals, I was stunned. I had been in such facilities many times, and they are depressing and dirty. And the youngsters, at least the American ones, were tough, often mean, and didn't care about how they acted or looked. I don't care how much polish the authorities put on the place or the kids; I would never have gotten on my hands and knees and touched their feet, much less washed and kissed them.

This guy has guts.

LIKE MANY OF my friends, I had been yearning for a Church I could believe in again. How many times over beers had my buddies and I lamented the disconnect between the church hierarchy and the foot soldiers—the self-sacrificing nuns and priests serving the poor all over the globe?

Lately, I had been needing my Church and my faith (the two, no matter how hard I tried, are as inseparable for me as they are for many Catholics) more than usual. My dad, Sargent Shriver, with whom I had a very close relationship, had died two years prior, on January 18, 2011. My mother, Eunice Shriver, with whom I was also very close, had died seventeen months before that, on August 11, 2009. Richard

Ragsdale, nicknamed Rags, who had worked for my mom and dad for my entire life and who was like a second father to me, had died just two weeks before my mom. And my one remaining uncle, Ted Kennedy, died two weeks after my mom. These losses were a series of mighty blows.

I kept up my Catholic routine simply because my father and mother's faith had had such a strong influence on me. Dad's faith and Catholicism had been on my mind even more since he had died. Whenever I went to mass, his spirit would end up sitting right next to me, squeezing in between my son and daughters and wife to prod me into emulating him. His faith was his animating principle, the fuel for his discipline, for his generosity, for his politics, and the source of his constant joy. I kept trying to imitate my dad's faithful habits in the hope that his outward practices would trigger a spiritual rejuvenation. But I just couldn't snap out of my funk.

My church wasn't helping my efforts. With each pedophilia scandal, with each corruption scandal, with each fumbling statement on homosexuality or the role of women or the status of Islam, I started to think that my father might have been mistaken, or at least too blindly loyal to the Catholic Church, if not the Catholic faith. One day at mass I reached my low point as a Catholic. I found myself, instead of trying to digest the homily with all my head and heart, thinking about what I would do to a priest who would dare molest my son, Tommy, sitting next to me in the pew. *I would shoot the priest, I really would.*

My mind started to wander: *If a bishop, a man in charge of priests, had known of the priest's sickness and still sent him to our church, well, I'd kill that bishop, too.*

I grew so enraged that, as I caught myself clenching my fists, I wondered if I had been speaking aloud and looked around. Tommy glanced over with concern, but I realized I had managed to keep my terrible thoughts to myself.

This was the personal context in which Pope Francis entered my consciousness: skeptical, disillusioned, and uncertain whether the Church remained a force for good in the world. You may have had your own moment of sudden fixation with this Argentine. Perhaps you are reading this book because of our mutual fascination with Bergoglio, or at least with the man whom we meet through the media. Our interest arises from a need and a want. We need a spiritual leader who restores the gospel's message to feed the hungry, to clothe the naked, to shelter the homeless. We all, regardless of our religion, long for an authentic leader who reaches out and helps others, who truly believes in the Jewish call of Tikkun Olam, to repair the world, or the Islamic call to Islah, to improve, to better the world, to make peace. And we want that leader to be warm, accessible, and hopeful.

As Pope Francis's first year progressed, I found myself starting to follow his speeches, trips, and writings more than I did those of any political figure in my hometown of Washington, D.C. Francis was single-handedly answering my needs and wants, and I started to make his thoughts and reflections a part of my daily prayers and reflections. I started to emerge from my Catholic funk.

And I realized that as Francis half-danced his way through our troubled world, hand in hand with the poor, the sick, and the shunned, he was lifting my spirit along with theirs. I know firsthand how adept some world leaders are at manipulating symbols and events to present a media persona far different from the real person who lives offscreen. So I kept warning myself not to believe unconditionally in a guy who, I kept reminding myself, headed a very flawed institution and would need to execute some serious reforms before I could truly consider him "the real deal."

But two of Francis's recurrent themes kept uplifting me, inspiring me to imitate them, to improve my own practice of them. Humility and mercy—it seemed that Pope Francis ingested these ideas at his famously meager breakfasts and then used them as fuel for spreading his mission in our world. From that balcony scene overlooking St. Peter's Square, to the picture of him paying his own hotel bill after being elected pope, to his choosing to live not in the Apostolic Palace but alongside fellow priests in Santa Marta, the Vatican guesthouse—from his now famous utterance "Who am I to judge a gay person of goodwill who seeks the Lord? You can't marginalize these people" to his first official visit as pope to the island of Lampedusa, where he denounced the "globalization of indifference" to migrants—the way Pope Francis turned these simple actions into badges of his mission to invigorate the gospel message kept pushing me to practice humility and mercy better myself.

Slowly, I also started to succumb to the contagion of a third theme—or rather a third way of thinking, seeing, and living: joy. I would eventually discover that this outward display of joy was new in his life, too.

Then on November 9, 2013—what would have been my father's ninety-eighth birthday—I opened an email and saw a picture that startled me: the pope hugging a man with a face so pocked and distorted with sores and growths that all I could do was stare, repulsed. I snapped out of it after thirty seconds. "What kind of Catholic are you?" I scolded myself. Red-faced, even with no one there to witness my sin, I turned back, looking at the sores and growths and then at the pope embracing the man and pulling him to his chest. *How does he do that? There's no way I could touch the man.* I stared and stared, almost unable to breathe.

Then, after what seemed like an hour, I smiled.

I couldn't see Francis's face but I felt as if he were smiling at me, smiling straight through to my soul.

I grew up as a witness to the awesome influence one person can have on our planet if the message and the messenger both strike that connective human chord. My uncle Jack Kennedy was a master of making you feel he could touch your inside, touch your heart and gut, touch you so much that it determined your mood, behavior, and, yes, actions. He marshaled the hopes of millions of people with his substance, but also with his style. So long ago I grew comfortable with the seemingly contemporary idea that, in the rare human being, style could be substance.

Pope Francis seemed like the right messenger with the right message, a man of substance with an endearing style. His public humility, austerity, the smile, the joy all seemed to emanate from a deep reservoir of peace and self-knowledge. I wanted to dig in and learn more.

Then, in June 2014, not long after I had written a book about my dad—a book that explored how faith and hope and love underpinned and permeated his work—I got a call asking me to consider writing a similar book about Pope Francis.

I thought an elaborate joke was being played on me.

Pope Francis? Me? Seriously?

I was flattered to be asked, yet overwhelmed with the immensity of the task.

I was in the first few months of creating a new organization, called Save the Children Action Network, aimed at mobilizing Americans to put children at the top of the political agenda. This was a major undertaking—politicians often say that children are our most valuable resource, but budget decisions don't reflect those words. My wife, Jeanne, and I have three children, two of whom are in high school and one in elementary school. We are busy.

But then, not yet knowing how fundamentally prayer and discernment inform Francis's every step and word and decision, I attempted to do what so many of my great Jesuit teachers had taught me to do—I prayed and tried to discern whether this project, this adventure, was right for me. I thought back to a five-day silent retreat I did with the Jesuits when I was at the College of the Holy Cross. It was one of the most peaceful, rewarding, and enriching events of my life. I had never heard my own deepest, innermost, wisest voice so clearly as during those five silent days, and I didn't hear it again with such clarity until the days after my dad died.

For weeks, I tried to channel that powerful silence again, to be attuned to what Ignatius called movements of the soul. The result of my own Ignatian process of decision making is this book. But the reason for doing it, I must admit, was basically selfish: I needed and wanted more of Bergoglio in my life. I needed him to help remedy my own distance from the Church and faith I was born into. I wanted to explore the warts and moles and failures as well as the virtues and good words and successes. *Can I believe him? Can he help me? Is he for real?*

. . .

HE WILL AWAKEN again—if he is able to get back to sleep—in two hours, even on a Saturday, to pray. He had fun in his youth—he would go dancing with friends, and he had a girlfriend—but he never partied the way these university students do.

He arises and prays like a Jesuit, not asking for specific blessings or benefits but trying to discern, through rigorous reflection, what Jesus Christ would do and how he would act in the day's anticipated situations. He exits his room in Córdoba and walks below a stone arch into a small, deserted courtyard in the Spanish colonial building where the Jesuits live. An arbor hangs over the courtyard, and grapes and the gorgeous leaves of Santa Rita trees dangle above his head.

On this Saturday, he will once again care for the old, ailing Jesuits in the infirmary. He will bathe them, cook for them, feed them— forkful by forkful—and read to them the way his grandmother read to him back in Flores, the paradise-like middle-class barrio of his youth in Buenos Aires. Later, he will walk to his favorite church, La Virgen de la Merced, to hear confessions.

After hearing confessions, he will kneel and pray again. Prayer for him is still all about discernment, as it was for Saint Ignatius. He is trying to figure out whether to accept the offer from Cardinal Antonio Quarracino of Buenos Aires to return to his beloved hometown as auxiliary bishop—or to stay in the Jesuit order and stay in Córdoba.

While becoming a bishop is seen by most as a promotion to a powerful, influential job, Jesuits promise not to seek episcopal offices and accept them only under obedience to the pope. They are to focus on those who are forgotten, those who live on the fringe. In fact, if a Jesuit suspects that a fellow Jesuit is angling for a position of authority, then he must report that suspicion. For Bergoglio to become auxiliary bishop means that he will have to live a profoundly different life, apart from his beloved Jesuit community. He will have to change the way he has lived for thirty-four years, but the cardinal back in the big city knows how good this Bergoglio is—how, despite his authoritarian style, his rigorous commitment to discipline, and his old-school approach to teaching and Jesuit formation, he is renowned as well for inspiring people, energizing parishes, managing budgets, giving brain-tingling and heart-touching homilies, and devotedly serving the poor.

He may very well be trying to discern what God wants for him by meditating on the Parable of the Talents. His friends and students know how much he loves Jesus's parables; they even say his way of speaking—simple, listener-friendly, concise, story-driven—is modeled on the parables.

This parable about what we are to do with God's gifts surely hits close to home for him. Jesus tells the story of a great landlord who is going to a faraway land for a long time and gives talents, or parts of his estate, to three servants to safeguard. One man gets five talents, invests them, and turns the five into ten by the time his master returns. One man turns three into six. But the third servant, who receives just one talent, buries it for fear of losing it. The master praises the two who made profitable use of their talents and banishes the man who buried his.

The lesson: We are responsible for using the gifts God has given us for the good of ourselves and others, and we are expected to take some risks in serving others.

The young Bergoglio—charismatic, intelligent, faithful, driven—had been the man who turned five into ten—or more. He had always had important roles and he must have known that his leadership skills were wasting away in Córdoba.

He is still wholeheartedly committed to Ignatius's call to "go forth and set the world on fire for the Lord." But he is still human, and he longs, this Saturday as each Saturday before, to go home to Buenos Aires. He is at heart a Porteño, as natives of the city of Buenos Aires are called. He is still a Jesuit, but one whose talents may require a step outside the order in which he was trained and has flourished.

As he walks home, the rain may turn to hail, as it sometimes does in Córdoba. He walks along the street where the drunken students awoke him earlier that morning. The stone structure of the Jesuit residence is marked by two huge metal doors. He leans to push them open as he inserts his key. The cold, dark foyer opens into an empty reception area. He walks to his room. His sins of heavy-handedness and self-certainty from the days when he was provincial and rector for the Jesuits fill him with regret. He is certain of nothing as day turns to dusk and then to darkness, except for one thing—that he needs to serve, that he is still on fire to serve, that it is his obligation to God the Father to serve in the most dynamic way he can.

When you stand in the middle of the Plaza de la Misericordia, in the Flores barrio of Buenos Aires, and see the kids playing soccer, and watch the rickety old carousel spin, and smell the fragrance of the purple jacaranda tree; when you see the statue of a mother embracing a child with the inscription "May the son that is brought up by the mother, with infinite tenderness, to be a source of love and peace, never become an instrument of hatred that generates destruction"; when you look at the tall, slender palm trees whose spiderweb of shadows dots the red gravel paths—you have got to believe in something. Be it God, or merely the grandeur of nature or the goodwill of mankind, the park elicits an irresistible feeling of goodness.

Jorge Mario Bergoglio's childhood home, about two blocks away, today is a simple two-story semidetached house with a nondescript white concrete balcony running the length of the second floor. The second floor is made of bricks; the first floor has faux marble covering what must be cinder blocks. The garage takes up about one-third of the first floor and is covered with wood panels. A sign is nailed to the house: IN THIS HOUSE LIVED POPE FRANCIS. LEGISLATURE OF THE AUTONOMOUS CITY OF BUENOS AIRES, MARCH 2013.

Just a block down from the Bergoglio house is a small triangular park, Herminia Brumana Square, which was under construction when I visited. When Jorge was young, this small area was a place to kick a soccer ball. If you wanted more space, you went two blocks up to the Plaza de la Misericordia.

The plaza is where, as a boy, Jorge played soccer and no doubt paused every once in a while to sniff the jacaranda's fragrance.

The people who label neighborhoods by economic categories today call Flores lower middle class. When Jorge was a boy there in the 1940s, they would have called it middle class, as that socioeconomic category was much more pervasive during Argentina's wealthier heyday. As I stood there in November of 2014, I called it bliss.

Flores lies between two distinct sides of Buenos Aires—a part that people say reminds them of central Paris and a part that reminds them of some neighborhoods of Lima, Peru. That is to say, to the northeast are the gorgeous buildings from Argentina's Belle Époque glory days, the wide boulevards that resemble those of Paris, and the coffee shops and steakhouses. To the southwest are slums that rival the worst urban pits of Latin America—multilevel apartments slapped together almost upon each other, separated only by tiny alleys. Trash fills the gutters, and the sidewalks teem with people waiting for buses and makeshift food vendors. Razor wire sits on top of many walls to keep would-be thieves away, and there are police decked out in riot gear at random checkpoints.

ANYONE SEEKING TO understand the zealous faith and socioeconomic commitments of Pope Francis, as well as his geniality and discipline, must visit his homeland, stopping first in this barrio called Flores where he grew up and where his heart and imagination still wander.

I have spent more than two years visiting Jorge's haunts, reading his letters and speeches, and thinking about his life and its effect on our world. Each of us is formed in the cauldron of our experiences; for Francis, at least six experiences from his boyhood in Flores helped define the man who would bring me, and I believe much of our world, to rethink our lives and faith.

First, he grew up in the enchanting, almost magical realm created by his charismatic Italian grandmother, Rosa. Many of us can relate to this experience, and it is worth understanding the first and most powerful influence on young Jorge in order to grasp the uniqueness of his youth.

Second, from his schools to his streets, from his family to his friends, Jorge experienced a fundamental and privileged serenity that has powerfully shaped his demeanor and perspective. I first felt it at that park in Flores, but I experienced it again and again as I moved through his world. Though his youth was not a privileged one financially, it surely was emotionally, psychologically, and spiritually secure.

Third, Jorge was raised at a moment in Argentine history when a sociological, as much as a political, phenomenon called Peronismo was born. Of course, Juan and Eva Perón were at the center of this cultural earthquake. Peronismo continues to undergo many iterations, but the era during which the Bergoglios and millions of other hardworking immigrant families embraced Peronismo heavily influenced Pope Francis's worldview.

Fourth, there are more Italian immigrants in Argentina, and particularly in Buenos Aires, than there are people from any other country. Pope Francis grew up in the golden age of Italian immigration to Argentina. The people of Buenos Aires are called Porteños. The word, meaning literally "people of the port," feeds the notion of Buenos Aires not so much as a capital but as a city-state, a stand-alone realm apart from, if not superior to, the rest of Argentina and especially Latin America. And the customs and culture of Buenos Aires, more unique and powerful than those of any other place I have ever been, are illuminating, for they help explain how a pope like no other comes from a place like no other.

Fifth, Jorge was a budding man of science. His job in a chemistry lab in Flores and his first mentor, Esther Ballestrino, his boss at that lab, impressed him with the value of scientific thinking and logic and shaped his rational worldview and practical approach to being a leader.

Sixth, so many of the stories in the history of Catholic experience, from Saint Paul to Thomas Merton, from Saint Augustine to Saint

Ignatius of Loyola, entail a conversion, an often sudden, startling event that transforms the trajectory of a life. Jorge heard his life-changing call at age sixteen in Flores, and a view of it from the very confessional in the basilica where it occurred sets the stage for Jorge Mario Bergoglio to become Pope Francis.

By opening these six windows and looking at his boyhood through them, we can better comprehend how and why an eighty-year-old man is joyfully reforming a two-thousand-year-old institution, one person at a time.

PILGRIMAGE

1 Rosa

MANY OF US who have an interest in our families' immigrant pasts have visited the port or the town where our forebears arrived, lived, worked, and struggled. We try to imagine the day of their arrival, the weather, the smell, the crowds, the anxiety. I have wandered the streets of Boston looking at the same sights my Irish maternal relatives must have seen; I have wondered what they must have felt when they read signs that said IRISH NEED NOT APPLY.

I have also walked through the rambling homestead of my German-Irish paternal forebears, a place nested in the rolling hills of Union Mills, Maryland, alongside a rushing creek that powered a gristmill employing generations of Shrivers. I wondered how they came to such a site, and how they survived the Battle of Gettysburg just a few miles up the road—how Shrivers fought on both sides of that bloody conflict yet somehow remained a united family for generations to come.

Argentina has a great deal in common with the United States of America in this way—millions upon millions of Europeans made the long, stormy voyage there in search of a better life. In the case of Pope Francis, his paternal grandparents, Rosa and Giovanni, came accompanied by their only child, Mario.

Like most families whose ancestors immigrated to the country where we live now, the Bergoglio family has its myths and amazing stories. Indeed, the Bergoglios almost didn't live to see

Argentina. The family had purchased steerage tickets on a ship, the *Principessa Mafalda*, which sank off the coast of Brazil, killing three hundred fourteen people. They exchanged those tickets only because there was a delay in selling their coffee shop in Turin, Italy.

The ship on which they did embark, the *Giulio Cesare*, docked in Buenos Aires on January 25, 1929, in the thick of the South American summer. Rosa and her family disembarked alongside hundreds of other Italians seeking a better life in America, albeit not the North America of Ellis Island fame. The heat and humidity did not daunt this mythic grandmother, however, and she kept her fox-fur coat tightly wrapped about her ample flesh while she waited in line. The family's entire net worth, generated from the sale of the coffee shop, was stitched into the lining of that winter coat.

Rosa was born into a peasant family in Val Bormida in northern Italy in 1884. On August 20, 1907, she married Giovanni, and they settled in Asti, in the Piedmont region of northwestern Italy. Their son, Mario, was born in 1908. Giovanni fought in World War I before they moved to Turin in 1920, where they ran the coffee shop that helped put Mario through school so he could become an accountant at the Bank of Italy.

During the 1920s, Rosa protested against Benito Mussolini as a member of Acción Católica, or Catholic Action. In a letter written while he was in exile in Córdoba in 1990, Bergoglio wrote that his grandmother "would give talks everywhere." He also recalled that his "grandmother said things that did not sit well with the politics of her time. Once they closed the hall where she was to give her talk so she gave it in the street standing on a table."

With unrest at home, with Italy's economy in ruins, and with Argentina's economy booming—and the very real feeling that another world war was fast approaching—Rosa and Giovanni traveled across the Atlantic Ocean with Mario.

Despite its distance from home, Rosa must have found Argentina familiar, for it was swarming with Italian immigrants. The economy was based on the export of raw materials, agricultural products, wool, and, of course, beef, and Jorge's grandparents had come not out of desperation, the way many Irish and Italians came to America, but rather to get in on the boom. Giovanni already had three brothers living in Paraná, where they had set up a successful paving company, so the family headed there immediately.

Another reason it must have felt familiar was the strong presence of an order of Catholic priests called the Salesians of Don Bosco. Saint John Bosco, often referred to as Don Bosco, was born in the Piedmont region in 1815. Fr. Joseph Boenzi, a Salesian of Don Bosco and professor of theology at the Dominican School of Philosophy and Theology, told me:

> Don Bosco chose Francis de Sales—a late sixteenth / early sev-
> enteenth century saint known for patience and gentleness—as a
> model for his work among the poorest and most marginalized
> immigrant young people who were otherwise neglected at best,
> and exploited at worst, in Turin during the middle of the 1800s.
> The Salesian Society, also called the Salesians of Don Bosco,
> continues his work in one hundred and thirty-three countries.
> Argentina has a long Salesian tradition, as Don Bosco sent his
> spiritual sons and daughters there in 1875.

In that letter he wrote from Córdoba in 1990, Bergoglio recalled that his father had befriended many Salesian priests while he lived in Italy and was a "part of the 'Salesian family.'" When Mario arrived in Paraná, he went to work for his uncles as the company accountant. According to Bergoglio, his dad "moved between Paraná, Santa Fe, and Buenos Aires. When he arrived in Buenos Aires he stayed with the Salesians on Solis Street, and it was while he was there that he met Father [Enrico] Pozzoli, who immediately became his confessor. He joined the group of young men that were close to Father Pozzoli and it was there that he met my mother's brothers and, as a result, my mother."

Mario met Regina Maria Sivori, an Argentine whose family was originally from Italy, at mass. They were married twelve months later, on December 12, 1935, and just twelve months after that, Jorge Mario

Bergoglio was born, on December 17, 1936. He was baptized eight days later, on December 25, 1936, by Pozzoli. Jorge was followed by a brother, Oscar, a sister, Marta, another brother, Alberto, and finally another sister, Maria Elena.

Bergoglio recalls being raised in such a devout Catholic family that not only did the family say the rosary before dinner, but they also had their priest as a frequent guest for meals. Pozzoli was not only responsible for introducing Mario and Regina but also played a critical role in the family's financial, educational, and spiritual histories. Bergoglio called him "the spiritual father of the family."

When Jorge's great-uncle, the president of the company in Paraná, died and the family lost everything, Pozzoli rescued them by introducing Jorge's grandparents to "a person who loaned them two thousand pesos with which my grandparents bought a store in the Flores neighborhood and Dad—who had been the [manager] of the Bank of Italy . . . and the accountant of the company—had to go around with the basket doing the delivery for the store."

Rosa was Jorge's godmother as well as his grandmother. Almost every morning, Rosa picked up Jorge and took him around the corner to her home, where he stayed until late in the day. She took him to church and taught him to pray. As Bergoglio said in a 2012 radio interview, "She had a big influence on my faith. . . . She'd tell me stories about the saints. She left a deep spiritual imprint on me."

The family also abided by the Church's teachings on divorce and on other religions. Bergoglio told his longtime friend Rabbi Abraham Skorka in their book *On Heaven and Earth*, "If someone close to the family divorced or separated, they could not enter your house; and they believed all Protestants were going to hell." Rosa, however, left a different and lasting impression on him. Bergoglio recalled that when he was a young boy, he saw two women from the Salvation Army and asked his beloved grandmother "if they were nuns, because they were wearing that little hat they used to wear. She responded to me, 'No, they are Protestants, but they are good.' That was the wisdom of the true religion. They were good women who did good things."

Rosa gave young Jorge his formation in the Catholic faith, a particularly earthy version of it that stressed the value and solace of ritual. From saying the rosary to accompanying Jorge to mass, from reading to him about the lives of the saints to demonstrating open-mindedness, she instilled in him not only a devotion to the healing, guiding rituals of the Catholic faith but also a commitment to compassion. Faith and ritual and compassion, in her view, were inseparable, and young Jorge soaked up that perspective.

When Jorge was ordained a priest on December 13, 1969, his two brothers and one of his sisters were present, as were his mother, Regina, and his first grade teacher. And his eighty-five-year-old grandmother.

Rosa gave him a letter that she had written, in a mixture of Spanish and Piedmontese, in case she died before he was ordained, a letter that Francis keeps with him every day:

> On this beautiful day in which you can hold in your consecrated hand Christ our Savior and on which a broad path for a deeper apostolate is opening up before you, I leave you this modest gift, which has very little material value but very great spiritual value.

The "modest gift" was more words, including this beautiful paragraph:

> May my grandchildren, to whom I gave the best of my heart, have a long and happy life. But if one day pain, illness, or the loss of someone they love should afflict them, let them remember that one sigh before the Tabernacle, where the greatest and most venerable of the martyrs is kept, and one glance at Mary at the foot of the Cross, will cause a drop of balm to fall on the deepest and most painful wounds.

ON JANUARY 18, 2015, Pope Francis spoke at the University of Santo Tomas in Manila. Speaking extemporaneously, he commented on the lack of female representation at the event: "And the small . . . the small representation of women. Too small! Women have much to say to us in today's society. Sometimes we are too 'machista'; we don't make room for women. Women are able to see things differently than men. Women can ask questions that we men just don't get. Pay attention." Pointing to a young woman who had asked why children suffer, he said, "She today asked the one question that doesn't have an answer. And she couldn't say it in words. She had to say it with tears. So that, when the next pope comes to Manila, there should be more women."

I have a hunch that Pope Francis had the image of his strong, sensitive grandmother in mind when he spoke those words.

Gender can influence one's way of seeing, and I believe that in general, a woman's perspective is more compassionate. I say "in general" because the disparate reactions of Rosa and Jorge's mother, Regina, to his decision to enter the seminary illustrate the trouble with such stereotypes. Rosa understood Jorge's faith even better than his own mother did, we know, for he also recalls to Francesca Ambrogetti and Sergio Rubin in *Pope Francis: His Life in His Own Words: Conversations with Jorge Bergoglio* that while his mother did not look favorably upon his decision to enter the seminary, Rosa, his first professor of the faith, gave him her wholehearted support. "When I told my grandmother, who had already known but pretended not to, she replied, 'Well, if God has called you, blessed be!' And immediately she added, 'Please never forget that the doors to this house are always open, and no one will reproach you for anything if you decide to come back.'"

That kind of unconditional love, of limitless compassion, clearly had a profound impact on Jorge. How could it not have? To spend every day with such a devout woman, to hear her stories about the saints, to pray the rosary with her, to be fed and nurtured by her seems like a story from a different century.

Today, for too many of my generation, interactions with our grandparents consist of a long summer weekend or a four-day Thanksgiving holiday or, if we are truly lucky, a couple of weeks a year. We hear their stories, we see their actions, we may even try to emulate them when we are together, but the time together is often too short and the impressions do not last long.

My paternal grandmother, Hilda, born in 1882, and my maternal grandmother, Rose, born in 1890, both went to daily mass and prayed the rosary daily as well. I clearly remember Grandma Rose taking her daily walk holding her rosary. Their devotion rubbed off on my mom and dad, both of whom went to daily mass and both of whom carried rosaries. And it rubbed off on me, too. A bit.

I remember asking Grandma Rose one day if she believed that the Shroud of Turin was really the burial cloth of Jesus Christ, as many thought it was. We were visiting her during Christmas break and I was lucky enough to accompany her on her afternoon stroll. We were walking down the street, slowly but surely; I was holding her left hand, and in her right hand was her ever-present rosary. She took a few steps and said, "If the Shroud of Turin encourages people to pray more, to believe in God more, then it is a good thing. Whatever brings people closer to God is good."

Jorge was with his grandmother every day of his young life, and he clearly values that relationship even today. By the time I realized how much Grandma Rose could teach me, she had suffered a series of strokes and was unable to communicate.

Two thousand years after Jesus chose Saint Peter as the rock on which "I will build my church," the two hundred sixty-sixth successor to Peter is a man whose faith is built upon what he learned from an Italian-born peasant, a woman who stood up against a dictator's regime, who emigrated to a foreign land, whose family went broke and had to take a loan arranged by a priest, a woman who, despite it all, maintained a devout Catholic faith that nevertheless allowed her to see the goodness in people of other faiths in a very closed-minded culture.

When Rosa died at the age of ninety, Jorge was at her bedside. The British writer Austen Ivereigh beautifully described the scene in his excellent biography, *The Great Reformer: Francis and the Making of a Radical Pope:*

"He adored her, she was his weakness," recalls one of [the Italian nuns who cared for Rosa,] Sister Catalina. "She only ever paid attention to what he said." As Rosa lay dying, Jorge kept vigil by her bed, holding her body until life left it. "He told us, 'At this moment my grandmother is at the most important point of her existence. She is being judged by God. This is the mystery of death.'" A few minutes later, said Sister Catalina, "he got up and left, as serene as ever."

Rosa, that rock of faith and love and compassion, built a solid foundation in her eldest grandchild, a foundation that, I learned, would come to be tested over and over again—just as she had foreseen.

2 Serenity

ACROSS THE STREET from the Plaza de la Misericordia is Jorge's first school, Colegio Nuestra Señora de la Misericordia (Our Lady of Mercy). As I walked into the foyer of the school, I had that same sense of serenity, of goodness, that I had felt in the park a few minutes earlier. On one side was a beautiful stained-glass image of the Virgin Mary and on the other side a stunning stained-glass image of Jesus. I didn't have an appointment, but the pleasant receptionist told me that if I would come back the next morning between ten o'clock and noon, Sister Martha Rabino, the mother superior of the school, would see me. Time is a relative thing in Buenos Aires, as people are, it seems, always late as a result of traffic, political demonstrations, a family matter—or something. Nobody seems upset when you are tardy or when you show up unannounced.

The next day, the receptionist welcomed me back with a warm smile. She led me to a seating area just off the main hallway where schoolchildren walked quickly from classroom to classroom. Sister Martha appeared about ten minutes later wearing a traditional gray habit. She was tiny. She smiled as she shuffled into the room and asked me if I would like to go to a more secluded place where we could chat. The quiet room was cluttered with supplies being collected for struggling families—stacks of water bottles and oil jugs, boxes crammed with clothes, toys and games spilling out of overstuffed bags. School sports

trophies crowded several display cases. In the midst of all this organized chaos stood the petite, serene nun.

Sister Martha, who is seventy-five years old, has been in charge of
the school since 1994 and knows its history well.

"The Holy Father completed his first level of schooling here, his
kindergarten. He started kindergarten when he was five, but because
this was an all girls' school then, he had to leave. His sisters continued, and his family, because they were from this neighborhood, came
to mass here on Sundays, and he did, too, and he prepared for his first
communion and confirmation here. In those days both sacraments
were held on the same day. He was eight. He was born in 1936, so
that would have been in 1944."

We chatted about the age when children receive first communion
and confirmation in America, and then I asked her if she had known
the pope when they were children. "No, not at that time," she said.
"After, I did, because he continued to come to the school. Many times.
He is a very grateful person. He was always very grateful for the sister
who prepared him for his first communion. Her name was Dolores."

Sister Martha told me that Sister Dolores died at the school and
that her wake was held in the school chapel. "We had a wake and he
stayed all night. He did not want to have anything to eat or drink
because he is very austere and selfless. We had the door open all night
and the only one who came was him."

After telling the story, she smiled and said, "He knew many of the
sisters here, the older ones, from his childhood and he came to visit
them every year. He would also give lectures to the sisters when he
was Archbishop of Buenos Aires, in the hall that we have in the basement, which is very nice, and three hundred or so sisters would attend. After the talk, he would have tea with us, and after that he would
celebrate mass. He would spend all afternoon with us. He did this
until 2012.

"We had a sister who was one hundred and one years old, Sister
Rose. Her mind was very sharp but she could no longer walk and was
confined to her bed. Bergoglio would ask her, 'What was I like when

I was a child?' She would say, 'A demon,' and he would find this very funny and would ask her again and he would laugh.

"When Bergoglio had left, I asked her, 'Why did you say he was a demon?'

" 'No,' she said, 'he was a good boy, but I say that because it makes him laugh.'

"She liked the joke. A demon, she would say. They say that he was a regular boy, very polite. He liked playing. A regular, wholesome child."

The best word to describe the school is "idyllic." Out back there are basketball and volleyball courts and swings. There is a small soccer "field"—not grass or artificial turf or even dirt, but concrete. The kids play, laugh, and scream as children do.

As Sister Martha walked me through the school and up to the big doors that connected the school to the parish church, I felt that young Jorge surely must have associated his first taste of organized religion with joy, community, and beauty. The ritual of the school day, of childhood religion and study, was full of serenity, just like Sister Martha.

But there was something more to his childhood, something one could not see by walking around his old haunts, something that did not become known until one of Pope Francis's letters, written in 2013, was released publicly in 2015.

In that letter, Pope Francis thanked Fr. Alexandre Awi, who was his interpreter at World Youth Day in Brazil, for an article that the priest had written on Francis and the culture of encounter. The letter stunned me:

In my family, there was a long history of disagreements and quarrels. Uncles and cousins quarreled and separated. As a child, when one of these fights was discussed or when we could see a new incident was about to take place, I cried a great deal, in secret, and sometimes I offered a sacrifice or a penance so that such events might not occur. I was very affected. Thank God, at home, Dad, Mom, and my five siblings lived in peace. But these events left a deep mark on me in my childhood and created a desire in my heart for people to not fight, to remain united. And if they fight, that they return to better feelings.

I read and reread Pope Francis's words. *Had I misunderstood his childhood? It was filled with quarrels and disagreements, so much so that people separated?*

Over time, as I pictured him crying in secret and praying for the quarrels to end—or not to happen at all—I started to see that perhaps only a man who had experienced both peace and serenity *and* such wounds as a child could show such extraordinary compassion and mercy as an adult.

As I TRIED to picture young Jorge and tried to imagine what it must have been like to be a boy in this part of Buenos Aires during the glory days of Perón, I realized how much I had been hearing about Perón on my visit, now forty years since his death and more than sixty years since the death of his idolized wife, still affectionately referred to as Evita. Jorge grew up in an era that was defined by the serenity I had glimpsed at his first school, in his favorite park, and on the street where his family house still stands. And I realized, however paradoxically or illogically, that that serenity was inseparable from its era, the pinnacle—some true believers would even say the golden age—of the Juan Perón era.

3 Peronismo

THE TINY TAXI had been stuck in traffic for thirty minutes. It was early November, the beginning of summer in Argentina, and the heat and humidity made it even worse. The taxi didn't have air-conditioning—the cramped car felt like a small sauna.

"The Plaza de Mayo is up there on the right," the taxi driver said, "and the Pink House is in the plaza. Up there a bit farther. Can you see it now?"

I opened the window, but two trucks ahead blocked the view. Horns blared. We didn't move.

"Wait a minute," he said before pulling the car hard to the right and almost T-boning the car next to us. The other driver waved his hands in exasperation but let us move ahead of him.

"Now can you see?" he asked.

Yes, I can see it, and it really is pink. And it's huge—four stories high and the length of a New York City block. There are six lanes of traffic, a cacophony of horns, jaywalkers everywhere. Complete chaos.

The Casa Rosada, or Pink House, is the executive government office. It sits on one end of the Plaza de Mayo, surrounded by other imposing buildings: the Metropolitan Cathedral of Buenos Aires, the Cabildo (the place where the first Argentine government was formed in 1810), and Buenos Aires City Hall. The plaza is where most political demonstrations occur.

As the car pulled alongside the Pink House and into the Plaza de Mayo, I caught a glimpse of the balcony where Evita stood and gave speeches to tens of thousands of Peronist faithful, urging them to support her husband. The balcony is a striking perch from which to see the Metropolitan Cathedral of Buenos Aires—the church that Jorge Mario Bergoglio would someday call his parish.

When Jorge was growing up, schools had a daily pledge of allegiance to Eva and Juan Perón, not to the country, and Evita's book, *La Razón de mi vida*, was mandatory classroom reading. In it, Evita wrote that "Perón is the face of God in the darkness. . . . Here the case of Bethlehem, two thousand years ago, was repeated; the first to believe were humble."

As outrageous as that statement sounds, one has to remember the history of a close relationship between the Catholic Church and the Argentine government. A constitutional requirement that one had to be Catholic in order to be elected president wasn't repealed until 1994. The constitution still requires the Argentine government to support the Catholic Church. The requirement does not specifically state how the government should do so, but the Catholic Church is the only religious institution mentioned and, as a result, the government has paid for the construction of buildings for the Church and subsidized the Church's operating expenses. In 1948, when Perón nationalized the rail system, he placed a statue of Mary in each station.

A few years later, when Jorge was a teenager, the Catholic Church that had once been Perón's platform, his foundation, had become one of his staunchest critics, questioning the authenticity of Perón's commitment to Catholic teaching. The conflation of Perón and Christ made explicit by Evita and implicit in the party's message, combined with attacks by Peronist-inspired mobs against Catholic churches in the mid-1950s, eventually led to a split between the Church and Perón, when Jorge was on the verge of entering the seminary.

But when Jorge was a boy, Peronismo meant one clear, shining thing to families like the Bergoglios: the marriage of church and state in an alliance that fought for the lowly. Like most immigrants, the Bergoglios embraced what might best be called Peronist Catholicism as a vehicle to bring about change that would benefit the underprivileged in the poor urban areas of Buenos Aires. From Perón's emphasis on human dignity, economic opportunity, and the need for social justice to his aggressive insistence on the rights of workers and the socioeconomic obligations of government, Perón co-opted the message of the gospel. To a family as faithful as Jorge's, the double message had to be meaningful, for Perón was identifying with the poor and working class and professing to be their salvation.

"There was a growing middle class at that time in Argentina, but it was small," Fr. Gustavo Morello, an Argentine Jesuit and a sociologist at Boston College, told me. "There were a few rich people, but most people were poor or working class. They didn't have access to what so many of us today take for granted. The so-called good life. That was what Evita and Juan Perón promised, and they used Catholicism to support this promise. There was the strong sense that it was the elites versus the people and Perón was on the side of the people. And to understand this helps one to understand Francis."

I met with Cardinal Leonardo Sandri, a seventy-two-year-old Argentine who attended seminary with Bergoglio and today is the prefect of the Congregation for the Oriental Churches. Like Bergoglio, his family immigrated to Argentina from Italy. His older sister was born in Italy, while he and his younger brother were born in Argentina. He grew up speaking Italian and Spanish. When I asked about life under Perón, Sandri answered in halting English, "I remember that Perón was a champion of social initiatives, for workers, for old people, for young people. The period of Perón was very important for these social initiatives in favor of workers and also the vote of women."

Fr. Julio Merediz, a Jesuit contemporary and lifelong friend of Pope Francis, told a friend of mine, "To understand Jorge, you have to understand that very particular moment in Argentine history during which he came of age. Jorge, all of us, still identify with the purity of that moment. Peronismo became many things to many people, but it was first and foremost a progressive embracing of hardworking people, faithful people, who were struggling to improve their lives. But you must realize how important a role Catholicism played in it. The separation of church and state did not exist. The Catholic faith was not only the faith of the government but also the practical vehicle through which it was attempting to execute its social programs. This is the Church Jorge grew up in. This is the Argentina Jorge grew up in."

WHEN I WAS growing up, my dad would regale my friends and me with amazing stories like the one in which in 1928, as a thirteen-year-old, he drove with his mom from Baltimore to Albany, where he sat on Maryland governor Albert Ritchie's lap as they watched Al Smith accept the Democratic nomination for president. Al Smith was the first Catholic ever nominated for the presidency.

Ritchie was a Shriver family friend, a strong supporter of states' rights, local government, and religious freedom. Dad told us, "The political leaders of Maryland created a document called the Declaration of Rights that established religious freedom in Maryland. That was before the idea was in the federal Bill of Rights."

The lack of separation between church and state in Argentina—indeed, the strong constitutional connection between the two entities—shocks me. While the United States has a centuries-old tradition of separation of church and state, Jorge's homeland has no such tradition at all. It is understandable, then, that a young and impressionable Jorge, growing up in the mid-1940s and early 1950s with all of that Perón energy charging the environment, would develop a lifelong interest in the intersection of faith and politics, social justice and economic opportunity. Both his rootedness in the Perón era and his rejection of its excesses and corruption—as we shall see—explain much of what he tried to accomplish as a leader in Argentina and is now trying to achieve in transforming the global Catholic Church.

4 El Porteño

"You're going to love Buenos Aires," the old man said. I had met him in a coffee shop on my second day in the capital city. He spoke English well.

"You know," he said, "everyone says that Buenos Aires is the Paris of Latin America. Obviously, I'm biased, but I think Buenos Aires is more beautiful than Paris. And there is action in Buenos Aires! We are a port doing business with the world. The world comes through Buenos Aires."

He laughed and gesticulated, saying, "People say that Parisians are rude and arrogant. You will see soon that they have nothing on us Porteños! But we have good reason to be arrogant—we have the widest river in the world, the most beautiful city in the world, we are the eighth-biggest country in the world, and we have a rich history."

I never did catch the man's name, but his words stuck with me. He must have been seventy-five years old and was impeccably dressed, with silver hair parted perfectly and a warm, welcoming presence. He looked like a lifelong Italian.

Before the trip, I had been warned by a couple of friends from Buenos Aires that Porteños were arrogant and aloof, that they were a breed unto themselves. The old man's words—his sense of pride, almost arrogance, the inflection of his voice, the way he carried himself—may have proved my friends right, but his warmth and friendliness showed that Porteños are complex. Like their city, they are full of contrasts.

From the architecture that rivals the beauty of Paris to the cracked city sidewalks; from the countless people who told me that Argentina was the seventh-biggest economy in the world in the early twentieth century to the small-business owner who told me that the economy today is so unstable that he is constantly afraid that he will be forced into the same bankruptcy his father had declared in the mid-1950s; from the Four Seasons Hotel to the *villas miseria* (the misery houses, or slums) less than a mile downhill and within view of the hotel's expensive rooms; from the commercial banks that exchanged American money to the "blue market"—the illegitimate but widely accepted currency exchange where dealers pay almost two times the official number of pesos for dollars—within a block of each other; from the serenity of the Plaza de la Misericordia to the chaos of the Plaza de Mayo, Buenos Aires is filled with palpable energy and startling contrasts.

These contrasts did not develop overnight but were years in the making. I knew that if I wanted to understand the Francis of today, I needed to understand not only Peronism, but Buenos Aires as well, for the place is the most complicated, intriguing city that I have ever visited, and Jorge Mario Bergoglio is first and foremost a Porteño.

THE SPANISH STARTED to colonize the sparsely populated area that today is Argentina in the early sixteenth century. Navigators from Spain and Portugal explored the Río de la Plata, the river on which Buenos Aires sits, in hopes of finding a passage from the Atlantic to the Pacific. The river is more than one hundred thirty-six miles wide at its opening. The first time I saw it, I asked the taxi driver if it was the Atlantic Ocean.

"No!" His response was a cross between a loud laugh and a mild reprimand. "No," he said again, waving his hand toward the mighty river, "that is the Río de la Plata. It is wider than the Amazon. It is incredible, no?"

He was right—it is incredible, so wide that some in fact consider it part of the Atlantic Ocean. I couldn't see land on the other side of the river—it doesn't look anything like any river I've seen in America. The Mississippi and Missouri rivers are dwarfed by the Río de la Plata; my home state's Chesapeake Bay is minuscule by comparison.

Bolivia and Peru, with their silver and gold mines, dominated the development of South America; what is now Argentina was part of the Viceroyalty of Peru, which was in turn part of the Spanish empire. In 1776, Argentina separated from the Viceroyalty of Peru, and Buenos Aires was named the capital of what was known as the Viceroyalty of the Río de la Plata.

In 1810, the May Revolution started Argentina's fight for independence from Spain. The revolution lasted for eight years before independence was finally won and the Argentine Republic was created. The new government was based in Buenos Aires, but infighting—principally between the peoples of the port and of the interior—persisted until 1861. In other words, Argentina had a forty-three-year-long civil war.

In 1861, Bartolomé Mitre was elected the first president of the reunified country. He and the next eleven presidents all emphasized liberal economic policies. A massive wave of European immigration—second only to the wave of immigrants headed into the United States—resulted in a complete overhaul of the Argentine society and economy. By the early twentieth century, Argentina was considered to be among the wealthiest nations in the world.

"Argentina grew in the second part of the nineteenth century, based on large-scale livestock production that led to some limited range of products for export like hides, wool, and low-quality sun-dried and salted beef," Eugenio Diaz-Bonilla, an Argentine economist with a long career in international development, told me. "Later, technological changes in transportation, especially the British-built railway system, and refrigeration led to higher-quality beef exports and the expansion of grain production. The land was concentrated in large ranches, and demand for labor in the agricultural sector was less dynamic than in the United States, but there was enough economic expansion to ensure high growth during the last part of the nineteenth century and early part of the twentieth century. That growth certainly benefited mainly Buenos Aires, especially since, unlike the United States, Argentina does not have a series of efficient seaports along its coast. The transportation system funnels virtually everything through the port of Buenos Aires."

By 1908, Argentina's per capita income was 60 percent higher than Italy's, close to 90 percent higher than Spain's, and almost 400 percent higher than that of its neighbor Brazil. Diaz-Bonilla told me that although there is no reliable data, those relatively higher incomes were probably very concentrated, in line with the large inequalities in land holdings, and enough wealthy Argentines were fond of traveling to Europe and flaunting their wealth that at some point in the 1920s, "spending like an Argentine" became a common figure of speech.

My friend José was born and raised in Buenos Aires but moved to the United States ten years ago. "We Porteños have an edge," he said. "You have to remember, Buenos Aires is by far the biggest and most important port in Argentina. It is also the most important port in Latin America. We Porteños are successful immigrants; we focus on Europe, not Latin America, and we think Buenos Aires is more impressive than any city in Europe.

"You know," José continued, "in the 1940s and 1950s, Buenos Aires was known as the capital of an empire that never existed." He said it all so matter-of-factly that the arrogance didn't seem so, well, arrogant.

It seems as if almost every conversation I have had with an Argentine inevitably touches upon how different Buenos Aires is from the rest of Argentina—it feels as if the forty-three-year civil war, which officially ended some one hundred fifty years ago, is still being waged. Buenos Aires is the capital city, the most important port, the city of successful immigrants—it is always contrasted with the rest of Argentina, the rest of Latin America, even Europe. But it is not just the tension between the Porteños and the rest of the country that defines a Porteño—indeed, Porteños have had to live through social and political unrest and military interventions.

When commodity producers, such as Argentina, were badly hurt by the collapse of world prices during the Great Depression, political instability ensued. In 1930, President Hipólito Yrigoyen was overthrown by a military coup led by José Félix Uriburu, who ruled for only two years. An election rife with fraud resulted in Agustín Pedro Justo's becoming president. Argentina remained neutral in World War II until the final month of the war, when it declared war on the Axis powers.

Amid all of this confusion, chaos, and economic uncertainty arose Juan and Eva Perón. "During that time," Diaz-Bonilla told me, "the Argentine economy and society experienced a substantial transformation with the expansion of industry, changes in agrarian laws that weakened the power of large landowners, the female vote, and the political participation of previously marginalized groups. In a sense, we have been processing those tectonic shifts in our social fabric during many decades of political and economic instability since then."

Buenos Aires survived a revolution and a prolonged civil war; it quickly became the major port of one of the largest economies in the world at the turn of the century; it was teeming with immigrants and energy into the early twentieth century; and it survived numerous military-led overthrows in the twentieth century. No wonder Porteños have an edge.

That edge, though, is infused with a deep love of their city. At the end of my conversation with José, he said, "You know my line about Buenos Aires being the capital of an empire that never existed? Well, I still see Buenos Aires as the most beautiful capital city in the world."

Pope Francis shares that sentiment: "I love my home. I love Buenos Aires. . . . I'm a native of the city and I wouldn't know what to do with myself outside Buenos Aires."

But when I asked Porteños about the political corruption or the "blue market," almost everyone—man or woman—shrugged, sighed, and said something to the effect of "Nothing can be done about it" or "That's the way it's always been" or "Corruption is a part of life here."

Arrogance, warmth, love, resignation, wealth, dire poverty—and Buenos Aires is becoming even more complex, as the Porteño of today is changing. "In the early part of the twentieth century, the vast majority of immigrants came from Europe, primarily Italy and Spain. But more recently, Buenos Aires has seen a large influx of people from other parts of Argentina as well as from Bolivia, Paraguay, and Peru," Father Morello told me. "In fact, the city with the second-highest population of Bolivians is Buenos Aires."

I would learn that Jorge Mario Bergoglio's humility and his sense of mercy and joy, nurtured in him as a child by his loving grandmother Rosa, would develop over time and be heavily influenced by the contrasts, conflicts, and changing demographics of his beloved Buenos Aires. As an auxiliary bishop and later as a cardinal, and especially during and after the profound economic crisis in 2001, Bergoglio would spend much of his time with these new and very poor immigrants while calling upon all Porteños to change.

5   The Scientific Method

IN FEBRUARY 1948, Jorge's mother gave birth to her fifth and last child, a girl named Maria Elena, and was bedridden as a result. Bergoglio would later say that his mother "became paralyzed . . . although she recovered over time." Jorge, then a sixth grader, and his younger brother, Oscar, were enrolled as boarders at Colegio Wilfrid Barón de los Santos Ángeles in Ramos Mejía, about a twenty-minute drive from Flores. Father Pozzoli, the close family friend and family priest for both the Bergoglio and Sivori families, had reached out to his fellow Salesians and enrolled the children at the school.

Jorge would later write that the year he spent boarding at Colegio Barón not only prepared him well for high school and life but, more important, inculcated within him a "Catholic culture."

> Life at the School was a "whole." We were submerged into a web of life, prepared so as to have no idle time. The day would fly by without any time to get bored. I felt immersed in a world that, although artificially "prepared" (with pedagogical resources) was not artificial at all. The natural thing was to go to mass every morning, have breakfast, study, go to class, play during the breaks, listen to the "Good Night" teachings of the Father Director. One got the chance to live the various intertwined aspects of life,

and this created in me a conscience: not only a moral conscience but also a sort of human conscience (social, recreational, artistic, etc.). In other words, the School created, through the awakening of an awareness of the truth of things, a Catholic culture that had nothing of "sanctimonious" or "clueless." Study, social values of coexistence, social references to the most needy (I remember having to learn there to do without things myself in order to give to people who were poorer than I was), sports, competition, piety. . . . Everything was real, and everything directed at creating real habits, in its entirety. They created in us a cultural way of being.

I read that paragraph time and again. Everything seems so organized in this man's brain; even his school experience seemed highly structured and logical. I read on:

All things were done with a purpose. There was nothing that "made no sense" (at least as far as the fundamental order of things [was concerned], because there might have been the occasional lack of patience on the part of some teachers, or small everyday injustices, etc.). There, almost unconsciously, I learned to seek the meaning of things.

The daily "good night" teachings by the Father Director, the head of the school, had a profound impact on Jorge. Sometimes the Father Inspector, the head of the Salesians in Argentina, would visit and give the "good night" teaching. On one such occasion, Msgr. Miguel Raspanti, the Father Inspector, spoke to the boys after attending his own mother's funeral. The talk would become Jorge's "point of reference throughout the rest of my life to the problem of death. That night, without fear, I felt that one day I would die; and that seemed to me to be most natural."

Raised in a culture that denies death at every turn, I find this insight particularly startling. Clearly, though, the Salesians impressed upon him a Catholic culture of rituals and routines that structured his life and made him unafraid, even of death. The harmony, the fullness of the day, included studies and extracurricular activities and God; one didn't have just religious studies, or fun activities, or academics. No, for Jorge, all of these pieces needed to fit together in a disciplined, structured way in order for one to truly live life.

Given this enlightened worldview, I guess Bergoglio's love of science should not have surprised me. But it did, simply because I had always thought of my Church as somewhat backward or retrograde, even fearful, on the topic. Many associate the Catholic Church with scientific backwardness, citing the Church's trial and imprisonment of Galileo for teaching that the sun, rather than the Earth, is the center of the universe. The Galileo affair has long been a source of embarrassment for the Church, which actually has a centuries-old tradition of sponsoring research in astronomy, chemistry, and medicine. But I still had thought that Bergoglio, having been raised in such a devout Catholic family and in a Catholic country, in a school that reinforced Catholic rituals and routines and immersed its students in a "Catholic culture," would have wanted to study theology or philosophy or history. Those are the topics I thought priests and nuns studied to become, well, priests and nuns.

I grew up surrounded by men and women in religious life. Priests would come over for dinner on a regular basis and even take family vacations with us. My mom and dad both went to daily mass, and on many Saturdays, the priest who had said mass that morning would be eating breakfast at our dining room table when I stumbled downstairs. When Mom's sister Rosemary, who was living in a home for people with developmental disabilities, visited us, she was always accompanied by two nuns who lived with her twenty-four hours a day, every day of the year. Sister Paulus and Sister Margaret Ann dedicated their lives to taking care of Aunt Rosie, and their two or three visits a year, for ten days or so at a time, were a highlight for all of us, but especially for my mom.

I don't remember talking to any of them about science, though, and I don't know a nun or a priest who has an advanced degree in the sciences. I recently asked a close priest friend of mine whether he had studied the sciences, and he laughed and said, "I took a science class in college in order to graduate, but, no, I don't love it at all—and I don't know anyone in religious life who reads science journals for pleasure, either!"

But young Jorge was captivated by science; he was almost as passionate about it as he was about religion. After his year at boarding school with the Salesians, he enrolled at Escuela Industrial No. 12, where he was in a class of twelve pupils who, in addition to the national curriculum, studied food chemistry. This corner of his intellectual history fascinates me for what it says about him and the development of his faith and his later role as a church leader trying to negotiate the tricky balance between theology and science.

Jorge would study science and he would work, hard. His father told him, "Now that you're starting secondary school, you should also start working; I'm going to find you something over vacation." That "something" ended up being a job at a hosiery factory, where Jorge cleaned and performed clerical duties. He would work from 7:00 A.M. until 1:00 P.M., then grab lunch, and then go to school from 2:00 P.M. until 8:00 P.M. Reflecting on that time, Bergoglio mused, "I'm so grateful to my father for making me work. The work I did was one of the best things I've done in my life."

"It was clear to all of us that Jorge was not only the smartest among us, but the most industrious," one of Jorge's classmates and longtime Buenos Aires resident Oscar Crespo said. "We all were hard workers, but he was tireless. Between his jobs and school, I wonder still where all his energy and discipline came from."

After three years at the hosiery factory, while still studying science, Jorge went to work at the Hickethier-Bachmann chemistry laboratory. "In the laboratory I got to see the good and the bad of all human endeavor," Jorge later said. "I had an extraordinary boss there, Esther Ballestrino de Careaga. . . . I loved her very much. I remember that when I handed her an analysis, she'd say, 'Wow, you did that so fast.' And then she'd ask, 'But did you do the test or not?' I would answer,

'What for?' If I'd done all the previous tests, it would surely be more or less the same. 'No, you have to do things properly,' she would chide me. In short, she taught me the seriousness of hard work. Truly, I owe a huge amount to that great woman."

Esther was from Paraguay and had a doctorate in biochemistry. Persecuted under the military dictatorship of Higinio Moríñigo, she fled to Argentina in 1947. She was an avowed Marxist and atheist with whom Jorge engaged in regular political discussion and debate. Her lab was devoted to the scientific method, but she seemed to live her life according to the Socratic method—questioning and debating with her employees and colleagues regardless of religious creed or political belief. Many years later, during the dark days of the Argentine Dirty War, which raged from 1976 to 1983 and resulted in the "disappearance" or killing of an estimated fifteen thousand people, Esther helped start a group called Mothers of the Plaza de Mayo. The Mothers were composed of mothers and grandmothers whose children had disappeared. At great danger to themselves and their families, they rallied every Thursday in that prominent square, demanding information about their missing loved ones.

In 1977, Esther and two nuns, who were meeting at Santa Cruz Church in Buenos Aires, were abducted and never seen alive again.

In 2005, shortly after Esther's remains were discovered and identified, her daughter, Mabel, asked then–Cardinal Bergoglio if her mother could be buried at Santa Cruz Church. Bergoglio agreed.

Ultimately, for Bergoglio, choosing the religious life did not mean shunning his scientific background. "Science and faith are not incompatible for Bergoglio," Fr. Juan Scannone, an Argentine Jesuit and renowned theologian, told me. Scannone, now eighty-five, was one of Bergoglio's teachers and maintains a good relationship with him. "In fact, his training in science has given him a strong sense of reality, of the superiority of experience over ideas. He favors the 'lived' experience over ideology."

Indeed, when Pope Francis addressed the Plenary Session of the Pontifical Academy of Sciences in 2014, we saw science and faith hand in hand:

When we read the account of Creation in Genesis we risk imagining that God was a magician, complete with an all-powerful magic wand. But that was not so. He created beings and He let them develop according to the internal laws with which He endowed each one, that they might develop and reach their fullness. He gave autonomy to the beings of the universe at the same time in which He assured them of his continual presence, giving life to every reality. And thus Creation has been progressing for centuries and centuries, millennia and millennia, until becoming as we know it today, precisely because God is not a demiurge or a magician, but the Creator who gives life to all beings. The beginning of the world was not a work of chaos that owes its origin to another, but derives directly from a supreme Principle who creates out of love. The Big Bang theory, which is proposed today as the origin of the world, does not contradict the intervention of a divine Creator but depends on it. Evolution in nature does not conflict with the notion of Creation, because evolution presupposes the creation of beings who evolve. . . .

But at the same time, the scientist must be moved by the conviction that nature, in its evolutionary mechanisms, hides its potential, which it leaves for intelligence and freedom to discover and actualize, in order to reach the development that is in the Creator's design. So then, no matter how limited, the action of man partakes in the power of God and is capable of building a world adapted to his twofold physical and spiritual life; to build a humane world for all human beings and not only for one group or one privileged class. . . . But it is also true that the action of man, when his freedom becomes autonomy—which is not freedom, but autonomy—destroys Creation and man takes the place of the Creator. And this is a grave sin against God the Creator.

When I read these comments, I thought that the Catholic Church had found a leader who saw science not as a threat, but, at its core, as a gift from God, a field in which that sense of wonder that faith provides could be discovered.

"We all knew how religious he was," his old friend Oscar Crespo remarked. "But his commitment to the truth, to what the schoolbooks call the 'scientific method,' was almost innate. He reconciled the two, and it in no way surprises me that he still, for the most part, does. He is one of those guys who will frustrate you by saying, 'Well, then who caused the Big Bang?' And he leaves you believing in both God and science."

Pope Francis sees the divine very much involved in creation and in the ongoing revelations of science. He sees creation as a gift to man— God has given creation to man and made "him the steward of creation, even that he will rule over creation, that he develop it until the end of time."

Some see the biblical text reading, "Let us make human beings in our image, after our likeness. Let them have dominion over the fish of the sea, the birds of the air, the tame animals, all the wild animals, and all the creatures that crawl on the earth" and interpret Francis's statement above as meaning that nature exists for humanity's sake alone.

On the contrary, Francis holds the opposite view:

We are not God. The earth was here before us and it has been given to us. This allows us to respond to the charge that Judaeo-Christian thinking, on the basis of the Genesis account which grants man "dominion" over the earth (cf. Gen 1:28), has encouraged the unbridled exploitation of nature by painting Him as domineering and destructive by nature. This is not a correct interpretation of the Bible as understood by the Church. Although it is true that we Christians have at times incorrectly interpreted the Scriptures, nowadays we must forcefully reject the notion that our being created in God's image and given dominion over the earth justifies absolute domination over other creatures. The biblical texts are to be read in their context, with an appropriate hermeneutic, recognizing that they tell us to "till and keep" the garden of the world (cf. Gen 2:15). "Tilling" refers to cultivating, plowing, or working, while "keeping" means caring, protecting, overseeing, and preserving. This implies a relationship of mutual responsibility between human beings and nature. Each community can take from the bounty of the earth whatever it needs for subsistence, but it also has the duty to protect the earth and to ensure its fruitfulness for coming generations.

Francis sees the relationship between man and nature as carefully balanced and altogether complete. It sounds like what the Salesians taught him nearly seventy years earlier: "Everything that we did and learned also had a harmonious unity. We were not 'compartmentalized' but rather one thing would relate to the other and one thing complemented the other. Unconsciously we felt we were growing up harmoniously, something which, of course, we could not put into words at the time, but were able to do so later."

Jorge's love of science shows the uncanny way in which Pope Francis's life challenges expectation and cliché. Not only was his early life dedicated to scientific thought and learning, but one of his key intellectual mentors was a female scientist, who worked at a time in Argentina when very few women worked, let alone in a scientific field.

And yet, despite the allure of chemistry and biology and a mentor who made both seem magical, there was also an influence that was even more magical, something that took him even closer to the mystery of faith, the mystery upon which he would decide to build his life.

6 The Decision

I HAVE ALWAYS thought that "basilica" was merely a fancy name bestowed on a church that was historic or large or beautiful—or all three.

When I lived in Baltimore, I would go to early morning mass at the Basilica of the Assumption on Charles Street, the first Catholic cathedral in the United States, built between 1806 and 1821. I also remember the basilica well from my adolescence— when my dad used to drive us to Baltimore Orioles baseball games, he would weave through the streets of Baltimore, always passing by the basilica. Dad had been born and raised in Maryland, and the basilica had been his favorite church since he was a child.

He would inevitably say the same thing every time we drove up Charles Street: "Do you kids know what's coming up on our left?"

One of us would say, "It's the Basilica of the Assumption, Dad. You ask us that all the time."

He would smile, undaunted. "Correct! Good answer! And someone must know who designed it?"

Before anyone could answer, he would blurt out, his voice filled with awe and pride and excitement: "Benjamin Henry Latrobe designed that beautiful church. Latrobe also designed the U.S. Capitol. Jefferson hired him to do that one. John Carroll, a Jesuit, the first bishop of the United States and founder of

Georgetown University, commissioned Latrobe to build the basilica. And Bishop Carroll's cousin was Charles Carroll of Carrollton, Maryland, the only Catholic to sign the Declaration of Independence."

The basilica is indeed a beautiful, stately building with columns out front, high ceilings, and beautiful artwork throughout it. Inside the basilica is a painting of James Cardinal Gibbons, the second cardinal in America. He went to the seminary with Dad's grandfather Thomas Herbert Shriver, who became seriously ill not once but twice and saw those sicknesses as a sign that he was not called to be a priest.

I had assumed that not all basilicas were as beautiful as the one in Baltimore, but when I got off the subway at Flores, I was expecting a massive, magnificent building, a place befitting not just Catholic Argentina but also the moment on September 21, 1953, when sixteen-year-old Jorge Mario Bergoglio, a student at Escuela Industrial No. 12 and a part-time employee at the Hickethier-Bachmann lab, would hear the voice of God and change his life.

I squinted in the sunlight as I emerged from underground—cars were everywhere, horns were beeping, and buses were moving through the traffic. To my right was the Plaza Flores, a square block with big beautiful trees and a merry-go-round.

To my immediate left was the Basilica of San José de Flores, wedged between two buildings with small alleys separating the church from her neighbors. In the alleyway to the right was a mattress and plenty of pigeons.

As I walked up the cracked steps, the cars and taxis and buses zipped by close enough that I could almost touch them.

The façade of the basilica includes four pilasters with a main door in the middle and two equal-sized doors on either side. Four saints stand atop the building, separated by a central steeple with a clock and a cross on the very top.

The Basilica of San José de Flores doesn't have the majesty or the beauty of the Basilica of the Assumption; it doesn't look as well maintained, either, but it did have people in and around it. A lot of people.

At 10:00 A.M., it felt like a busy bus station. People pushed the front door open, walked directly to their favorite pews, and sat down to pray. This went on all morning—commuters about to catch their buses in Plaza Flores rushed in, knelt and prayed, and rushed out; mothers pushing baby carriages struggled through the door, sat at the end of a rear pew and huffed, then closed their eyes and prayed; old men looked to nearby visitors for help with the door, then shuffled in, leaning on their canes, before sitting down in a pew, looking up at the ceiling, and praying.

I have never seen this kind of display of people praying in the United States.

The inside of the basilica was more impressive, but dark, even gloomy. The pews were made of plain wood with no cushions; the kneelers had no cushions, either. My knees hurt when I knelt.

The ceiling was covered with paintings of angels and scenes from the Bible, and the gold paint lightened the mood. From the middle of the church rose a pulpit.

Small altars dedicated to various saints lined both sides of the nave, with people kneeling in front of them to pray to their favorites.

I made my way to the main sanctuary where a large marble altar stood, flanked by candles on both sides. At the back of the sanctuary, six columns reached up to the ceiling, surrounded by more candles. The Argentine flag hung in a corner.

I asked a man to direct me to the confessional where Pope Francis had his moment. He pointed to the front of the church, where I had entered.

I wandered over and sat in the pew closest to the confessional.

And stared at it.

This is it?

The confessional was made of dark wood and was poorly lit, situated close by one of the small side altars. It was empty.

This is where Pope Francis had his life-changing moment—this small, simple confessional?

Now, there are many legendary conversions in the history of Christianity, perhaps the most famous of which is the story of Saul, on his donkey headed to Damascus to persecute early Christians. The story goes that he was knocked off the animal, blinded by light, and stunned by the voice of God asking, "Saul, Saul, why do you persecute me?"

Saul replied, "Who are you, sir?"

The reply came: "I am Jesus, whom you are persecuting. Now get up and go into the city and you will be told what you must do."

Saul was blind for three days and did not eat or drink. When he regained his sight, he was baptized immediately, took the name Paul, and became God's "chosen instrument of mine to carry my name before Gentiles, kings, and Israelites."

Then there is the story of Saint Ignatius of Loyola, the soldier and playboy who went on to become one of the best-known leaders of the Catholic faith, which I recounted in the prologue.

Young Jorge's encounter was different. He was on his way to meet up with his girlfriend and other students when

I looked, it was dark, it was a morning in September, maybe 9:00 A.M., and I saw a priest walking, I didn't know him, he wasn't one of the parish clergy. And he sits down in one of the confessionals, the last confessional as you're looking down the left side at the altar. I don't quite know what happened next, I felt like somebody grabbed me from inside and took me to the confessional. Obviously I told him my things, I confessed . . . but I don't know what happened.

When I had finished my confession I asked the priest where he was from, because I didn't know him, and he told me: "I'm from Corrientes and I'm living here close by, in the priests' home. I come to celebrate mass here now and then." He had cancer—leukemia—and died the following year. Right there I knew I had to be a priest; I was totally certain. Instead of going out with the others I went back home because I was overwhelmed. Afterward I carried on at school and with everything, but knowing now where I was headed.

In his official biography, he said, "Something strange happened to me in that confession. I don't know what it was, but it changed my life. I think it surprised me, caught me with my guard down."

This epiphany occurred while sixteen-year-old Jorge was working under the tutelage of Esther Ballestrino at the Hickethier-Bachmann laboratory. He told no one for a long time, continuing to seek spiritual direction from the priest he had met in the confessional at the basilica that day. But just as his interest and expertise in science were growing, so, too, was his faith blossoming. We tend to see faith and logic as incompatible, but in Jorge's head, faith and scientific thought developed at the same time.

"But I knew that if he had to pick, even then, it would be faith and social justice," his childhood friend Oscar Crespo said. "We had a boy in our class who everyone knew was, let me say, a bit slower. And Jorge always took him under his wing, not just tutoring him but always encouraging him. His concern for the poor wasn't just for the poor of pocketbook but the poor of soul. Even as a teenager, he devoted himself to his fellow man."

As Jorge's social conscience grew, he struggled to reconcile Marxism and social activism with a faith-based spiritual life. His career as Jesuit provincial; as rector of the Jesuit formation house, Colegio Máximo, in Buenos Aires; as auxiliary bishop; and even as cardinal would be marked by the unyielding tension between faith and social activism. They would clash in his life, as we shall see, tugging him toward social justice one day and toward spirituality the next. He would struggle with how to reconcile the two; indeed, he would get in trouble with his fellow clergy, with Argentine politicians, and with his students over his struggle to reconcile them.

As I sat looking at the plain confessional, I began to realize that young Jorge's conversion made total sense because it was so profoundly simple: no fireworks, no hyperventilation, no dramatic scene. It also seemed completely fitting that his moment happened not in some magnificent cathedral but rather in an ordinary basilica comfortably nestled in a thriving, lively neighborhood filled with ordinary working-class people. And perhaps best of all, it happened in a church named after San José, Saint Joseph, the father of Jesus, a man who was ready to leave his pregnant fiancée, Mary, but stayed with her because he had a dream in which he heard the small voice of God tell him to marry the young woman.

I'm not saying that Jorge Mario Bergoglio is on the level of Saint Joseph, but they both made huge decisions in a similarly calm, prosaic way. God reached out to both of them—an ordinary sixteen-year-old boy in Argentina and a young Jewish man two thousand years earlier—and both made a simple decision. It seems logical, if such a term can describe a profound, faith-filled moment. It doesn't have to happen in a big, fancy, historical church, I learned; it rarely does, actually.

As I learned more about Jorge Mario Bergoglio, the merging of logic and faith seems, well, almost natural.

7 Seminary

THERE IS A majestic building atop the crest of a steep hill in northwest Baltimore that my dad would drive by on our way to visit Grandma Shriver when she was gravely ill. Looming at the end of a winding, tree-lined driveway, its elegant façade features six massive pillars framing three arched entrances. It is huge— two stories high and longer than a big city block. When I first saw it, I was reminded of some sort of beautiful but forbidding imperial palace, a place with hidden passageways and secret rooms, something that should have been in the popular game of the day, Dungeons and Dragons. It is far off the main road and faces a huge front lawn the size of a football field, making the building appear even more remote and mysterious.

The building is St. Mary's Seminary, the first Catholic seminary in the United States, but it did not elicit the same energy and excitement from Dad as did the Basilica of the Assumption. Dad would point it out and say simply, "That is St. Mary's Seminary, where young men go to become priests." Maybe it was his deep respect for priests that subdued him, or maybe it was knowing that his beloved mother was failing; the result was that the imposing building scared the hell out of me.

Why does a guy become a priest, anyway? He can't get married. He can't have children. It looks like a fearsome castle. I never see anyone playing on that front lawn. What happens in there?

I was too afraid to ask those questions and Dad didn't offer more insights, so I was glad we always moved on quickly.

As I got older and discovered girls, the building came to symbolize for me the solitariness of priests. If you are a boy who goes to Catholic school, attends mass on Sundays, and grows up immersed in the Catholic tradition, sooner or later, if only for a few days, the idea of becoming a priest will either cross your mind or be brought to your attention. That building, not a girlfriend or a first kiss, was the primary reason for my rejection of the priesthood. The isolated appearance of the seminary—and the presumably isolated lives of the young men inside—haunted me. I assumed that despite the general garrulousness and good nature of most priests I knew, they ultimately, at the end of their long, faith-filled day, went home alone. The very idea terrified me, and so the beauty of St. Mary's was, as the Irish poet William Butler Yeats wrote about a far different subject, a terrible beauty.

I never really knew what went on at seminaries, the place where young men went to study and prepare themselves to become priests. If you are a doubter of the Catholic way, you might be skeptical of celibacy and think of the seminary as the place where it is officially embraced and enforced. Worse, you might see the seminary as the breeding ground for the sexual crimes perpetrated by some Catholic priests. So many young men, who should be flourishing, going forth and procreating as God instructs in Genesis, are instead locked into monastic rooms.

One of my oldest friends, Bill Byrne, a classmate in high school and a roommate in college, entered the seminary a few years after we graduated from Holy Cross. Bill's decision didn't surprise me—I remember discussing the priesthood with him a number of times during our senior year, and though he went to teach elementary school after graduating from Holy Cross, it was the same Catholic elementary school he had attended from sixth through eighth grade. He was living and working—and praying—at a place he knew and loved, trying to figure out if he was being called to the priesthood.

When he told me he was headed to Rome to go to the North

American College, I knew that that was a great honor; only a few—the best and the brightest—are assigned to study in Rome. The rest study at a local seminary like St. Mary's. And I knew that he was studying to be a diocesan priest; in other words, he was not joining an order like the Jesuits or the Salesians.

A diocesan priest is trained to be a parish priest; he is usually assigned to a local parish and lives with one or two other priests. His "boss" is the local bishop or, if he is in a major city, an archbishop or even a cardinal, of which there are only seven active today in America. Diocesan priests take a vow of chastity and obedience but not poverty or special allegiance to the pope as do Jesuits.

A Jesuit, on the other hand, usually lives in a community with many other Jesuit priests. In most cases, each Jesuit has a different job—one may teach at a local high school, another at a local college, while another might work in a parish and another at a hospital. The Jesuit provincial is the "boss" of each Jesuit in his region, telling each man where he can work and whether he can change jobs.

All priests in America are trained through the program of priestly formation, which is formulated and continually revised by the U.S. Conference of Catholic Bishops. Seminarians take standard courses, regardless of whether they have joined an order or chosen to be a diocesan priest. If they choose an order like the Jesuits or Salesians, that order can supplement their coursework.

I guess I was too busy back then pursuing my own career, trying to find the perfect girlfriend, trying to get ahead, to ask Bill for more details. I was proud of him but, I'm embarrassed to write, I never took the time to have an in-depth conversation about what he would do at the Pontifical North American College.

Maybe it was that his decision to forgo an ordinary life with a wife and kids was so shockingly different from the path I had chosen that I never wanted—or was afraid—to dig in and understand.

I had known Bill since we were both fifteen-year-old sophomores at Georgetown Prep. When I transferred into the school that year, we hung out on weekends, went to parties together, went on dates together. We took French and math and history together. (Luckily, the two-year requirement to study Latin was waived for me. I don't know why—maybe the Jesuits didn't want me to take classes with the freshmen? But I am grateful to this day that I didn't have to take Latin. A couple of my friends who failed out of Prep because of it still have nightmares about that language.)

My son, Tommy, though, a student at Georgetown Prep, is taking Latin and loving it. Through him, I have been reminded of one of the many benefits of a Catholic education: the emphasis on language and, more specifically, the roots of words. So when Tommy's ninth-grade Latin class commenced, simultaneously with my investigation of the life of Pope Francis, I soon wondered what the heck the word "seminary" really meant, not just since I was going to visit young Jorge's seminary in Buenos Aires, but because I had begun to aspire to think in the systematic way of the Jesuits who taught me and who now teach my son.

I learned that the root of the word lies in the Latin *seminarium*, which means "seed plot." I further discovered that the deepest origin of the word is the Latin *semen*, which of course means "seed."

The etymological investigation instantly helped me to understand Jorge's and Bill's experiences as nascent priests. They were, quite simply, there to begin their training as the seeds of Jesus Christ, as young men who would learn and grow to become fertile spreaders of the faith, of hope, love, and joy.

After graduating from Escuela Industrial No. 12, Bergoglio entered the diocesan seminary of Buenos Aires in March 1956, fully intending to become a parish priest. The seminary, often referred to as Villa Devoto after the barrio where the seminary is located, does not look at all like Baltimore's St. Mary's—rather, it is in the thick of things, on a tree-lined street in the middle of a busy Buenos Aires neighborhood.

In the mid-1950s, Villa Devoto had a "minor seminary" for young students ages twelve to eighteen who were trying to discern whether or not to become priests, and a "major seminary" for older students, typically ages seventeen to twenty-seven, who either had finished the minor seminary or, like Bergoglio, had studied elsewhere and discovered their vocation later in life.

Cardinal Sandri, the prefect of the Congregation for the Oriental Churches, was a twelve-year-old enrolled in the minor seminary when Bergoglio studied at Villa Devoto.

When I asked Sandri if he remembered anything about Bergoglio, he told me in halting English that Bergoglio was "the prefect of the younger students. I remember more his attitude, his person, how he was passing through us and watching us."

"Was he grumpy?" I asked. "Or happy, or—"

Sandri cut me off. "Very serious, serious, but we loved him." He smiled warmly, his eyes twinkling at the memory. "We loved Bergoglio, as he was very close to us," he said.

"Did he wake you in the morning?" I asked.

"Yes," he replied. "In the morning, he was passing by our beds."

"So you were in a big room?" I asked.

"A big, a huge dormitory," he replied. He went on to say that each boy had "only a bed and then a little drawer, a little armoire to put our things, yes, and one chair."

"How many in the room, twenty or thirty?" I asked.

"Oh, more, more, in this perhaps forty, and Bergoglio was passing through all this at six o'clock in the morning, and we become—"

"He woke you up at six o'clock?" I interrupted him.

"He was calling us by ringing a bell. The first who was awake would say, 'Kyrie eleison, Kyrie eleison, Kyrie eleison.' It means 'Lord have mercy' in Greek," Sandri said.

"You mean he walks through saying that? Or the boys say that?" I asked.

"Whoever woke up. The first one to get up said it." Sandri laughed.

"And does Bergoglio say something or just . . ."

"Bergoglio was approving all this."

"Was he yelling, 'Get up, boys'?"

"No, no. He was not, no. But if one was not respecting the time, yes, he would say, 'Please, please, go, please, please awake.'"

Sandri went on to tell me that what he remembered most about the daily routine at Villa Devoto was that wake-up prayer followed by daily mass.

"Every day?" I asked him.

"Every day," he replied.

"Every day," he said a second time. "And Bergoglio was following us, yes. . . ."

Breakfast followed mass and then there were "lessons," as he called their classes. Then lunch. In the afternoon, they played sports: soccer ("for soccer, I was not so brilliant," he said, laughing), basketball, and volleyball. Despite Bergoglio's love of soccer, Sandri did not remember him playing. Then they did homework and had a "very early" bedtime.

Sandri told me that the younger students were taught the humanities: "Latin, Greek, the Greek literature, Homer, all these things of ancient Greece. The major seminary is three years of philosophy and four years of theology."

During his first year at Villa Devoto, Bergoglio had his reckoning with the decision to lead a celibate life, and, more courageously it seems to me, run the risk of the loneliness that celibacy may bring.

Bergoglio later recalled:

When I was a seminarian, I was enchanted by a young woman at my uncle's wedding. I was surprised by her beauty, the clarity of her intellect . . . and, well, I kicked the idea around for a while. When I returned to the seminary after the wedding, I could not pray during the entire week because when I prepared to pray, the woman appeared in my mind. I had to go back to thinking about what I was doing. I was still free because I was only a seminarian, I could have gone back home and said *see you later*. I had to think about my choice again. I chose once again—or allowed myself to be chosen for—the religious path. It would be abnormal for these types of things not to happen. When they do happen, one has to rediscover his place. He has to see if he reaffirms his choice or if he says, "No, what I am feeling is really beautiful, I am afraid that later I will not be faithful to my commitment, I must leave the seminary."

What I find so interesting in Bergoglio's explanation of his decision is the ruthless logic of it. It may not be surprising, given my impression of his generally rational approach to life, but I still find this striking in one respect. Bergoglio, you see, was also a great lover of literature, the opera, and of dancing the *milonga;* and his ability to think so clearly in terms of "either . . . or" instead of "both . . . and," even at the age of twenty, demonstrates not only a self-mastery but, more impressively, a keen awareness that life is about choices and that choices entail both embracing one option and rejecting another.

As I walked around Villa Devoto trying to capture the sense of enthusiasm and zeal that Bergoglio surely felt, I came to see celibacy in a new light. For my entire life, I had brushed aside the seminary as the origins of clerical loneliness. I could not imagine life without the hugs and companionship of Jeanne and the joys and struggles of our three children, so my admiration for anyone strong enough to try to live without these fundamental satisfactions is boundless.

But I came to see that a seminary can be a vibrant place, full of young priests eager to nurture the world. It is my sense that Bergoglio was very much aware that he was studying in a "seed bed," that he was being watered and fertilized, as the metaphor would have it, in preparation for his service to God's people under the auspices of the Archdiocese of Buenos Aires. He had a sense of his budding fertility, albeit an untraditional one in many people's eyes, which would manifest itself in his looming ability to propagate the faith through consoling, healing, and leading the faithful.

I remember something a missionary priest told me many years ago: "My parishioners give me more hugs than I could ever have gotten from a single woman in a marriage. These hugs give me almost divine consolation."

Bergoglio's decision to turn his back on romantic love should not be interpreted the easy way, the way I had looked at it, the way most non-Catholics and many Catholics do. Clerical celibacy does not equate with a renunciation of intimacy. It depends on how one defines intimacy and what one expects from it.

When I walked the streets of Buenos Aires searching for Pope Francis's past and seeking out his spiritual secrets, I was struck by all the hugging and kissing going on around me. Infants were in the arms of their parents; teenage lovers, of course, were everywhere on the spring days; I saw women and men hugging elderly mothers and fathers, and young children on blankets snuggling their parents. This was all so foreign to this Irish American who grew up with familial love but few outward displays of affection.

When I watch Pope Francis light up as he hugs a person with developmental differences or a child, when I see the joy in his face as he celebrates the weddings of twenty couples in St. Peter's Basilica at the Vatican—including some couples who had lived together before marriage and one who had a child out of wedlock—I think back to the streets of Buenos Aires and to Bergoglio's decision to forgo the pursuit of the smart, pretty girl at the wedding and return to his seminary. The man is rooted in intimacy—in his Argentine culture, among his friends, and especially in his spirituality—and he knew he would get enough of it, was wise enough to know that even at age twenty. By renouncing sexual activity, he was able to embrace a wider intimacy.

8 Illness

In August 1957, an inflammation of the lining of Bergoglio's lungs worsened despite a heavy dosage of antibiotics. He was rushed to the Syrian-Lebanese Hospital near Villa Devoto, where surgeons removed three pulmonary cysts and part of his upper right lung. He spent five days in an oxygen tent and then a brutal month of painful recovery during which doctors pumped saline solution into his chest to wash away the dead tissue of his lung lining.

It is difficult to imagine the robust Pope Francis of today in a fevered, anguished state as a young man, but Dr. Fabian Garcia, who specializes in internal medicine in Buenos Aires, can picture the scene:

> The first thing you have to know is that Syrian-Lebanese Hospital was originally started as an assistance center, a place where immigrants with no money or no place to go could find shelter. It was turned into a hospital about thirty years before Bergoglio went there. It was a middle-class public hospital then and now, so he was not in the best hospital in Buenos Aires.
>
> I have seen many older patients today who had the same radiology as Pope Francis did, and they had tuberculosis— it was a common diagnosis and treatment in those days, but many doctors did not call it tuberculosis.

And what he had was not common at all for a healthy twenty-year-old male—he had to have known that he was close to death. It was a common cause of death in those days.

I asked him whether the illness would have been painful.

There was medication, but in those days patients who complained at all were looked down upon by doctors. It is only in the last ten to fifteen years that doctors in Argentina have focused on managing pain. Pain management is a new approach in our country.

Garcia's comments are particularly revealing when you hear Pope Francis talk about this illness. He credits a nurse who tripled his dose of medicine for saving his life because "she was daringly astute. She knew what to do because she was with ill people all day." The doctor, according to Pope Francis, "lived in a laboratory," while the nurse "lived on the frontier and was in dialogue with it every day."

It is noteworthy that Pope Francis said that the nurse "lived on the frontier." That is an image the Jesuits use to describe their own work. At the age of twenty, he knew the Jesuits well, because even though Villa Devoto was a diocesan seminary, the Jesuits were asked to run it from its founding on March 29, 1623. "It is not uncommon for this to happen," Fr. Hernán Paredes, a Jesuit and former student of Pope Francis, told me. "Most Catholics know that Jesuits specialize in education, and the Villa Devoto administrators surely wanted Jesuits running the place because of their pedagogical skills." The Jesuits ran Villa Devoto until 1960, except for a time when they were suppressed in the late eighteenth century. Bergoglio would enter the Jesuit order in 1958. Perhaps he knew, lying in his hospital bed day after day, that he was imitating, by life's whims, the founder of the religious order he was soon to enter.

While Ignatius was recovering from his battle wounds, he read books on the lives of saints and Christ. He was drawn to *The Imitation of Christ*, according to Fr. John O'Malley in his book *The First Jesuits*, because of "the call to inwardness, to reflection and self-awareness. . . . *The Imitation* purported to speak to the heart and from the heart."

Ignatius's conversion would transform the Catholic Church with the creation of the Jesuit order and introduce to the world what is commonly called Ignatian spirituality. The idea of motion within Ignatius, of feeling his whole being go from a selfish, suffering state to a new and more joyful one, was always the most salient part of the story for me when I heard it at my Jesuit high school or Jesuit college. The idea that a person could feel an internal movement toward God, the almost physical sensation of it, was what I liked most.

My first experience with Ignatian spirituality took place at Holy Cross with an old Jesuit named Fr. Joseph LaBran, who had the thickest Boston accent I had ever heard. LaBran walked around campus with a cowboy hat on his head and a shillelagh in his hand. At night, he would wander into the student pub, sit down next to students, and talk. When he saw me, with his blue eyes twinkling, he would shout, "Shriiiiver!"

He would drag out certain vowels with that Boston accent for what seemed like minutes. "Are you coming to the reeetreeeat this month?"

Before I could answer, he would blurt out, "Noooo excuuuuses this time, young maaaan, you haaaave to come!"

I finally went during Christmas break of my senior year, and it was the best five days of my college experience. We stayed at a beautiful retreat center in Narragansett, Rhode Island. After welcoming us all, LaBran gave a five-minute talk and then told us to go off, in silence, to think about what he had said.

We reconvened a few hours later.

Again, LaBran spoke for a short time, then asked us to go off and think about these words, too. This routine of a short talk by LaBran, in which he would share a poem or a prayer or a short essay, filled our days and nights. We were not allowed to talk during the retreat; silence was observed at meals as well. But we were encouraged to meet with LaBran or one of the other priests on the retreat, if we were so moved.

Two days into the retreat, I finally went in to meet with LaBran. I felt at peace, yet confused about my future.

LaBran smiled widely, his eyes twinkling even more than usual.

"Yahweeeeh!" he yelled. The Old Testament word for God sat on his lips for a good ten seconds. "Yahweh is working in you!" He was more excited than ever. "Go back and listen to Yahweh, try to hear what God is saying to you, Mark. Yahweh is in everything and in everybody. Try to discern Yahweh's voice!"

That's it? That's all you're going to say to me, Father?

He raised his hands, fists clenched now. "Shriiiiverrrr," he shouted, "discern Yahweh's voice!"

He shook his fists and smiled. I got up and went for a walk.

What does "Discern Yahweh's voice" mean? How do you do that?

LOOKING BACK ON my time with the Jesuits, I suppose that there are three fundamental concepts that best define most of the Jesuits I have met and, I have a hunch, define Francis, too.

The first is the idea of formation, the long studying and training that take most Jesuits a minimum of eleven years to complete before they are finally ordained. By comparison, a diocesan priest goes to seminary for four years after graduating from college; if he has entered the seminary out of high school, he attends for eight years before becoming a priest.

The second is the notion of community, embodied in the little villages in which all Jesuits live side by side with other Jesuits, be it in missions in the Third World, university communities in America, or retreat centers where Jesuits engage in Ignatius's spiritual retreat, the Spiritual Exercises. These are not monasteries, nor are they diocesan homes where many priests live alone or with another priest or two. The Jesuit communities are active, bustling places where ideas, disagreement, and accomplishments are matched, measured, and refined.

But it is the third key Jesuit characteristic that most applies to Bergoglio's illness and his decision to leave the diocesan seminary for the Jesuit path. It's discernment—what LaBran implored me to undertake when I was twenty-one. Discernment is, in the words of the Jesuit priest Mark Thibodeaux, "the Ignatian way to discover God's will." This means that the best route to determine God's will is not to go out into the world and search, but to burrow deep inside yourself and listen for God there. Thibodeaux calls it "God's voice within," and hearing it requires a lot of practice and patience.

In his book *God's Voice Within*, Thibodeaux writes:

Ignatius was a keen student of human nature, a beloved spiritual master, and a superb decision maker. Through his own experiences (both in his daily life and in his prayer), he came to understand an important truth: God desires for us to make good decisions and will help us do so. All we need to do, besides having a good intention, is not only rely on our (literally) God-given reason but also pay attention to the movements of our heart, which was also given to us by God.

We all face a series of critical decisions every day of our lives, and every few years we likely face one as big as the one Bergoglio faced during his illness. I believe that through the pain of his illness, Bergoglio felt that movement of the heart, and it took him down a path that would seem to forever preclude him from becoming pope, for no Jesuit had ever been pope. The irony is that the very process he likely used to decide to leave Villa Devoto, forgo the idea of becoming a diocesan priest, and enter the Jesuit order—this Ignatian discernment—was both the cause and the result of his decision. During his process of searching for God's voice within, Bergoglio surely realized that he was going through the Ignatian process of discernment itself. He left one life for another because the interior spirituality of that new life led him there.

The grand result of this hospital-bed conversion—I don't think that word is an exaggeration, though it is hard to compare anyone's experience to that of Saint Ignatius—would play out over the next fifty-plus years. Bergoglio's relationship with the Jesuit order would have great highs and great lows, but the first step on that journey was a trip to the interior—the interior of Argentina and the interior of his own soul.

9   A Novice

When I was twenty-one years old and starting my senior year at the College of the Holy Cross, I lived with nine buddies in what was called a "triple decker"—a house that had three separate apartments, one atop another. One of my roommates was a fellow named Tim Royston, whom I had known since our senior year of high school.

Tim was a member of the Naval Reserve Officers' Training Corps (ROTC) program at Holy Cross. After his sophomore year, he elected the Marine option in ROTC, which involved extra training and prepared him to become a second lieutenant in the Marine Corps after graduation. He ultimately became an F-18 fighter pilot.

When we lived with Tim our senior year, his routine surprised all of us. The rest of the gang and I were used to staying up late, getting up late, and being disorganized. But not Tim.

The Marines trained him to be very well organized and extremely disciplined. His clothes were clean and folded in his drawers. He even put his initials on them, afraid that we would "borrow" them—and he was right, we did, a lot. His desk was impeccable; the books were always in their proper place, as were the pens and paper. And he was at physical training (PT) at 6:30 A.M. three days a week, without fail. Every other month, he went on a day-and-a-half-long field exercise, which meant that he was up at 5:00 A.M. Saturday and gone until Sunday afternoon.

By the time I awoke most Saturday afternoons, Tim had already put in a full day of hard work.

It took a while for me to realize it, but the Marines were changing Tim's approach to school and work—to life, really—and the change was fundamental. Tim was not just going through the motions to get his college scholarship. His body was changing—his five-foot-eight-inch frame was becoming more solid, his hair was now cut "high and tight"—not much more than peach fuzz on his head. As his routine changed, his thinking changed, too. He still played rugby and laughed and had a good time, but he was becoming a full-fledged Marine who knew that war and death were real possibilities.

The Jesuits have long been referred to as God's army or God's soldiers, willing to go anywhere at any time for God. Numerous Jesuits have told me that the Jesuits are trained to have "one foot up and a bag ready"—to be prepared to move, in other words, whenever the call comes. This willingness to go to "any frontier" was the vision of Saint Ignatius, who founded the Society of Jesus in 1540, a time when the immensity and variety of the world were just being realized. Ships were traveling the seas; new lands and peoples were being discovered; a rising merchant class was enlivening cities; the Renaissance was reinvigorating learning; and reform movements within the Catholic Church were picking up steam. These times demanded a new, movable kind of religious order, and Ignatius offered the people of his times a practical, down-to-earth spirituality that was open to all, meeting people where they were and committed to addressing needs no one else would. Ignatius wanted his Jesuits to be out and about, not in a monastery but on the road. They would be "contemplatives in action," as the first Jesuits put it, monks in the midst of the new worldliness that began with Columbus and other explorers and coursed through the Renaissance.

"I ultimately entered the Society of Jesus," Bergoglio told his biographers, "because I was attracted to its position on, to put it in military terms, the front lines of the Church, grounded in obedience and discipline. It was also due to its focus on missionary work. I later had an urge to become a missionary in Japan, where Jesuits have carried out important work for many years. But due to the severe health issues I'd had since my youth, I wasn't allowed."

The Jesuits' commitment to obedience, discipline, and missionary work all attracted Bergoglio, but there was another element: community. While the order nowadays is referred to as the Society of Jesus, the original name was the Company of Jesus—the term "company" signifying companionship. For Jesuits, this "company" means a group of friends living and working together, serving Christ and his people. That sense of togetherness clearly appealed to Bergoglio. In a September 2013 interview for *America* magazine, he explained, "I was always looking for a community. I did not see myself as a priest on my own. I need a community. And you can tell this by the fact that I am here in Santa Marta [the Vatican guesthouse]. . . . I cannot live without people. I need to live my life with others."

In 1958, as Bergoglio and his parents approached the door of the imposing Jesuit building called the Novitiate, on the outskirts of Córdoba, surrounded by empty fields, they surely knew the Jesuits' reputation. As a Jesuit novice, Bergoglio was committing to the first two years of at least a decade-long process of formation, of shaping one's mind and spirit. But the deeper reality was that he had come to begin a new life—to join the religious equivalent of the Marines—and in so doing, abruptly end his youth.

Jesuit novices knew that Ignatius wanted his followers to be mentally and spiritually disciplined; they needed to be grounded in their tradition, able to think on their feet, and ready to adapt to novel situations. This process began in the novitiate, under the tutelage of a novice master. In a centuries-old tradition, an unvarying routine of prayer, study, housework, local ministry, and living in community were critical to forming the Jesuit novice.

Central to the novitiate was a thirty-day, mostly silent retreat based on the Spiritual Exercises of Saint Ignatius that would take place six months in. The Spiritual Exercises are unique to the Jesuit order and distinguish a Jesuit from a Dominican or a Franciscan or a diocesan priest. Guided by the novice master or another spiritual director, the novice exercises his soul in a form of spiritual boot camp. As he confronts the reality of his strengths and limitations, as he reckons with his past and taps into desires for his future, the novice Jesuit discovers how God is calling him to live his life.

If all went well, at the end of two years, Bergoglio would profess vows of poverty, chastity, and obedience and then become a "scholastic," or a student, and enter the next stage of formation, the juniorate. The juniorate, designed for young men who join the Jesuits without university education, is usually two or three years of studies focused on the humanities.

After the juniorate, the scholastic completes three years of philosophy studies and then is sent to work in a Jesuit ministry, usually in a Jesuit high school, to learn how to balance prayer, study, and work, like any fully formed Jesuit. After this period of ministry in the "real world," the scholastic requests permission to study theology for three more years, in preparation for ordination. During his theology studies—more than seven years after setting foot in the Novitiate—Bergoglio would ask the Jesuit provincial to be ordained as a priest. Though the local bishop makes the ultimate decision on whether to ordain, the bishop often defers to the judgment of the Jesuit provincial. Should the answer be yes, Bergoglio would be ordained a priest and then be sent—somewhere.

Maybe it would be to get a Ph.D., or maybe to teach, or maybe to work in a parish. Whatever the assignment, after a few years as a priest, Bergoglio would enter tertianship. Tertianship is remarkably like the novitiate in that the wiser, older Jesuit goes back and studies the founding documents of the Jesuits, lives in a community, works with the poor, and makes another thirty-day, mostly silent retreat.

At the end of tertianship, which usually lasts about nine months, the Jesuit professes final vows. Some, but not all, Jesuits are called to profess an additional fourth vow prescribed by Ignatius—a vow of obedience to the pope with respect to missions. In Ignatius's time, this vow meant that the pope could literally send a Jesuit to another land as a missionary. Today, the pope relies on the fourth vow to "mission" the Jesuits to address pressing needs such as revitalizing the Church in Eastern Europe after the fall of the Berlin Wall or leading institutes of higher learning around the world. Wherever and whatever the need is, the Jesuits go. The fourth vow, which also enables a Jesuit to assume positions of leadership within the order, is a reminder of the Jesuits' vocation to be available, to have one foot up, ready to go to the next frontier where they are needed most.

With such a rigorous and prolonged path ahead of her son, it was no wonder that Regina wept uncontrollably as she said goodbye to him that day, March 28, 1958. Surely Bergoglio and his parents knew that, given the military-like regimen of the Jesuits, he wasn't just entering adulthood; he was enrolling in an order to which he would offer himself entirely. Bergoglio was joining another family, and Regina, no doubt, grasped it in her core, and so she wept like many a mother of a child stepping across a threshold into a new stage of life that permanently revokes the prior one.

Bergoglio and his superiors would say he was subjecting himself to God's will for the rest of his life, and yes, that was true. But God's will would be lived out in a community of men and mediated by men. This is key for a Jesuit—they profess their vows within a community, they share goods, they live and pray together, they work in a common ministry. And once he took the vow of obedience, Bergoglio would have to ask for permission for everything—to continue his studies, to take vacations, to travel. These men were about to train him, discipline him, shape him, and send him to all corners of the continent, or of the world.

WHEN I WENT to Córdoba—to the "interior," as Argentines call it—I had just spent a couple of weeks in Buenos Aires, and it was an abrupt change in both geography and style. Given the geographical difference and the blue-collar feel of Córdoba, especially compared to the cosmopolitan vibe of Buenos Aires, I have to believe that Bergoglio, who had never been to Córdoba, felt a similarly jarring sensation.

But Bergoglio also had to feel as if he was journeying to one of the intellectual capitals of Latin America. For centuries, Córdoba had thrived as a center of learning, of intellectual and academic life. The first university in Argentina and the fourth-oldest university in South America, National University of Córdoba was founded in 1613. Today, the city is home to six universities and several postsecondary colleges, with students from throughout Argentina as well as from neighboring countries.

"Córdoba, throughout Argentinian history, always had that cachet as a place for thinkers and writers," said Fr. Miguel Petty, a Jesuit priest and contemporary of Bergoglio who studied in England for three years. Born in Argentina, Petty is a tall man with a commanding presence, silver hair, a warm smile, and a strong British accent. He began his Jesuit novitiate in Córdoba in 1951 when he was eighteen years old. "I don't think it was a coincidence that the Jesuit order maintained its novitiate there. The location of the novitiate was removed from the bustle of Córdoba by distance, but not philosophically."

Petty described the building and its inner workings vividly:

The actual Jesuit Novitiate building was a stark and forbidding building on the outside, the thick brick walls lacking the typical Argentinian plaster. The house was composed of two cloisters; at the front was the juniorate and at the back was the novitiate. The novitiate had the form of a cloister, three boys to a room, with curtains separating cubicles for each one. In the novitiate cloister garden, there were four lovely palm trees. For an early morning shower we had to walk around one hundred meters to the big shower room and then dash back, whatever the weather. We had to go down one floor to the huge dining room, where juniors sat on one side and novices on the other. In the middle of the room, there was a pulpit from which readings took place during meals.

Apart from the formation of mind, heart, and soul rooted in the Spiritual Exercises, Bergoglio lived a life that few, save perhaps military service members, can fully comprehend. The regimentation of their time reflected the martial nature of the order in general. Each day at the Novitiate was structured around periods of prayer, both alone and with other novices. When not at prayer, Bergoglio would have read various spiritual classics and attended lectures on the history of the Jesuits, the founding constitutions that prescribe their way of life, and the ideals of poverty, chastity, and obedience.

Add to this regimen meetings with his novice master to discuss his spiritual life and discernment, manual labor around the house, and forays into the surrounding community to perform work in hospitals, schools, and homes, and you have two years' worth of intense testing of a young man's spiritual mettle.

I find a breakdown of Bergoglio's day useful to the imagination. As corroborated by Javier Cámara and Sebastián Pfaffen in their fine book on the role Córdoba played in Pope Francis's life and formation, his day looked like this:

6:00 A.M. Rise to the sound of a bell, kneel by his bed, and immediately pray the Te Deum (a traditional Catholic hymn of praise) in Latin. Wash and dress.

7:00 A.M. Rush to the chapel in silence and say communal prayer.

7:30 A.M. Morning mass, in Latin and with the presiding priest's back to the novices, as was the custom prior to Vatican II reforms.

8:15 A.M. Breakfast in silence, followed by one hour of manual labor. Bergoglio would read his assigned task—clean toilets, wash dishes, etc.—on a chalkboard in the dining room. The rest of the morning would be spent in classes in Latin, Greek, and public speaking.

12:00 P.M. The first Examen, a prayer of discernment.

1:00 P.M. Lunch. Bergoglio or one of his peers would read a spiritual lesson or passage of Jesuit history aloud while the rest of the novices and Jesuit priests listened and ate in silence. On Mondays, Wednesdays, and Fridays, to emphasize, or inculcate, the vow of poverty, some novices would not be served and they would have to beg for food from the others.

2:00 P.M. A brief prayer session in the chapel, followed by fifteen minutes of recreation in the courtyard. These would be the only minutes of the day when Bergoglio and his peers were permitted to speak Spanish. Even this activity was regimented: The young men had to walk in groups of three, one group facing the other, so one group always had to walk backward!

2:30 P.M. Thirty minutes for a nap.

3:00 P.M. A communal prayer, followed by two hours of classes on the constitutions of the Jesuit order, Jesuit history, and Church history.

5:00 P.M. A snack.

5:30 P.M. Soccer or basketball two or three times a week, followed by a cold shower and then an hour of spiritual reading, thirty minutes for prayer, and fifteen minutes for private meetings with the novice master or other staff.

8:00 P.M. Dinner, which always included a soup that the novices helped to serve. Bergoglio, or a colleague, would practice his rhetorical skills in front of the group while the others ate in silence. Dinner was followed by another short recreation period during which the novices would chat in the corridors.

9:30 P.M. The second Examen and one last visit to chapel for a final prayer.

10:00 P.M. Sleep.

More than a place, the novitiate is a state of mind, a spiritual and psychological passage for incoming Jesuits. And the orchestrator of it all—part drill sergeant, part teacher, part mentor and brother—would be his novice master, a Jesuit priest named Francisco Zaragozí.

Petty entered the novitiate under Zaragozí, too, and he grows wistful when he reflects on who Zaragozí was and what he meant to him:

Physically, he was short; his health was not always good. He would measure his words very carefully. When we had to report to him, he said very little, but whatever he did say was immensely important to us. We dearly loved him. We had great confidence in his assessments of us, and when he told us at the end of year two that we could make our first vows, we felt our vocation was assured.

He was a very austere man. He had to be very careful about his diet, but he was fun when he would sit around and chat with us. He would take us off to the hills to make holes in the ground, sometimes even through the bare rock, for later planting pine trees. It was tough work, in the cold early mornings, but we loved it. I remember he sent me to work in a brewery, and my job was to paste labels onto bottles. Nobody was supposed to know that we were novices, but I think now that most people must have known. He had a catchword—*está claro*—that meant he had everything under control.

But Zaragozí almost wasn't Bergoglio's novice master. It is uncanny to think about how Bergoglio's trajectory might have been different if he had not been. From one of those rare admissions of dislike on the part of Pope Francis, we know that the novice master when he arrived, Fr. Cándido Gaviña, was not to his liking:

Gaviña was a very reserved, serious, good, and tactful man. But I did not get along very well with him; also, at one point, later on, he even suggested I should consider leaving the novitiate. I remember that on one occasion, I told him I could not tolerate his way of being; he was very Colombian in his habits and I was very direct, so that is why we did not understand each other very well.

Petty explained that "to Argentines, Colombians can seem very formal, almost pompous. And that formal nature meant that Gaviña often beat around the bush."

The frankness of Bergoglio's statement is shocking—as is the key fact that Bergoglio's novice director suggested that Bergoglio give up his Jesuit aspirations.

But in July 1958, just four months after he began his novitiate,

Bergoglio got his first taste of how quickly Jesuits can be reassigned when Gaviña moved on to become provincial of Argentina, to be replaced by the more affable and spiritual Zaragozí. This change no doubt impacted Bergoglio's life as much as any other single twist of chance he would experience. Zaragozí would teach him the Ignatian way of life, would direct him in Ignatius's Spiritual Exercises, and would provide the spiritual coaching and information that Bergoglio absorbed as a young man and later used to transform himself and, eventually, his church.

"Bergoglio always talked about the impact Zaragozí had on him," Father Paredes, Bergoglio's former student, recalled. "He would tell us stories about how holy Zaragozí was, how he would pray with such sincerity and purity. We got the sense that Zaragozí awoke in Bergoglio not just the habit but the rage for prayer that he has to this day. I had never met a man who prayed as much and as deeply as Bergoglio. When he told us he didn't even come close to Zaragozí, well, I could only imagine how pious Zaragozí was and what an example he set for the novices back then."

"Piety" is a tricky word. Today, when you hear someone called pious, the adjective usually implies sanctimony, a holier-than-thou bearing. But it has its root in *pietas*, the Latin word for dutifulness. Bergoglio was taught the ritual and routine of prayer by his grandmother; the practice was nurtured by the Salesians and further refined by Zaragozí and the Jesuits. The "habit," the "rage for prayer"—clearly, both the novice master and the novice saw prayer as a welcome duty that gave meaning to their daily lives.

My friend Fr. Kevin O'Brien, dean of the Jesuit School of Theology at Santa Clara University, explained that comparing the relationship between a novice and a novice master to the one between a patient and a psychotherapist is a common but false analogy for the Ignatian spiritual director:

In therapy, the therapist usually takes an active approach in caring for the person, and the focus of care is on the person's mental and emotional health. In the Jesuit tradition, the role of the spiritual director—we don't call them novice masters nowadays, and they can be men or women—is to help the person grow closer to God, and he or she is careful not to interfere with that primary relationship. The focus is on the person's spiritual and religious life, but because one's faith is affected by and lived out in all aspects of life, they may discuss how one's emotional life, their relationships, their commitments at work and school, and their intellectual pursuits help or hinder their spiritual life. Every good spiritual director knows his or her limits and refers to other professionals when matters go deeply into mental and emotional health.

"Every good spiritual director also knows that formation is not an assembly line," O'Brien continued.

Surely there is a molding that takes place—you leave a former life and are introduced to a new one, and that requires being enculturated into a new way of life with other men in a new community, based on a centuries-old tradition. You have to learn the structure, the daily routine, and how to live in a brotherhood. Yet adaptation is key in Jesuit life. Trying to follow God's lead, the spiritual director knows when to stick to the rules and when to be flexible, especially with a group of novices from very different backgrounds and ages. He has to have good intuition and judgment, or in Jesuit language, he has to be very discerning in approach.

If Zaragozí provided the constant shaping of Bergoglio's mind and spirit in Córdoba, then another man's appearance, albeit brief, would provide a jolt of divine electricity to Bergoglio and his fellow novices. In 1959, the iconic Pedro Arrupe, who would become Superior General of the Jesuit Order globally in 1965, visited the novitiates in Córdoba.

Even though he had not yet attained the international fame that would accrue to him as Superior General, Arrupe already had a stellar reputation within the Jesuit order. He lived and worked in Japan prior to the Pearl Harbor attack; he was arrested shortly thereafter, imprisoned, and kept in solitary confinement for thirty-three days. On August 6, 1945, he was in Nagatsuka, just outside Hiroshima, where he was novice master, when the atomic bomb was dropped. He turned the novitiate into a temporary hospital, caring for more than one hundred fifty victims. In 1958, the Jesuits made Japan a province and named Arrupe the first provincial. His missionary courage and devotion would inspire millions and would make him one of the most famous Jesuits in history.

Arrupe embodied the Jesuitical ideal of the priest as frontiersman. If, as some theologians say, Jesus Christ was the second Adam, then Arrupe was the second Ignatius, fulfilling the vision of the original man and expanding it for the modern world. Arrupe, who almost completed medical studies before entering the Jesuits, embodied Ignatius's ideal Jesuit: a "contemplative in action." Arrupe was thoughtful but charismatic; loyal to his Basque origins but global in his spiritual and political convictions; a go-to leader yet an inspiring priest and pastor.

We know Arrupe gave a talk to the novices. We know Bergoglio emerged from that talk convinced that he wanted to go to Japan to minister there. Having spoken with many of Bergoglio's friends, I believe Bergoglio saw clearly that day in Córdoba not only the life he wanted to live, but the man he wanted to become. I have a feeling he heard words like these—a prayer attributed to Arrupe—and devoured them with all his head, heart, and soul:

Nothing is more practical than finding God, that is, than falling in love in a quite absolute, final way. What you are in love with, what seizes your imagination, will affect everything. It will decide what will get you out of bed in the morning, what you will do with your evenings, how you will spend your weekends, what you read, who you know, what breaks your heart, and what amazes you with joy and gratitude. Fall in love, stay in love, and it will decide everything.

As a young novice, Jorge Mario Bergoglio was taking the first steps to understanding the faith and love described in Arrupe's prayer. These days, when I read this prayer, I hear Bergoglio's voice, but as we shall see, it would take Bergoglio years to completely incarnate this prayer. He would shoot up the Jesuit ranks with startling swiftness, and he would have numerous encounters with Arrupe. But the next step on the journey for the young novice would be to stretch his soul in that most Jesuit of pursuits, the Spiritual Exercises.

10 The Spiritual Exercises

Six months after he had arrived in Córdoba, and now firmly under Zaragozí's tutelage, Bergoglio undertook a thirty-day journey deep into the self in search of God's voice: the Spiritual Exercises.

The Spiritual Exercises are not like other well-known spiritual classics that inspire by their reading. Instead, the book is like a cookbook or instruction manual for the soul. A collection of prayers and insights, some based on scripture, others derived from Ignatius's imagination, the Exercises were written over many months of intensive prayer and spiritual discipline. The content is not entirely new, as Ignatius draws on traditions familiar in his time. What is unique is how he puts it all together—bringing those traditions so compellingly to life that people are still making the Spiritual Exercises nearly five hundred years after Ignatius devised them.

The Exercises are to be experienced more than read. And they are life-changing for many. Many Jesuits have told me that the Spiritual Exercises are not about behavior modification but rather about developing a deep, heartfelt commitment to God. The best description of the Spiritual Exercises comes from Ignatius himself, who wrote that their purpose is "the conquest of self and the regulation of one's life in such a way that no decision is made under the influence of any inordinate attachment." The Spiritual Exercises provide a structure that facilitates an ongoing conversation with God, so that one is better able to discern God's will.

"The Exercises demand that the person fully engage them. They rely on the memory and the imagination, the mind and the heart. The Jesuit or anyone making the Exercises must both think and feel their way through them," Father O'Brien told me. That balancing of intellect and emotion is perhaps the definitive achievement of Ignatius. In Ignatius's view, these are two ways to approach God, and the Exercises embrace both. All the while, whether one is thinking intensely or feeling intensely, the retreatant experiences what Ignatius called movements of the soul.

Ignatius provided different ways of making the Spiritual Exercises. The most traditional form is what Bergoglio experienced as a novice: the thirty-day retreat. Other versions of the Spiritual Exercises can be given over a weekend, or over five days, as I experienced them at Holy Cross, or the full Exercises over eight months in the midst of one's daily life. Jesuits are required to make an eight-day silent retreat each year.

The thirty-day version is broken into four segments, which Ignatius calls weeks, though they are sometimes longer or shorter than calendar weeks. These "weeks" begin with some important preparation: The retreatant is to focus on God's goodness in creating and sustaining the world and on God's unconditional love for each person. This very hope-filled view of the world marks Ignatius's way of relating to others: God is at work in all persons, in all of their beauty and brokenness.

Yet Ignatius was not naive. He knew that we all have a darker side. In spite of God's goodness, we often choose selfishness and ingratitude. The retreatant has to grapple with this conflict in the "First Week" of the Exercises. It is the most self-centered time of the retreat. I don't mean this in a negative way. The retreatant does some real soul-searching, taking stock of patterns of sin and self-preoccupation, fears and failings, joys and hopes. As O'Brien told me, "Getting in touch with one's interior life is hard, especially with so many distractions and temptations that work against the solitude and silence necessary for such interior work. It is hard to face the truth of who we are: beautiful but broken sinners. But such examination leads to rich insights: With awareness comes freedom, liberation from all the baggage that holds us back from loving more generously and clutters our life's purpose. This is not navel-gazing or psychotherapy but real inner freedom that comes because the retreatant experiences God's merciful love."

I tried to discern interior movements when I went on the five-day retreat, and I believe I did. But toward the end of the retreat, I longed for my college buddies and college parties, and I didn't go on another retreat for twenty-eight years. It is difficult, and unnerving, work.

The "Second Week," or second phase, shifts from the analysis of the self to a study of the life and work of Jesus Christ. "The heart of the retreat is meeting Jesus, who invites each person—like the disciples—to join him on a mission," O'Brien said. "Energized by the merciful love of God, the person naturally wants to extend that mercy to others. This part of the retreat—the longest—challenges us to become like Christ's disciples, healing, serving, teaching, and helping others."

In this "week," Ignatius borrows from the medieval practice of using one's imagination to put oneself in the scene with Jesus. The retreatant is even given permission to imagine the scene beyond the exact written words of the Gospels.

This intense use of imagination carries over into the "Third Week," during which the reflections and conversations with the spiritual director focus exclusively on Christ's Last Supper, passion, and death. Now, these are clearly not groundbreaking topics for reflection, but what does make the Exercises unique is this continued insistence on intense imagining. I have spoken with Jesuits who tell me that they use their imagination so deeply that they can almost feel Christ's fear in the Garden of Gethsemane, his pain under the lashings, and his desolation on the Cross. Saint Ignatius was by no means the most beautiful writer or poet in religious history, but his insistent reliance on imagination has helped countless people in their faith life.

During the "Fourth Week," the retreatant meditates on Jesus's resurrection and his meeting with his disciples. Ignatius even adds a meditation on something not in the Bible: Jesus going to meet his mother, Mary, after the resurrection to console her. The word "consolation" is key for Ignatius. God wants to console us and help us, and Jesus does exactly that both in his earthly life and in his risen life.

The movement of the heart here, according to many people who have done the full thirty-day Exercises, replicates the sense of resurrection in that one often feels one's own self rising, lifting above the worldly concerns and ambitions that plague us. Father Petty described the thirty-day retreat as "living up in the clouds, and how strange it was to come back to the real world after the month's Exercises."

The first abiding lesson from the Spiritual Exercises is experiencing God's unconditional love and mercy and the desire to share that love and mercy with others. Ignatius concludes the Exercises with a simple yet profound observation: "Love ought to show itself more by deeds than by words."

This first lesson is critical to understanding Pope Francis. In one of his very first homilies as pope, he said, "I think we, too, are the people who, on the one hand, want to listen to Jesus, but on the other hand, at times, like to find a stick to beat others with, to condemn others. And Jesus has this message for us: mercy. I think—and I say it with humility—that this is the Lord's most powerful message: mercy."

When I first read those words, I saw "mercy" as an intellectual, theological concept and believed that Pope Francis simply wanted me to be nicer to people. But Pope Francis is talking about mercy at a completely different level: He sees mercy as a deeply personal, lived experience that changes the very essence of who we are and how we interact with others.

The Spiritual Exercises taught him to be aware of his own sinfulness, his brokenness, but the Exercises also taught him that God's merciful love was there not despite his sinfulness and brokenness but because of it. In other words, God's mercy and love are unconditional and endure forever.

The clearest example of this lesson for Bergoglio occurred on the morning of September 21, 1953, at the Basilica of San José de Flores.

September 21 is the feast day of Saint Matthew, who, before becoming a disciple of Jesus, was a hated tax collector. The story goes that Jesus saw Matthew sitting at work and said to him, "Follow me." Matthew got up and followed Jesus. When Jesus was later criticized for associating with the likes of Matthew, he said, "I desire mercy, not sacrifice. I did not come to call the righteous but sinners." Much has been written about Jesus's gesture, but the words of an eighth-century English monk, the Venerable Bede, resonate most with Bergoglio. Bede wrote that Jesus's call to Matthew was *miserando atque eligendo*," which means "because he saw him through the eyes of mercy and chose him."

Bergoglio felt that on September 21, 1953, when he was confessing his sins, Christ reached out with mercy and chose him to become a priest just as Christ had reached out with mercy to Matthew, a sinner, and chose him to be one of the twelve disciples.

In the *America* magazine interview, Pope Francis said he often visited the Church of St. Louis of France when he was in Rome, where he would "contemplate the painting of *The Calling of St. Matthew* by Caravaggio." I visited the church when I was in Rome in 2015 and was surprised to find such a masterpiece in a dimly lit area. I dropped some change into a box to turn on the light above the painting and stared at the image of Jesus pointing to Matthew. Matthew is pointing at himself as if to say, "Who, me?"

"That finger of Jesus, pointing at Matthew. That's me," Bergoglio said in that interview. "I feel like him. Like Matthew . . . It is the gesture of Matthew that strikes me: He holds on to his money as if to say, 'No, not me! No, this money is mine.' Here, this is me, a sinner on whom the Lord has turned his gaze. And this is what I said when they asked me if I would accept my election as pontiff. . . . I am a sinner, but I trust in the infinite mercy and patience of our Lord Jesus Christ, and I accept in a spirit of penance."

Mercy is revealed in personal, concrete, tangible ways—in deeds—

and for Bergoglio, the call to the priesthood was real; it was God's mercy in action despite his own personal sinfulness and hesitation. So, too, was the call to be pope a tangible, mercy-filled action of God directed at him, a sinner.

When Bergoglio was named an auxiliary bishop, he chose Bede's words *miserando atque eligendo* — "because he saw him through the eyes of mercy and chose him" — for his episcopal motto to remind himself, and all of us, that God's loving mercy endures forever. He has kept that motto as pope.

And in early April 2015, Pope Francis officially announced the Extraordinary Jubilee Year of Mercy, to begin on December 8, 2015. At first this didn't mean much to me, because I had no idea what a "Jubilee Year" was, but I soon learned that Jubilee Years are typically called by the pope every twenty-five years. When a special occasion arises outside that cycle, a pope calls an Extraordinary Jubilee. The 2015 jubilee was not in the twenty-five-year cycle. Pope Francis was obviously making a point, and he said so quite simply: "Mercy is the very foundation of the Church's life. The Church's very credibility is seen in how she shows merciful and compassionate love."

The December 8, 2015, date is highly symbolic. It is the fiftieth anniversary of the end of the Second Vatican Council, otherwise known as Vatican II—a pivotal moment that brought the Catholic Church into the modern world. Pope John XXIII convened Vatican II on October 11, 1962. In his opening address, he spoke about how, in the past, the Church dealt with errors of faith "with the greatest severity. Nowadays, however, the spouse of Christ prefers to make use of the medicine of mercy rather than of severity."

Pope Francis clearly chose the date to reinforce the importance of mercy.

A Jubilee Year of Mercy might appear to be little more than a theological concept, far removed from "concrete deeds." To underscore his true purpose, one month into the Year of Mercy, Pope Francis released a book entitled *The Name of God Is Mercy*. In it he explains why he proclaimed the Jubilee Year and shares stories. It is his examples of seemingly small, insignificant gestures—deeds—of mercy to others that strike me the most. He gives an example from his time as rector of Colegio Máximo:

> I remember a mother with young children, whose husband had left her. She did not have a steady job and only managed to find temporary jobs a couple of months out of the year. When there was no work, she had to prostitute herself to provide her children with food. She was humble, she came to the parish church, and we tried to help her with Caritas (our charity). I remember one day—it was during the Christmas holidays—she came with her children to the College and asked for me. They called me and I went to greet her. She had come to thank me. I thought it was for the package of food from Caritas that we had sent to her. "Did you receive it?" I asked. "Yes, yes, thank you for that, too. But I came here today to thank you because you never stopped calling me Señora."

This was not about being nice to the woman, or even feeding her; no, this was mercy at a different level: entering into her situation, into her chaos, and reading her heart's deepest needs—and responding accordingly. By praying and pondering on God's unlimited, loving mercy—and forgiveness—the retreatant is propelled to a new and deeper relationship with God, and with his fellow human beings.

The second key lesson from the Exercises is balancing the heart and the head. The Jesuits are known as an intellectually elite order, and they do indeed stock the faculties of some of the best universities and high schools in the world. But the Exercises are as much about listening to movements of the heart as refining one's intellect. Ignatius writes about a heartfelt kind of knowing, the type of knowing that we experience in friendships. In this case, he asks us to consider our relationship with God as a friendship of sorts. We see that throughout his life, Bergoglio has had deep respect for the hearts of people—yes, he can move in the highest theological circles, but he has long given equal attention to the movements of the heart. I believe the Exercises taught him this balance and led him to develop the strong connection with the people, *el pueblo*, that we will soon see in his work at Colegio Máximo and throughout his life.

Third, because Ignatius insists on the development and use of the imagination in approaching Christ during the Exercises, Bergoglio, I believe, realized the power of imagination in the religious experience and started to hone it for future use in homilies, in giving his own spiritual direction to young Jesuits, and on the public stage. Indeed, when I watch him gaze out at the adoring crowds during his addresses, he seems to be imagining what the world could be like if we all strove to live the gospel message more fully. I believe Francis, apart from insisting on mercy for the world as it is, also urges us to imagine along with him how it could be.

Ron Hansen, an award-winning novelist and professor at Santa Clara University, says it best when discussing the use of the imagination in the Spiritual Exercises:

> The method for each hour's meditation is generally the same. We begin with a preparatory prayer and as a prelude to the meditation consider the history of the subject, such as Jesus appearing to seven of his disciples as they fished (John 21:1–17), reading the gospel passage several times until we can develop a mental representation of the locale and the people in it. We then ask for a grace; in this case, it is to be consoled at seeing Christ on the shore and to feel the joy and comfort of his resurrection. We see the fishermen hauling in their nets on the Sea of Galilee, hear the smack of waves against the boat's hull, feel the sunshine on our skins, smell seaweed and brine, taste the water we scoop up in our palm. With all five senses wholly engaged, we become part of the scene and can be as shocked and happy as Peter was when he recognized that it was the risen Christ who was roasting a fish on a charcoal fire on the shore and plunged into the sea to wade to him. We hear Christ's instruction to Peter, and we also enter the conversation—or as Ignatius puts it, colloquy—inquiring, perhaps, on how we ourselves can feed his sheep or just saying, like Peter, "Lord, you know that I love you."

Last, a critical point of the Exercises is learning the movements of consolation and desolation. These are perhaps the most repeated words during the retreat. Father Thibodeaux, in his book *God's Voice Within*, defines these two concepts succinctly. Desolation, he writes, is "the state of being under the influence of the false spirit. . . . The false spirit [is] the 'inner pull' away from God's plan and away from faith, hope, and love. The false spirit is also referred to as the 'evil spirit' or 'the enemy of our human nature.'" In contrast, consolation is "the state of being under the influence of the true spirit. . . . The true spirit is the 'inner pull' toward God's plan and toward faith, hope, and love. It is also referred to as the 'good spirit.'" Throughout the Exercises, the retreatant learns very practical rules to discern these competing spirits at work in the person and within groups of people.

The notion of movement or motion runs throughout these definitions; we all experience these sensations moving within us as we live our lives, and as we shall see, Bergoglio would be no different. In his 2013 Apostolic Exhortation *Evangelii Gaudium* (*The Joy of the Gospel*), Pope Francis would write: "We need to distinguish clearly what might be a fruit of the kingdom from what runs counter to God's plan. This involves not only recognizing and discerning spirits, but also—and this is decisive—choosing movements of the spirit of good and rejecting those of the spirit of evil."

He would struggle with the movements of good and evil spirits throughout the coming years. But the recognition of them and the tools for discerning and managing them were developed here in Córdoba as a young man; as a middle-aged man in exile, he would come back to the place where he first made the Spiritual Exercises to regroup and try to discern the pull of that true spirit again.

Years later, in 2003, Cardinal Bergoglio told a politician: "Manuel, you've got to live your own exile. I did. And afterward you'll be back. And when you do come back, you will be more merciful, kinder, and you're going to want to serve your people more."

The Exercises, finally, are a sort of exile. Self-enforced, yes, but they entail an aggressive setting of oneself apart from the world, from habits, from routines. The retreatant encounters silence and solitude.

Coming out of them—or, better said, moving out of them—brings the sort of complex richness and depth Bergoglio refers to here. And though Ignatius prescribed that a Jesuit set aside time twice a day for discernment in a prayer he called the Examen, the deepest joy in Bergoglio's life came, I believe, when he realized he could continuously make a version of the Spiritual Exercises, all day long, every day of his life.

11 Colegio Máximo

On March 12, 1960, Bergoglio professed the vows of poverty, chastity, and obedience. He then spent a year in the juniorate in Santiago, Chile, reading Jesuit texts, studying the humanities, and expanding upon what he learned in the novitiate. In 1961, he entered Colegio Máximo in the town of San Miguel.

The drive to Colegio Máximo was supposed to take thirty to forty minutes, but as with almost everything else I had experienced in Buenos Aires, the timing was off. Forty minutes became fifty, and fifty became sixty.

The drive was not particularly scenic. The grand tree-lined boulevards of downtown Buenos Aires gave way to a nondescript highway, which gave way to smaller, tighter roads lined with fast-food joints and strip malls. As the time dragged on, I saw car repair shops and industrial parks.

"How much longer?" I whined to Miguel Calculli, the driver.

"Soon," he replied. "Very soon."

I liked Miguel. He always pointed out the sites in Buenos Aires: a government building here, the polo grounds there, a university building over that way. But Miguel was hardly ever on time for morning pickups, and he had a knack for finding every major traffic jam in the city. Or so it seemed. And he never gave a specific time for our arrival. But he always smiled and did not complain when the day dragged on and he worked later than he was supposed to.

The car repair shops and industrial parks were now giving way to clothing stores, knickknack shops, and fast-food places again. We were approaching a town—maybe Miguel was right after all.

"Is that it to my left?" I asked hopefully. A black fence had appeared, enclosing many well-landscaped acres. I could see a couple of buildings on the grounds.

We hit a red light.

"No." Miguel's answer was short. There was a pause. "No, that is Campo de Mayo. That is where the army trains. It is a huge military compound."

He paused.

"That is where many people were jailed in the 1970s and some of them disappeared. There were other bases that were bad, too, but Campo de Mayo wasn't a good place. There are no nice memories of it."

The car went quiet. I was embarrassed that I had asked the question, and Miguel clearly wasn't his normal chatty self. The light turned green. We moved forward. I looked out the window and saw soldiers marching in unison past jeeps and military barracks.

If only I had kept quiet another minute, I would have avoided asking that stupid question.

We drove on for what seemed like another hour but was more likely only a couple more minutes.

"Here is Colegio Máximo," Miguel said. He turned in to a long driveway and headed toward a grand building.

Colegio Máximo de San José, the place Jorge Mario Bergoglio would first call home in 1961 and that would be his home, on and off, for the next thirty years, was practically next door to the infamous Campo de Mayo.

After being in Argentina for only a few days, I had come to believe that Colegio Máximo was the place that defined Pope Francis more than any other—more than even the Flores neighborhood in which he grew up, more than the novitiate in Córdoba, more than his time in Buenos Aires when he was bishop and then cardinal, and even more than the pope's office in Rome.

How could it not? This is where he spent seven years studying, this is where he lived for four years when he was provincial; he would then become rector of this institution for six years and come back to teach here even when he was no longer rector. Indeed, his teaching here in the late 1980s—almost thirty years after he first entered the building—would be the final straw, causing such internal strife within the Jesuit community in Argentina that he would be banished to Córdoba.

When I spoke with Father Petty, Father Paredes, Father Morello, and other Jesuits in Argentina about Colegio Máximo, their eyes twinkled and their voices alternated between reverence and joy whenever they spoke those five words: Colegio Máximo de San José.

It sounded as if the ancient Romans had named the place—it sounded big and fancy, powerful and mysterious. I pictured St. Mary's Seminary in Baltimore and thought this place was going to be at least twice the size and twice as mysterious. I pictured some grand building teeming with Jesuit gladiators who were being trained to go to the ends of the earth to fight on God's behalf.

I was partly right: Colegio Máximo is a huge building, four stories high, one hundred meters long, and sixty meters wide. It is rectangular in shape and has seventy-eight rooms, fifty-three of which have private bathrooms and twenty-five with shared bathrooms. Set on one hundred twenty acres, it can sleep almost two hundred people. It was built in stages—construction started in 1931, when the land was a plant nursery and the surrounding region was rural. The roads were poor; most visitors arrived by train and walked just over a mile to Colegio the school. The final construction project was a library in 1982 under the direction of the rector, Father Bergoglio.

Today, Colegio Máximo is clearly in a state of disrepair. The driveway is potholed, the grass needs to be cut, and the grounds are not well maintained; there is moss growing on the building, whose walls are crumbling in places.

The big doors that graced the imposing building opened to a dark, musty, and quiet foyer. Straight ahead, an impressive wraparound staircase led up to the second floor. A water cooler was off to one side and a small security window fronted a nondescript, empty little office.

A plain-looking six-foot-high bookcase held some religious books and rosaries for sale. A large banner with a picture of Pope Francis was propped up in the corner. It detailed his time at Colegio Máximo—as a student, provincial, and rector. There was no energy, no color, no action. It felt like an old, rarely visited museum.

The rector of Colegio Máximo, Fr. Juan Berli, greeted me in the foyer. As Berli led me to his office, we passed through a lovely sunlit courtyard. The large space was well maintained with green grass, trees all around, and a goldfish pond in the middle. I heard a gong and deep voices humming. Surprised, I looked at Berli, who explained that a Buddhist retreat was being held at the school that day.

A Buddhist retreat was being held at Colegio Máximo de San José?

I later learned that while Jesuit scholastics still study philosophy and theology at Colegio Máximo, they live in a nearby community called Casa Arrupe. Today, only thirty Jesuits live at Colegio Máximo—a small fraction of the number who lived there when Bergoglio was a scholastic. The many empty rooms are frequently used by outside groups, such as the Buddhists who were there that day.

When we arrived at Berli's office, he offered me a seat and then stepped into a side room. He reappeared a moment later holding a tray with two hollow wooden gourds and a thermos.

"Would you like some maté?" he asked.

Ah, maté. I had heard a lot about the drink—it is a favorite of Pope Francis—but I had not yet had any. I don't drink caffeine and was concerned that maté, known for its energizing effects, would stimulate me so much that I would not be able to sleep.

But there was no way around it here in this small room an hour outside Buenos Aires—the rector had made maté and he was serving it. I had to say yes.

Berli opened the thermos and poured hot water into the gourds. Each gourd was filled to the top with a powdery substance. As I later learned, maté leaves are dried, chopped, and ground into the powdery mixture in front of me.

As the water seeped into the mixture, he poured more. Then he smiled. He must have detected my hesitation. "Have at least one sip," he said. "We drink till the end, little by little, slowly. But you only need to try it."

He took a slim silver straw called a *bombilla* and put it into one of the gourds. The straw had only a tiny opening so that one could drink the maté without getting any of the powder in one's mouth.

There was one gourd for me and another for Berli but only one straw. We were supposed to share the drink.

As I later learned, maté is a communal drink. Typically there is only one maté gourd and one straw, regardless of the number of people in the room.

Before I took a sip, Berli poured sugar on the leaves.

"Let the sugar soak in first," he said.

I waited. I really didn't want to drink this unknown liquid, nor did I want to suck from the same tiny silver straw as another person, but I had no choice.

I took a sip.

"It's a little bitter," I said, "but I can taste the sugar."

Berli explained that Jesuits discovered maté in the interior of the continent, in the area that would be Brazil or Guairá. "The Jesuits started to cultivate and produce it because it would get rid of hangovers and would give people the strength to work."

"It's good, actually," I said.

"It contains a lot of vitamin B. It's an energizer."

The conversation turned to Berli's childhood. He grew up in Santa Fe, Argentina, about four and a half hours by car from Buenos Aires. His mother is Italian and still lives in Santa Fe. Berli almost casually mentioned that his mother had had a stroke the day before. I was surprised that he had agreed to meet with me anyway. My mother had a few strokes and I could not imagine having meetings the next day. He said that she was getting better and that he was going to see her in a few hours. I thanked him for seeing me. There was a silent pause as his mother's plight sank in for both of us. There was a knock on the door.

"Juan?" a voice said.

"Come on in, Marito! Brother Rausch!" Berli was clearly happy to see Brother Mario Rausch.

So was I. I had been hoping to meet Rausch. Petty and other Argentine Jesuits had told me about him. He had worked at Colegio Máximo for years and enjoyed a very close relationship with Bergoglio.

"I am Mark Shriver."

"It's a pleasure," Rausch said. He was about five feet eight inches tall and reed-thin, with glasses. He wore black pants, a black jacket, and black shoes; he had a warm smile and a firm handshake. He seemed genuinely happy to meet me. He had a gentle, welcoming air. I liked him immediately.

We exchanged a few more pleasantries before Berli said that when he first met Bergoglio, they went for a walk. "In the middle of the walk, he put the clothes in the washing machine, and then we continued walking. And after, I helped him to hang up the clothes. This was very natural behavior for Bergoglio. Even washing the plates. But he would do this naturally. It's not as though he was making a sacrifice to go wash, but rather he was a practical man."

We talked for a few more minutes before I asked whether they had ever heard the expression that Jesuits needed to have "one foot up"—in other words, a Jesuit should always be ready to be sent on a mission. "Is that true?" I asked.

Rausch replied, "Bergoglio would say 'have your suitcase ready.' He would insist on availability—like, be ready to go to Japan."

Then Berli interjected, "I heard Bergoglio talk about a Jesuit, Father Sojo, who was the superior in Córdoba, and he went to visit him and said, 'Ecuador is asking me for a Jesuit, to collaborate spiritually.'

"And Father Sojo picked up the cross and said he had taken vows of obedience. 'I am at your disposal.'

"And Bergoglio was surprised that, even though Father Sojo was a superior, he could assign him to go to Ecuador for one year, two years. Bergoglio would tell us that story here as an example of the need to have 'one's suitcase ready.'"

I had already overstayed my welcome with Berli. He was busy, I knew, and he was going to see his mother. We said our goodbyes and I headed out to explore with Rausch. Our first stop was Bergoglio's old room.

We walked down the hallway a few yards before Rausch came to a stop in front of a door. He fiddled in his pockets until he found the right key. "This is where Father Bergoglio lived," Rausch explained as he opened the door and signaled for me to go in.

A single bed with a plain wooden frame was tucked into a corner. Beside the bed was a small three-drawer nightstand; on top of the nightstand were a cheap little lamp with an even cheaper-looking off-white lampshade and a framed picture of Bergoglio and his mother eating a meal.

Next to the night table was an armoire and off in another corner was a place to kneel and say prayers. Beside the kneeler was an ugly brown chair with a bright red cushion on it. Behind the chair, I noticed a gap in the wooden flooring; I looked up at the ceiling and saw water damage in the corner.

A small altar flush against the wall, covered with a simple brocade cloth, held a crucifix on a stand. Nearby stood two chairs.

The bedroom area opened to a small room that Bergoglio had used as a work area, with a plain wooden desk, a lamp, and a bookshelf. Today the bookshelf is mostly bare except for a couple of books, a few knickknacks, and two framed pictures, one of Bergoglio baptizing a baby and the other of him surrounded by young children. A window let in natural light. A plain wooden-framed picture—it looked like a copy of an etching—of Ignatius of Loyola hung on the wall. Ignatius was not smiling.

I stood there looking around, in silence, for about two minutes.

"Thank you for showing me the room."

I couldn't think of anything else to say. Usually when I am shown a room, I can make small talk about the unique headboard, or the beautiful comforter, or the fancy mirror in the corner, or the gorgeous nineteenth-century French bureau, or the view of the ocean from the king-sized bed.

But not in this room. Clearly decor was not a priority for Bergoglio.

We walked back into the hallway and looked through one of the arches at the courtyard. At least that was a beautiful sight.

"Come this way," Rausch said. "I want to show you the rest of Colegio Máximo."

Rausch then took me behind the building. He pointed out the clothesline mentioned in Berli's story; it was still in use. A few yards away, he showed me a freestanding building that was the old library; twenty yards or so beyond that were a decrepit basketball court and two handball courts that had seen far better days. The hum of crickets and insects was loud. The backyard had countless large trees that provided shade to a couple of wandering dogs.

Rausch pointed farther back behind Colegio Máximo and said, "This is where we raised the cows and chickens and bees and grew crops. In these two big fields." Off to the side, I saw rusty, broken-down field equipment.

What was once a tree-lined "road" is now a grass-covered path running down the middle of the field. "My brother helped plant those fruit trees on the road there," Rausch said. "He is a Jesuit brother, too. He lives in Córdoba and will show you around the Jesuit community if you go there."

He had taken off his jacket. His dark blue shirt was short-sleeved but he had started to perspire. It was hot. But he could not have been more patient and pleasant.

A barbed-wire fence and locked gate divided the school grounds from the fields. "The fields have been sold," Rausch said. "We no longer own them."

"What is that building?" I asked, pointing to a structure on the other side of the fence.

"That is the San Miguel Astronomical Observatory," Rausch said. "Jesuits used to live there—it was not part of Colegio Máximo, although some of the professors from here would teach there. The Jesuits sold it to the Air Force in 1976."

The Jesuits sold a building to the military during the Dirty War? So close to their spiritual and intellectual headquarters . . .

We went back inside and saw the long, rectangular dining room that used to be filled to capacity. Dozens of tables, each of which could seat five men, surrounded a long, narrow serving table. The industrial kitchen that prepared hundreds of meals every day looked like something one would see in a high school cafeteria, complete with ovens, stoves, heat vents, refrigerators, sinks, and bulletin boards.

"Bergoglio would cook here," Rausch said.

We wandered through the second floor hallway to the "new" library, built in 1982. Small, comfortable-looking reading rooms held a few chairs, a couple of desks, and tomes on philosophy and theology, but other sections of the library looked sadly run down—the lighting was poor, books were water damaged, and pools of water sat unattended. It was beautiful in some areas, depressing in others.

Colegio Máximo looked like the Argentine version of a once grand Southern plantation, its beauty and dignity still radiant beneath the dusty veil of time. With those spacious classrooms and beautiful courtyards and brick archways, it felt like the religious version of a grand space of learning—a somewhat faded version of Harvard Yard or the Lawn at the University of Virginia. I had the very real feeling that I was in a place like few others.

BERGOGLIO FIRST ARRIVED at this majestic institution set amid beautiful fields to take the standard next step in his Jesuit formation—three years of studying philosophy. He must have felt the charm, the uniqueness of the place, but also felt the continued emphasis on discipline and structure. All conversations were supposed to be in Latin, and he would read Saint Thomas Aquinas and philosophers like Kant and Heidegger to develop a systematic way of thinking about the world from their dense and rigorous texts. He would spend his days discussing and debating with learned Jesuit professors from around the world.

"Here you continue a life of study and prayer," Petty told me. "Now you study philosophy and metaphysics and logic and ethics. And, of course, you develop your spiritual life."

I asked Petty whether all conversations at the college were actually conducted in Latin. He laughed. "They were supposed to be but it was impossible to do so. Classes started in Latin, but we often carried on in Spanish."

As I walked the grounds of Colegio Máximo and imagined young Bergoglio there during its bustling days, I got the sense that he was living in a thriving mini-society defined by its unique devotion to the demands and guidance of Saint Ignatius. Walls and fences surround the property; each part of the property has its defined function—library, kitchen, garden, chapel—forming its own self-contained religious ecosystem. The place feels as if it could get along quite well without the world outside, even while it trained men to go out into that world to serve its people.

It was here that Bergoglio would begin to interact with Fr. Miguel Fiorito. Father Fiorito was the dean of philosophy, a worldwide expert on the Ignatian principle of discernment—a topic already clearly dear to Bergoglio—and, quietly, the intellectual godfather of a generation of Argentine Jesuits.

"He was a brilliant teacher," Petty told me. "He made us love his course. He was writing profusely on the Exercises and was considered an authority on the question of discernment. I think Bergoglio, like many of us, found [in him] the model for his intellectual and spiritual life."

Father Scannone, an Argentine theologian and one of Bergoglio's teachers, remarked, "Father Fiorito was a very profound person, very clear, a very good philosopher. But, above all, he was very interested in Ignatian spirituality. When he directed the Spiritual Exercises—I did Spiritual Exercises with Father Fiorito several times—he also gave us his writings, sometimes pages that he had written, about spiritual discernment, or prayer. He had a great influence on all the Argentine students."

Fiorito's achievement was singular in that he took some of the heaviest, most intellectually challenging material from the history of human thought and turned it into as much of a spiritual as an intellectual experience for these young Jesuits. That trait, I think, is keenly apparent in Bergoglio—an acute mind, but one that prizes the spirit above all.

APART FROM FIORITO, with his intellectual power and timeless spirituality, the faculty at Colegio Máximo was mainly composed of older, foreign-born Jesuits who were seen by some younger students as out of touch with the ambitions and needs of a new generation of Jesuits. Vatican II was in the air; the Catholic Church was about to undergo a massive philosophical and practical restructuring the likes of which few Catholics had ever imagined possible; and priests were about to leave their profession in droves worldwide because of the turmoil. But at Colegio Máximo, a nineteenth-century approach to pedagogy, and to life, still prevailed, often defiantly.

"We were definitely being instructed in what you would call an old-school pedagogical method, and yes, some young Jesuits who were well aware of what was going on out in the world started to resist that," Petty told me. "But I always enjoyed it. It kept me in touch with our origins, with the way Ignatius wanted us to develop our minds and hearts. You can't throw all that out, you know? You just can't. Change for its own sake was becoming the order of the day, and that never really leads to anything productive."

Bergoglio began his studies in philosophy alongside twenty-five other young Jesuits, six from Uruguay, nine from Chile, and ten others from Argentina. Looking out at those fields, I could only imagine that they were well trodden at that time by perplexed young men who were trying to make sense of the brewing crisis of the Jesuit order and the larger Catholic Church.

"The real action at the Máximo in those years," the British writer Austen Ivereigh wrote, "was in the small groups who formed to discuss what it meant to be a Jesuit in these new times. It was a process of self-questioning that would lead many to leave; for Bergoglio, it shaped his ideas about the Society's renewal."

Despite the sense of an incoming cultural tsunami, Bergoglio kept his focus. I met a former Jesuit who had studied at Colegio Máximo and doubled as the school's secretary. He told me that he had access to the secret grades of all the Jesuits who studied there. No one had ever been told his own grades, as a matter of policy. You advance or you repeat, or, if the talent isn't there at all, you look for another line of work. Only one person at Colegio Máximo had ever earned perfect tens in every course he had taken. Bergoglio, of course.

The studiousness and academic excellence that Bergoglio demonstrated during these three years confirmed the breadth of his intellect. For a man originally devoted to science, he clearly demonstrated a brain that was just as agile in complex philosophical thought. "He is very, very smart. And focused and disciplined," the man told me with great admiration. "Everyone knew it and admired him greatly."

These years, then, show the development of a young man who would be able to walk forever in two worlds because of his ability to combine two talents prized by the Jesuits. Seated in the high-ceilinged classrooms at Colegio Máximo, he secured his reputation as a first-rate, even world-class, thinker and writer.

The other talent—the charisma of a compassionate priest with a common touch—had its roots back in the humble, lively barrio of his birth, Flores, but would next be tested and proved in the venue where most young Jesuits spend at least three years of their lives—at the front of a high school classroom.

12   Teaching Borges

BERGOGLIO LEFT COLEGIO Máximo to teach at Argentina's old-est and most prestigious secondary school, Colegio de la In-maculada Concepción in Santa Fe, four and a half hours northwest of Buenos Aires. Here Bergoglio would act in the role that unifies "Jesuit products" (this is both how we refer to ourselves and how we are often referred to by our former teach-ers) like me worldwide. Our first contact with Jesuits usually comes in high schools, where they teach us courses as varied as calculus, Latin, religion, and literature. The latter was to be Bergoglio's domain despite his background in the sciences, and his time in Santa Fe emphasized two characteristics that were now coming to the fore of his personality—charisma and intel-lectualism. The two don't necessarily go hand in hand, as we all know. But the best Jesuit teachers—and there are countless leg-endary ones at high schools and universities around the world, men whom thousands of students remember with tremendous fondness and gratitude—combine these two qualities.

In Bergoglio's case, he did something quietly radical to get his students to appreciate the classics, his personal literary pref-erence. In his first year there, 1964, he was to teach Spanish literature. He began with the study of the twentieth-century Spanish poet Federico García Lorca. García Lorca's sensual, blood-and-guts subjects and progressive, inventive poetic style had made him, after Cervantes, Spain's best-known literary export. He was assassinated by pro-Franco forces in 1936 at the beginning of the Spanish Civil War. His writing was sure to grab the attention of a group of adolescents who were discovering the range of human emotions, impulses, and desires.

"We knew when he arrived that he had never taught school," Yayo Grassi, a former student of Bergoglio's, told me one morning over coffee in Washington, D.C. "When he started the class with the modern writers, it was unheard of at that time." Grassi smiled and shook his head, seemingly still surprised that his teacher would do such a thing. "We didn't know any teacher who would do that. Remember, this is 1964–1965 in Argentina. He somehow knew that we would want to start with modern writers—they were more accessible, it was more of what we wanted to read. He was so attuned to us."

But disregarding the chronological syllabus that traditionally began with the Spanish classic *El Cid* or perhaps Cervantes's *Don Quixote* was not the most radical part of Bergoglio's pedagogical decision. Rather, it was the symbolism of García Lorca more than his substance—he was an openly homosexual writer under the rule of General Franco in intensely conservative Spain—that makes Bergoglio's opening weeks at the strict, elite boarding and day school in Santa Fe so telling. Argentina would soon tumble into civil war, and Bergoglio's critics, during the battle for the country's soul, would often label him too "conservative" and cautious. Simultaneously, a battle for the soul of the Jesuit order would take place in Argentina, and many so-called progressive Jesuits would consider Bergoglio backward-thinking and inflexible for his insistence on devotion to the original Ignatian principles of formation.

But there, in that high school classroom in Santa Fe among the children of Argentina's elite, Bergoglio was showing his true self— a man with a curious, open mind, who tried to merge the old with the new, who tried to adapt the best of the intellectual and political past with the needs and styles of the present, and who, above all, cherished excellence and quality above any cultural or personal traits such as sexuality or social class. In fact, I think his most famous words as pope—"Who am I to judge?"—have their roots in that classroom in Santa Fe.

Just a few lines from García Lorca's poem "City That Does Not Sleep" demonstrate the radicalness of young Bergoglio's decision:

> But forgetfulness does not exist, dreams do not exist;
> flesh exists. Kisses tie our mouths
> in a thicket of new veins,
> and whoever his pain pains will feel that pain forever
> and whoever is afraid of death will carry it on his shoulders.

García Lorca wrote about death and love and loss in such a visceral way, it is stunning that Bergoglio, a future priest, would discuss such ideas and expressions, especially in a conservative Catholic country in 1964, with the teenage sons of the wealthy and elite.

Bergoglio then went way back in time to the foundation of Spanish literature—to Cervantes and Quevedo—and showed his students how and why García Lorca cherished them. The artistic roots of the avant-garde García Lorca led naturally back into classical Spanish literary history. "When we later studied the classics, we did so eagerly and happily," Grassi told me.

Bergoglio's pedagogical trick had his students hooked. A savvy, charismatic first-time teacher used an innovative gambit to bring his students to an understanding of and pleasure in older books. Those first few weeks in that high school classroom among boys dressed in jackets and ties may have been the best response to Bergoglio's looming accusers a decade later—here was a man open to radicalism, self-expression, and liberal thought at the same time that he was devoted to the fundamentals, to rigorous moral thinking, and to God.

Grassi and another former student, Jorge Milia, described Bergoglio similarly. "He was a strict teacher, but he was very good-natured. He would encourage us to read what interested us the most so that we would love literature. He was very organized, too," Milia told me.

Grassi agreed. "All of us had a wonderful memory of him. And it is not a polished memory because he became pope. We genuinely loved him even though he absolutely pushed us."

But it was a single project in August 1965 (his next year of teaching, devoted to the expanse of Argentine literature) that raised his time in Santa Fe to the level of local legend. Bergoglio, like many Argentines, adored the short stories of the Buenos Aires resident Jorge Luis Borges, a writer whom many experts and ordinary readers alike place in the pantheon of great writers in the history of world literature. In another gesture that combined intellectualism with charisma, Bergoglio pulled off a minor miracle by persuading the world-famous Borges to come to his classroom for a few days to teach not just his own writing, but also the popular genre of gaucho literature.

Almost every conversation I had in Argentina touched on gaucho literature—the poems and prose written about the lives and struggles of Argentine cowboys in the eighteenth and nineteenth centuries. I asked Grassi to explain gaucho literature and its influence on Argentina.

"We all loved gaucho literature," he told me. "The gauchos were real human beings, humble people we believed in. They worked the land for little pay. Sometimes they were illiterate and did not have any resources, but they struggled and they tried. Some were abused by the power structure, and when they continued to push ahead, that made them even more admirable for us.

"The most famous piece of gaucho literature was, and still is, a long poem called *Martín Fierro* written by José Hernández. It is the story of a gaucho narrating his own hard life. Everyone in Argentina read *Martín Fierro*—we all knew about his hard-luck life, how he worked hard and persevered. To have Borges come and talk about his own writings—which we struggled to understand, but we tried—and to talk about the gauchos—it was amazing. Really amazing. I have no idea how Bergoglio got Borges to come to Santa Fe. He was one of the greatest writers in the world at that time." Grassi smiled and shook his head. "Bergoglio has this amazing capacity to pull people together. He convinces them that he is serious and dedicated to the effort and people just want to follow him."

Borges's secretary, María Esther Vázquez, had taught piano to the Bergoglio children, and Milia thought that connection "may have been the key to establishing direct contact with the writer." However it happened, the fact that Borges visited was a coup. "Thousands of literature professors from prestigious universities, not just teachers from some secondary school, would have given anything to be in Bergoglio's position," Milia wrote in a 2013 article for *La Stampa*.

Milia recalled that "Bergoglio went to pick [Borges] up from the old station on Via Mendoza in front of the post office. No aeroplane for him. The six-hour coach journey from Buenos Aires must have been exhausting. I was a bit surprised as I thought a man of his age would have preferred to come by plane. What was I saying! Forget about the age, I just thought the coach wasn't an appropriate form of transport for a Nobel Prize nominee."

Milia went on, "[Bergoglio's] zeal did not stem from sudden rapture but from a methodical preparation that is typical of him. We, his uncomplaining pupils, struggled with Borges, his stories and his poems. Maybe that was what won Borges over. He did say on a number of occasions, even to me personally, that what had surprised him, fascinated him almost, is that teens like us had read so many of his works. Borges must have been aware that a group of young people could only have grasped such reading material through methodical and well-planned guidance. It must have brought him great joy to learn that a handful of secondary school pupils—not students from an academic environment, as he would have expected that—had been introduced to that world and were reading, studying, and discussing it. It showed there was something deeply mystical about their education."

Grassi told me, "A small group of us got to read our stories to Borges. He was almost blind, so we read to him—I read to Borges!" Grassi didn't raise his voice, but it was filled with excitement—almost fifty years after the event took place. "And Borges said, 'These are very good stories.' Then he said to Bergoglio, 'If you get them published, I will write the prologue.'"

Bergoglio seized on the unique opportunity and compiled the eight best pieces in a bound book entitled *Original Stories*. Borges wrote what Milia called "probably the most generous preface ever: 'This preface is not just the preface to this book but to each of the indefinite number of works each one of the pupils here present may write in the future.'"

THE BORGES ADVENTURE also pointed to a sensibility and style that I think Bergoglio wanted to imitate even then. In 2010, Bergoglio said that "Borges had a genius's knack for talking about any subject without ever bragging." I can't think of a better description for the mode and manner of Pope Francis than that. Borges was a humble genius, a man of the promenades and cafes of Buenos Aires who shunned fame and microphones.

In a highly publicized series of interviews that Borges gave to the Argentine writer Fernando Sorrentino in 1974, Borges, among many memorable lines, said this: "Before I ever wrote a single line, I knew, in some mysterious and therefore unequivocal way, that I was destined for literature. What I didn't realize at first is that besides being destined to be a reader, I was also destined to be a writer, and I don't think one is less important than the other."

Borges had become a celebrity, yet he was a diffident one. He was a writer who wrote for himself and his readers as if they were friends, or partners, or even co-conspirators in the intellectual journey that each of his stories constituted. I cannot help but apply this quote to the man Bergoglio would become—novice master, provincial, bishop, then pope—for, according to so many people, Bergoglio rarely distinguished between shepherd and sheep, between pastor and parishioner. He calls himself a sinner; he calls himself flawed; he calls upon God for help with the same authenticity, love, and desperation as any member of the Church he now leads, or any true seeker of any faith. Predisposed to emulate Borges in style, temperament, and intellect, Bergoglio was surely a student among his students during those glorious few days, digesting the paradoxes that Borges lived out—the genius with the common touch, the humble literary star, the seemingly distant but amazingly close friend.

13 Vatican II

BERGOGLIO WOULD SPEND a year teaching at another prestigious high school, Colegio del Salvador in Buenos Aires, before
returning to Colegio Máximo in 1967 to spend the next three
years of his life studying theology.

The period of time from when he entered the Jesuit order in
March 1958 to his return to Colegio Máximo in 1967—in his
twenties—was incredibly tumultuous on many fronts.

"The 1950s and 1960s were a time of great change for the
Catholic Church, but one has to look at Vatican I to truly understand what happened at Vatican II," Dr. Massimo Faggioli,
director of the Institute for Catholicism and Citizenship at the
University of St. Thomas in Minnesota, told me.

"In 1864, Pius IX issued a document called the Syllabus, a list
of eighty errors of modern culture. Among other things, the
Church stated that the separation of church and state was an
error, as was the concept that the pope was no longer a king.
Freedom of conscience and freedom of religion were also considered an error.

"Called by Pope Pius IX, the First Vatican Council was held
from 1869 to 1870. It is best remembered for declaring the in-
fallibility of the pope. Vatican I showed the Catholic Church at
odds with modernity. For example, the Church was against religious freedom for non-Catholics. If a non-Catholic lived in a
Catholic country, that person could be tolerated, but did not

have freedom to practice his or her religion. But if a Catholic lived in a non-Catholic country, he or she had to have the right to practice Catholicism, according to the Catholic Church, because the Catholic Church alone was 'the true Church.' And the Church believed that only Catholics could go to heaven; Protestants and Jews—anyone else, really—could get to heaven only if they converted to Catholicism. And only the new covenant was seen as valid, which meant that the Jews were not a part of the people of the covenant. This meant that the Jews were ostracized."

A priest friend of mine once told me, "the Catholic Church hunkered down after the Reformation."

I laughed. "The Reformation happened in the early fifteen hundreds. That's impossible."

"I am serious," he said. "The Church had essentially locked itself behind closed doors for all those years."

Faggioli said it succinctly: "The Reformation turned the Catholic Church inward, in a defensive mode. The counterreformation period lasts more than three centuries, and Pius IX's attack on modernity is part of the Catholic reaction to the Reformation and to the Enlightenment.

"By the mid-1950s, though, there were so many strains of thought and experience that the Church's façade was cracking. Bishops and theologians had lived through, and some had fought in, World War I and World War II. Everybody now knew of the Holocaust. There was the rise of the Soviet Union and the Cuban Revolution. There was debate about nuclear war and [about] the just war theory no longer being valid.

"When Pius XII died in 1958, the cardinals elected Angelo Giuseppe Roncalli to be a caretaker of the Church, to stabilize the Church for the next stage. Roncalli, who became John XXIII, was seventy-six when he was elected pope, the same age Jorge Mario Bergoglio was when he was elected pope. John XXIII started planning for the Second Vatican Council almost immediately. It took three years, from 1959 to 1962, to decide what would be discussed. Vatican II itself would begin on October 11, 1962, and conclude on December 8, 1965."

The sixteen official documents published as a result of Vatican II were approved by the bishops with majorities close to 99 percent of the vote. "They didn't want a simple majority. It was basically unanimous," Faggioli said. He laughed. "That's pretty incredible, especially when you realize that Vatican II was the largest gathering of bishops in recorded Church history. There were more than twenty-six hundred bishops there."

EVEN BEFORE ROME was enmeshed in Vatican II, Argentina was experiencing its own dramatic political and social unrest. "In 1954, when the Argentine Congress passed a divorce law, Catholic congresspersons who did not vote against it were excommunicated," Father Morello from Boston College told me. "That caused an uproar, and then in 1955, Perón was overthrown in a coup. He had become a bully, he was persecuting his opponents. The military wanted him out. In fact, they banned Peronism—it was against the law to even *say* the word 'Peronism.'

"In 1957, the military called for an election, but the Peronists were not allowed to run a candidate. President Arturo Frondizi was elected with twenty-five to thirty percent of the people participating in the process. There was no legitimacy in the political system. In 1962, there is a sort of coup."

"A sort of coup?" I asked Morello.

"Well, Frondizi realized that the situation was untenable, so he tried to ease the ban on Peronism. The military opposed that, so they threw out Frondizi and the vice president and installed the third-highest-ranking official, José María Guido. But this situation doesn't last, either. Within a year, Guido calls for an election and Arturo Illia is elected. Illia soon tries to ease the ban on Peronism. The military again disapproves, so in 1966, there is another coup and General Juan Carlos Onganía becomes president."

"So there is a coup in 1955, an illegitimate election in 1957, another 'sort of' coup in 1962, and yet another coup in 1966?" I asked.

"Yes," Morello said. He continued smoothly, as if such turmoil wasn't that unusual. "Onganía had a lot of support from the national-istic conservative Catholics. They thought he would be an Argentine version of General Franco in Spain, the leader who would be the one to restore Catholic values. Onganía banned all political activity—not just political parties, but student associations, too. The only place he allows people to get together is in the churches—he thinks that the churches are all on his side and will support him. The irony is that this happens at the same time Vatican II is calling for openness, for Catholics to be more involved in determining their future than ever before. Vatican II wanted Catholics to reach out to the world."

I knew that Vatican II had famously thrown open the windows of the Vatican to let in fresh air. I knew that there had been fundamental changes to the mass—it was no longer said in Latin but in the local language, and the priest no longer celebrated mass with his back to the parishioners. But I knew that Morello was talking about the impact of Vatican II on a much deeper level than I had ever understood it.

"Vatican II revealed two basic problems in Argentina: one political, one religious," he continued. "President Onganía wanted the people to stay at home so that the country could be run by the bishops and the military. The bishops thought they could control the people, but that was changing dramatically. The bishops didn't really know what was happening in their parishes. The local priests for the most part wanted more openness, and they didn't support the bishops. And the people, encouraged by Vatican II and their priests, wanted to be more in control of their own lives. They wanted to elect whomever they could, including Perón. This was a huge political problem for Gen-eral Onganía. Perón was in exile in Spain. It was compounded by the fact that Onganía thought the priests were fomenting the problem. He soon began to split from the Catholic hierarchy."

He paused. "That's a lot of information, I know," Morello said. He laughed. "Argentina is complicated, and this was a very complicated time."

"And what was the religious problem?" I asked.

"That happened on a couple of levels," Morello replied. "Vatican II ushered in many changes, but perhaps the most important change was the relationship between the laity and those in religious life. Prior to Vatican II, one had to be a priest or a nun or a brother to assume a leadership role in any part of the Catholic Church. Catholic school principals were all priests or nuns or brothers, for example, but that changed—the laity became much more empowered. Some would say that they were empowered at the expense of the clergy. This change caused confusion.

"Within the Jesuits, the conservatives wanted to focus on their inner life, their religious life, and educating the children of the elites like they had done in the past. The progressives wanted to work with the poor in the *villas.*"

With all this social and political change, there was a precipitous drop in the number of Jesuits. Argentina had twenty-five novices in 1961, but just twelve years later, there were only two. In 1965, the Jesuit order claimed some thirty-six thousand members worldwide; by the mid-1970s, that number had sharply declined to around twenty-five thousand.

"I think many Jesuits left the order then because it was previously considered a mortal sin to do so, and now it was no longer seen as such," Father Petty told me. "At the same time, as Vatican II made the work of laypeople more esteemed and important, these men could still serve the Church and their faith without having to be Jesuits. Some good things came out of it for the Jesuits—to me, we changed from being the 'elite' bunch in the 'perfect society' to being 'chosen to serve' in and among the 'people of God.' In that sense, the message of Vatican II was well understood—we, Jesuits and everyone else, were to serve the people, not the other way around. But it opened up so many possibilities that many of us lost our heads. In Latin America, the various liberation theologies grew out of this new freedom, thrived on it, and really, I think, strayed from the message of Vatican II by leading with [political] elites and priest elites instead of letting the people lead."

Vatican II seemed to sanction a degree of creativity and free thought that had never been imagined. This played out in Latin America with the emergence of a new movement called liberation theology, which emphasized a commitment to the poor and called for social change. Some critics, including the Vatican, saw liberation theology as overtly Marxist.

The tumult was in its early days and was starting to manifest itself in political schisms in Argentine society. Two more seminal events would help shape the theological and social course that Bergoglio would steer steadfastly for the next forty years.

The first was the Latin American Episcopal Conference in Medellín, Colombia, in 1968, which brought together Catholic bishops from around the region, essentially including all the countries south of the United States, from Mexico and the Caribbean through Central and South America.

After Vatican II, each church was supposed to apply the council's decrees locally; the Medellín conference was the only one that tried to apply the principles of Vatican II to an entire region.

There were three major outcomes of the conference. For the first time, the Church in Latin America stated that the oppression of the people in that region was an institutional sin. Church leaders also said that they could understand why people would resort to violence, though they did not condone it. And, finally, the bishops said the Church should align with the poor.

Though the Medellín document sternly warned against the political impulses and seductiveness of Marxism, the following quote from Bergoglio demonstrates the inevitable conflation of the Church's renewed emphasis on social justice with powerful social movements coursing through the continent at that time: "The option for the poor goes back even to the first centuries of Christianity. It is the gospel itself. If I, today, were to read as a sermon some of the sermons given by the first fathers of the Church, from the second or third century, about how to treat the poor, people would say this is Maoist or Trotskyist."

Just a few months later, in 1969, the Argentine bishops themselves gathered in San Miguel, Argentina. "The San Miguel meeting was meant to apply Medellín to the Argentine reality," Morello explained. "San Miguel said that popular Catholicism—popular religiosity—was very important for the future of the Church. Popular Catholicism—celebrating feast days, lighting candles, saying novenas, going on pilgrimages, placing flowers at statues of saints, touching those statues—was not second-class Catholicism anymore. This was a big step in the evolution of the *teología del pueblo*, the theology of the people."

Morello laughed. "Do you understand all that?"

Before I could answer, he went on, "Both documents emphasized faith first and foremost, but they also said that the Church should be building a more just society.

"Left-wing people, particularly in Central America at that time, tended to think that poor people were alienated from society. The poor were seen as people in need of some kind of elite—scholars or priests or intellectuals—who could lead them to liberation. Liberation theology emphasized what they lacked: power, leadership, economic justice, enlightenment," Morello told me. "*Teología del pueblo*, on the other hand, was based to some degree on Peronism. It's theological Peronism, if you will—the people already have the power, it lies in their faith and work, and it can be harnessed without Marxist structural violence. It is a uniquely Argentine theological phenomenon. And for people who grew up under the early years of Perón, like Bergoglio, the prioritizing of the working class and faith in the working class had to be appealing."

So, for Bergoglio, his Flores roots and Grandma Rosa's faith had found their intellectual apotheosis. Faith was the key to improving the lives of the poor, of the people. But the people didn't have to be taught faith by the Church; they already possessed it, they were its repository. And it wasn't a faith of creeds and professions and books—it was Rosa's faith of saints and relics and prayers. It was a visceral, grassroots faith that could save society, improve the lives of the poor and lower class, and help realize the kingdom of God here on earth.

This fundamentally Argentine view of change and power would struggle to take root during the civil war that was unfolding in the country. The theology of the people would be refined in the years ahead. And as a main proponent of it, Bergoglio himself would be tested and exiled and undergo dramatic change. But decades later, the theology of the people would form the crux of the message of change and hope and faith he would bring to the world as Pope Francis.

14 Father Bergoglio

ON DECEMBER 13, 1969, the almost thirty-three-year-old Bergoglio was ordained a priest in Colegio Máximo's chapel. He would graduate at the end of 1970 with a degree in theology. But the long and often grueling Jesuit road—twelve years of relocations, intense reading and discussion, training in Ignatian thought, teaching, and solitude—had to pass one more time through where it began: the Spiritual Exercises.

Bergoglio was sent to Spain, to a small town east of Madrid called Alcala de Henares, for his tertianship, the last stage of formation before he would make his final vows. Saint Ignatius himself studied and gave the Spiritual Exercises here in the 1520s, so it is fitting that that is where Bergoglio would make the full thirty-day Exercises for the second time. His footsteps would retrace those of the man who had lived more than four centuries before but whom Bergoglio must have felt to be as close to him as the shirt on his back.

The second time around, separated by more than a decade, scores of books and courses, and innumerable hours of prayer and discernment, is profoundly different from the first thirty-day retreat back in the novitiate in Córdoba. Although the retreat follows the same pattern, the person has changed. Father Morello told me that he himself was "much more aware of my own limitations, I was much more aware of my calling than when I was younger. I still vividly remember many of the prayers and insights that I had on that second retreat. I still reflect on them today."

"Have you done a third thirty-day silent retreat?" I asked.

"No," he said, "and if I want to, I would have to ask permission to do it again. We are told, 'You are a Jesuit, not a monk. The annual eight-day retreat is fine. Go out into the world and live.'"

He laughed. "You are a Jesuit, not a monk," he repeated.

I laughed, too. "That's funny," I said.

"It's great," Morello said, "it's great. We Jesuits are contemplatives in action."

But perhaps the most important part of this final stage was a side trip Bergoglio made to a little village in the north of Spain named Loyola—the birthplace of Saint Ignatius.

As he stood in the house where Ignatius grew up, now a small museum, and prayed in the church where Ignatius went to mass with his family long before his conversion during his convalescence, Bergoglio surely must have heard more clearly than ever the voice of the man who, after Jesus Christ himself, had provided him with the strongest direction, instruction, solace, and courage.

But that softer, feminine voice remained in his head, too, the voice he first heard growing up in Flores. His grandmother Rosa, now eighty-five, had summoned the strength to attend his ordination mass the prior year at the Colegio Máximo, and she gave him a heartfelt letter (described earlier) that he carries with him every day. A key paragraph from it reads:

May my grandchildren, to whom I gave the best of my heart, have a long and happy life. But if one day pain, illness, or loss of someone they love should afflict them, let them remember that one sigh before the Tabernacle, where the greatest and most venerable of the martyrs is kept, and one glance at Mary at the foot of the Cross, will cause a drop of balm to fall on the deepest and most painful wounds.

The personal and the professional—the boy from Flores was now a priest and man of the world—finally melded into one. The voice of the famed Saint Ignatius would forever fill his head; but so, too, would the faithful, God-charged words of Rosa. The rest of Bergoglio's life would in many ways be a dance with these two partners—a profound, ambitious, disciplined man who shaped the intellectual history of our world, and a humble, faithful, loving Italian grandmother who would forever sustain and shape Bergoglio with equal power.

In a document Bergoglio wrote just prior to his ordination, which he called his creed, we see the influence of Ignatius and Rosa shine through:

> I want to believe in God the Father, who loves me like a son, and in Jesus, the Lord, who infused my life with His Spirit, to make me smile and, in so doing, lead me to the eternal Kingdom of life.
>
> I believe in the Church.
>
> I believe in history that was pierced by the gaze of the love of God, who, on the spring day of September 21, came out to meet me and invite me to follow Him.
>
> I believe in my pain, made fruitless by selfishness, in which I seek refuge.
>
> I believe in the stinginess of my soul that seeks to take without giving.
>
> I believe that others are good and that I must love them without fear and without ever betraying them, never seeking my own security.
>
> I believe in religious life.
>
> I believe I want to love a lot.
>
> I believe in the daily burning death from which I flee, but which smiles at me and invites me to accept her.
>
> I believe in God's patience, welcoming, good, like a summer's evening.
>
> I believe that my father is in Heaven, next to the Lord.

I believe that Father Duarte is also there, interceding for my priesthood.

I believe in Mary, my Mother, who loves and who will never leave me alone.

And I look forward to the surprise of every day in which love, strength, betrayal, and sin will accompany me always until the final meeting with that marvelous face, whose countenance I do not know, a face that I continually escape from but that I want to know and love. Amen.

When I first read this creed, it confused me—it made me feel warm and comforted and hopeful but at the same time sad and confused.

I am accustomed to prayers that are full of either praise or pleas—or both. I was raised to praise God, Jesus, and the Holy Spirit, saying daily Our Fathers and Hail Marys. The Hail Mary, for example, is a prayer of veneration to Jesus's mother filled with reassuring phrases such as Mary's being "full of grace" and that "the Lord is with" her, and that "the fruit" of her "womb" is blessed and that she is "holy" and the "mother of God." And yes, there is a plea that Mary "pray for us sinners now and at the hour of our death." But that sinfulness is a general concept, not a personal acknowledgment of specific wrongs.

In Bergoglio's creed, I am comforted by the vision of being loved by God like a child and the idea that the Holy Spirit infuses one's life with smiles and eventually eternal life. But then jarring reality: There is pain in life. Bergoglio confesses his own selfishness, his stinginess, his propensity for taking without giving, before pivoting back to love and faith. Then, most astoundingly and poetically, Bergoglio writes about "the daily burning death, from which I flee, but which smiles at me and invites me to accept her."

Reading and rereading this document made me feel as if I were on a roller coaster—and despite the last few lines of the creed, which left me feeling hopeful and positive, I needed some more reassurance.

I went into the basement of our house, pulled out my file on my father's funeral, and read the back page of the funeral mass booklet. It was my father's own creed:

> I am a man who was born and has tried to live committed to being open to all people, no matter their differences in nationality, race, religion, or geography.
>
> I am a man who is full of energy and health.
>
> I am a man who takes his responsibilities seriously. I am committed to doing everything I can to succeed.
>
> I am a man who is original and creative.
>
> I am a man who is unencumbered by the past and by existing hierarchies.
>
> I feel free to invent.
>
> I believe the world was and is created by God. I believe the world is good beyond description.
>
> I believe that we human beings who seek life, liberty, and the pursuit of happiness do so because God has given us these things. They are a gift.
>
> I believe that we have a responsibility to God to do whatever we can to do good things for people, especially the poor.
>
> I believe in ideals. I believe that the world can be better if only we focus on achieving our ideals.
>
> I believe that any failure to achieve our ideals should only result in a rededication to them.
>
> I believe in faith, hope, and love. I believe that they have power.

I love my dad's positive outlook on life, his faith in humanity and in God. Bergoglio's creed was positive and hopeful, too, but it had pain and his own specific sins, front and center. He didn't use generic terms like "sinfulness" to mask his shortcomings—no, he used clear, descriptive words: stinginess, selfishness, taking without giving.

Yet I soon began to realize that Bergoglio's honest-to-the-core words—his acknowledgment of his own flawed humanity—should not be jarring at all, for he sees himself, first and foremost, as a sinner called through mercy to God. His acknowledgment of his sins makes him fully human, makes him more accessible, actually, than some idealized saint. Or even than my own father.

For Bergoglio, because of Rosa and Ignatius, faith in God was the consuming love of his life. His charisma and intellect would quickly land him in leadership roles, but his all-consuming faith would set him apart as much as those two worldly talents.

He would need every ounce of that faith and more as he would soon be thrust into a firestorm of political, cultural, and religious issues threatening to tear apart the nation of Argentina, the Argentine Catholic Church, the Argentine Jesuits, and many of his friends.

15 Novice Master

BERGOGLIO RETURNED TO Argentina, where, in April 1971, he made his final profession of "solemn" vows, including the fourth vow of "obedience to the Supreme Pontiff [pope] for the missions." That same day, he also professed the five "simple" vows in private, pledging not to change the Jesuit constitutions regarding poverty (unless to make them stricter), not to seek higher office within the Jesuit order, not to seek higher office within the larger Catholic Church, and to report anyone who appeared to have such ambitions. As the fifth simple vow, Bergoglio also committed to continue to take advice from the superior general if he were to become a bishop.

The call to take the fourth solemn vow—obedience to the pope—was a sign of Bergoglio's talent to serve in a variety of ways and of his potential for leadership, since only those who are selected to take that vow can hold important positions of authority within the Jesuit hierarchy. And the order did not waste time in appointing him to his first important position within the province: novice master.

Novice master may seem like a position of lesser power and importance than provincial or rector. Novice masters are in charge of the men who have just signed up to become Jesuits; the rector of Colegio Máximo is in charge of all the Jesuits studying at the formation house (many more than just the novices); and the provincial is in charge of all the Jesuits in the province. But the job of novice master is strategically reserved for some of the most talented, savvy, and intellectually astute men in the order.

"The provincial sends the names of three candidates for the position of novice master, in order of preference, to the superior general, and the superior general makes the decision. It was a big move to appoint someone so young. Bergoglio was only thirty-four when he was made novice master in 1971. There was a lot of hope for him," Father Morello of Boston College told me. "Thirty-four is very, very unusual."

The placement of such a young and inexperienced man in a position of such influence was surely a tribute to Bergoglio's talents—but also a commentary on the sickly state of the Jesuit order in Argentina at the time. Overall, the numbers were startling. From the early 1960s to 1973, the number of Jesuits in the Argentine Province dropped from more than four hundred to just two hundred and forty-three. In that same period, the number of young men in the process of formation dropped from more than one hundred to only nine; similarly, the number of novices declined from twenty-five to two. The numbers were declining around the globe, but Argentina was one of the most alarming cases. "Many priests left the order at that time," Morello said, "and there were not as many men to pick from. Bergoglio was in the new generation, and he had a lot of promise, so the decision made sense."

At the time Bergoglio was made novice master, Argentina itself was seething. "Some people say that the Dirty War was from 1976 to 1983—from when so many people started to disappear to the open elections in 1983—but many Argentines say that the Dirty War started in 1969," Morello told me. "There was a group called the Montoneros that formed around that time to overthrow the military government of General Onganía. They wanted to bring Perón home. There were many bombings, demonstrations, and killings in the early 1970s."

Bergoglio was an active supporter of the movement seeking Perón's return. In 1971, he began serving as a spiritual adviser of sorts to the leaders of a Peronist group at Universidad del Salvador, the Jesuit university in Buenos Aires. The group's core tenet—the preservation of the original "worker-based, social-justice Peronist platform of the 1940s"—should come as no surprise, given Bergoglio's Peronist inclinations during his youthful days in the middle-class Flores barrio. But Peronism had become a mélange of ambitions and manipulations, some right-wing, some verging on Marxism, and others, like Bergoglio's, loyal to the original working-class vision.

The Jesuit order was also splintering. Fr. Ricardo O'Farrell, the provincial, was presiding over a situation that paralleled that of the larger Argentine society. O'Farrell initiated two reforms that would soon involve, and dramatically impact, not only the order but Bergoglio himself. The first was to alter the Jesuit formation courses. "There was a lot of experimentation at that time," Morello told me. "Saint Thomas Aquinas and traditional Catholic doctrine were no longer the priority. New theological trends, including sociology and modern political thought like Marx and Sartre, were introduced. Things were evolving, and the result was that there was much uncertainty." O'Farrell surely saw the need to adapt by making the course of study more contemporary and accessible, but the faculty at the Colegio Máximo weren't sure what to do. And many resented the reforms.

Second, O'Farrell made the provocative decision in 1970 to allow the same man who led the curriculum reform, Fr. Orlando Yorio, to move out of the Jesuit community in which he lived in order to form a satellite Jesuit presence in an impoverished barrio called Ituzaingó in Buenos Aires. Community is a fundamental premise of the Jesuit order. Saint Ignatius envisioned all Jesuits living with other Jesuits, sharing meals, prayers, and diversions. To break with that model of community was to rupture a foundational principle of Jesuit life. Yorio, a native of Buenos Aires who was four years older than Bergoglio, had persuaded O'Farrell of the necessity of political involvement, social action, and an aggressive, even radical, push for structural and economic change. Faith, the bedrock of Bergoglio's being, was being pushed into the background.

The stage was set for a civil war inside Argentina—and within the

Jesuit order, too. O'Farrell quickly became a casualty when he was removed as provincial in 1973 after serving only four years of his six-year term. Fr. Luis Escribano, his perceived successor, had been killed in a car accident, so there was no clear succession plan.

The names of three potential provincials were sent to Superior General Pedro Arrupe. Arrupe chose the man he first met in Córdoba some fourteen years earlier, the rising star of the next generation, Jorge Mario Bergoglio.

16 Provincial

AFTER VISITING ARGENTINA and reading countless pages about what happened in that country in the 1970s and speaking to many people who lived through that decade, I still find the history of the nation very blurry.

One night in Buenos Aires over plates of Spanish hams and cheeses, a former high-level government official told me, "It was sheer chaos. There were so many different groups doing so many different things—the army didn't know what the hell the navy was doing, and the navy didn't know what the hell the army was doing. People were walking down the street, grabbed and thrown in a car, and they disappeared. They were gone! Gone! Never to be seen again. Some were supposedly Communists who wanted to overthrow the government. Some were supposedly leftists who wanted to overthrow the government. Whoever they were and whatever they believed was never clear—they just disappeared. And priests and nuns were killed. For what reason?"

He paused. I could tell by his voice and his face that the memory still haunted him.

"For what reason?" he repeated. "For living with the poor? For being Communist guerrillas? For being Marxists? For not being loyal to the government? For being too loyal to the army? Or to the navy? Who knows? It was complete chaos."

"What did the police do?" I asked. "Wasn't there some authority in place?"

"They didn't know what the hell was happening, either," he said. "It was total chaos."

I just couldn't fathom that level of confusion. Surely there had to be a clear series of events like the scenarios from the history books of my school days. Cause and effect; miscommunication; somewhat logical causes for human behavior. So I went back to Father Petty, Bergoglio's contemporary, a Jesuit priest just like Bergoglio who had also lived through that time, to get clarity.

"No one knows, Mark, what was really going on during the seventies," Petty told me. "No one. And any historian who tells you that he or she knows for sure, is wrong.

"Perón came back to Argentina in June 1973 and was elected to his third term as president a few months later. He took office in October 1973, with his third wife, Isabel, as vice president, but he died less than a year later, in July 1974. Isabel became president and was an absolute calamity. After almost two years under her rule, we welcomed the military coming in and throwing her out. We all thought that at least the military would bring law and order. But the military lost their heads. They became the worst dictators in Argentine history."

He shook his head. "It was a terribly complex time. The Jesuit Center for Social Research and Action published an article against torture. Shortly thereafter, bombs placed in our house blew out all the windows on the ground floor."

He paused. I didn't say anything.

Petty broke the silence with a laugh, but it was not a laugh of joy. "Let me tell you what happened to me when Bergoglio was my provincial," he said.

"I had gone to the University of Chicago to study education. I came back and was living in Buenos Aires, running the Belgrano Education Research Center. We were doing wonderful work studying the grade schools in Argentina. We studied the dropout situation and technical schools as well. We wanted to figure out how to improve the education system. We had support from the Ford Foundation, and the foundation was very happy with our work. We were not a threat to the military at all.

"One day, Bergoglio visited us and he said to me, 'You have to leave this place and go to Córdoba. The university needs your help. There is a priest that is going to die soon and you need to replace him.'

"I nearly died right on the spot myself! I was really enjoying my work and it was good work and I didn't want to go to Córdoba. And I knew the priest was just fine—he lived another ten years!

"I later found out that two girls who worked for me disappeared, never to be seen again. And one man who worked there, an ex-Jesuit who became a guerrilla, was killed. And another young lady had a boyfriend there who was a suspected guerrilla. I didn't know all of this. All I knew was that Bergoglio was moving me and I was very mad at him at the time. Very mad.

"I am positive today that he did it to save my life. But I had no idea at the time. No idea whatsoever."

I had dinner a few days later in Buenos Aires with Miguel Mom Debussy, who entered the Jesuits in 1973 and was ordained in 1984. He served at times as Bergoglio's driver when Bergoglio was provincial, and he underwent a painful separation from the order in 1986. Today, he is a vocal critic of Bergoglio. When asked to describe what it was like in Argentina and within the Jesuit order under Bergoglio in the 1970s, he said, almost offhandedly, "At that time, political issues were of vital importance. I will tell you something which I didn't tell Bergoglio. My family does not know this. I was part of armed organizations. I was a Montonero before entering the Society. In the middle of '72 and '73, when the dictatorship was already ending and Perón was already returning to Argentina, within the Montoneros, there was a great discussion as to whether or not the armed warfare should continue. And most of us disagreed with continuing the armed warfare because it no longer made sense. But there were others who said, no, the armed warfare had to go on. So those were the ones that continued [fighting], and they were the ones that were annihilated by the dictatorship."

One of Bergoglio's closest colleagues had been a member of the Montone-ros? And Bergoglio knew nothing about it? The confusion and deceptions are unfathomable to anyone who did not live there then—and even to those who did.

"Bergoglio had forbidden us from talking politics with the older Jesuits," Mom Debussy went on. "We would follow that order. But he had also forbidden us from talking about politics in the barrios, in the *villas*. But I would talk politics outside the school, and I would have contact with the union leaders, or the union members, and in other spheres as well, in San Miguel, and in other surrounding areas. I did not take this [restriction] kindly. But with a certain perspective, know-ing how cruel, brutal, and terrible the dictatorship was, and consider-ing that, among the older Jesuits, there were several that were military chaplains who were in agreement with the dictatorship, and that in the barrios there were many infiltrated people [informers], [I can see that] Bergoglio was protecting us. This is something I have to say. I realized that later."

Even Mom Debussy, the man who probably spent more time with Bergoglio than any other at the time, didn't know how decisions were made and for what reason!

Petty's words echoed in my head again: *No one knows for sure what went on.*

BERGOGLIO WAS MADE provincial on July 31, 1973, at the young age of thirty-six. He wanted to stay true to the early Ignatian principles of formation and wanted young Jesuits to be reading the foundational documents of the Catholic faith, while reformers like Fr. Orlando Yorio wanted to shift some of the curriculum to sociology, liberation theology, and more contemporary theologians, including some Marxist-leaning ones. For Bergoglio, faith was ahistorical, as were the great texts and Ignatian principles that informed his version of it.

There was a split on another level. Yorio and others believed their obligation was to free the poor from the economic and social shackles gripping them. They embraced social change as a complement to faith, if not a more urgent demand. For them, this approach still meant, in the theological sense, living the gospel, but in the cultural sense, it meant potential revolution and even prioritizing politics over faith if need be. Bergoglio, on the other hand, believed that faith was primary; he came to be characterized as conservative, dogmatic, and inflexible. This was a major point of disagreement over the future of the Jesuit order in Argentina.

Such conflicts were playing out all over the world. In an effort to address this schism, the leadership of the Jesuit order—two hundred thirty-seven Jesuits from all over the world, including Bergoglio—met in Rome from December 1974 to March 1975 for the thirty-second General Congregation, often referred to as GC32. A General Congregation is usually called to elect a new Superior General of the Jesuit Order; GC32 was called by Superior General Pedro Arrupe to come to agreement on the future direction of the order.

Before the meeting began, though, an immediate issue had to be addressed. A group of Jesuits from Spain, who wanted the order to look much as it did in the 1800s, had petitioned Pope Paul VI to be allowed to break from the order and report directly to the pope himself. That petition was rejected, but the group of dissidents headed to Rome to push their perspective.

Arrupe sent Bergoglio to the Termini train station in Rome to intercept the group. Bergoglio ordered their leader, Fr. Nicolás Puyadas, a Spaniard who had joined the Argentine Province, to leave Rome—or leave the order. Puyadas did as ordered and left Rome; the remaining dissenters left as well.

GC32 is most remembered for Decree Four, which is best described by the writer Austen Ivereigh: "Decree Four incorporated the pursuit of social justice as a key part of everything Jesuits did. The original purpose of the Society of Jesus in the sixteenth century had been the 'defense and propagation of the faith.' Now, at GC32, this became 'the service of the faith, of which the promotion of justice is an absolute requirement.'"

The resulting call for justice "appeared to have few safeguards against being turned into an ideology." Without clear direction and adequate safeguards, individual Jesuits were free to interpret the decree as they saw fit. Though GC32 and Decree Four were meant to clarify the direction of the Jesuit order, the result was a strong difference in opinion on how the Jesuits should fulfill this new decree.

Yorio, who had moved to the Ituzaingó barrio in 1970, had been forced to move back to the Jesuit community. In late 1972, Father O'Farrell again gave him permission to move out of the community. Along with a few other Jesuits, Yorio created another satellite community in an apartment on the Calle Rondeau. In early 1975, Yorio moved again, this time to Villa 1-11-14 in Bajo Flores. He was joined by fellow Jesuits Fr. Franz Jalics and Fr. Luis Dourrón. The move resulted in "a very dangerous situation," according to Petty. "The military had to ask themselves, 'What is a theologian doing living in the slums?'

"Asking for trouble is the answer," Petty said.

In such a chaotic time, this type of behavior was perceived as dramatically different from how priests had lived and taught their parishioners for thousands of years. Indeed, Catholic doctrine had been taught by theologians to priests, who in turn passed it along to the people. Now priests were living with ordinary, everyday people who were taking a more active role in the Church, weighing in on its teachings, on scripture, and on societal issues. This was theology from below—a very new and different approach in the 1970s.

The dictatorship in Argentina considered such activities a threat. When Bergoglio was asked in 2010 about the dictatorship's view of liberation theology, he said, "There were Latin American points of reference that the people of the dictatorship considered demoniacal.... They tended to see it solely as something revolutionary, Marxist, leftist, and a renouncement of the Gospels. ... There were some [priests] who engaged in theology with a Marxist hermeneutics, something that was considered unacceptable by the Holy See. Others sought to have a pastoral presence among the poor in accordance with the Gospels. The upper echelons of the dictatorship demonized all of liberation theology, both those priests with a Marxist hermeneutics, who in Argentina were few compared to other Latin American countries, and those priests who simply chose to live among the poor as their priestly vocation. They put them all in the same bag."

When Bergoglio was asked about Jalics and Yorio's stance regarding liberation theology, he answered, "They had a balanced, orthodox view." However, the two men, along with Dourrón, wanted to go in a different direction from the Jesuits. After they tried unsuccessfully to form their own religious congregation, they were given an ultimatum by Arrupe: Return to the Jesuit community or leave the order. The men decided to leave. Jalics had taken a solemn vow of obedience to the pope, so only the pope could grant his request, but Dourrón's and Yorio's resignations were accepted on March 19, 1976.

At the time, there were widespread rumors of a coup d'état. In his official biography, Bergoglio said, "In view of the rumors . . . I told them to be very careful. I remember I offered them the chance to come and live in the Company's provincial house, in the interest of their safety." But Dourrón, Jalics, and Yorio chose to continue living in Bajo Flores, and five days later, on March 24, 1976—the very day Bergoglio moved the Jesuit Curia from 300 Bogotá Street in Buenos Aires to Colegio Máximo in San Miguel—there was a military coup and Isabel Perón was deposed. A deadly, chaotic situation had become even more dangerous—especially for priests living among the poor. Two months later, on May 23, 1976, Jalics and Yorio were kidnapped by a military squad. Dourrón happened to be riding his bicycle at the time and escaped when he saw the commotion.

It has been suggested that Bergoglio notified military authorities that the three priests were no longer in good standing, which would have made them very vulnerable. There is no hard evidence that Bergoglio ever did such a thing, but Yorio stood by the claim until his death in 2000, telling a journalist, "I am sure that he gave the list with our names to the Marines." Jalics, however, issued a statement shortly after Bergoglio became pope in 2013 that said, "I myself was once inclined to believe that we were the victims of a denunciation. [But] at the end of the '90s, after numerous conversations, it became clear to me that this suspicion was unfounded. It is therefore wrong to assert that our capture took place at the initiative of Father Bergoglio."

The Dirty War was at its height—murders and disappearances were constant, chaos and confusion rampant. An estimated fifteen thousand people were disappeared or killed during this time. Many were murdered right in their homes and communities, including three priests and two seminarians of the Pallottine order who were found dead in St. Patrick's Catholic Church in the Belgrano neighborhood of Buenos Aires just six weeks after Jalics and Yorio were kidnapped.

It is unclear why Yorio and Jalics were eventually released on October 23, 1976. Yorio maintained that he had "no reason to think [Bergoglio] ever did anything to free us." But Bergoglio later recounted that they were released, "first of all, because they could not be accused of anything, and, second, because we wasted no time. The very night I learned they had been kidnapped, I set the ball rolling."

He went on to say:

I did what I could for my age and, with the few contacts I had, to plead for people who had been kidnapped. I got to meet with General Jorge Videla and Admiral Emilio Massera [in charge of the army and navy, respectively] twice. In one of my attempts to talk to Videla, I managed to find out which military chaplain celebrated the mass and persuaded him to say he was sick and to send me in his place. I remember that I celebrated mass in the residence of the commander in chief of the army, before the whole Videla family, one Saturday afternoon. Afterward, I asked Videla if I could have a word with him, with the intention of finding out where the arrested priests were being held.

But a nagging question remains: Could Bergoglio have done more than he did during that decade? His preemptive actions with Petty and Miguel Mom Debussy surely saved their lives. I also read numerous accounts of other aid he provided to priests and laypeople alike, including hiding men and women in Colegio Máximo and helping others escape the country.

And it is a fact that not one Jesuit was killed while Bergoglio was provincial.

Still, that question—could he have done more?—remains, especially after I read Bergoglio telling Rabbi Skorka, "We all are Political animals, with a capital *P*. We are called to constructive political activity among our people. The preaching of human and religious values has a political consequence. Whether we like it or not, it is there. The challenge of preaching is to propose those values without interfering in that little thing called partisan politics."

Here is a man who understands politics, a man who, despite claiming that he didn't have much influence because of his age, clearly had enough contacts and was enough of a political animal to meet with the heads of the army and navy twice and to say mass for General Videla; who somehow had enough pull to get Petty and many others out of potential trouble; and who, a decade earlier, had persuaded the world-renowned and nearly blind Jorge Luis Borges to make the six-hour journey to Santa Fe to teach literature to a class of teenage boys.

"What did the Church do during those years?" Bergoglio said to Skorka. "It did what any organization does that has both saints and sinners. There were also men that are a mix of both. . . . Some Catholics made mistakes, others moved ahead correctly. There were Catholics who justified their actions with the argument that they were fighting against Communism. . . . In the Church there were Christians from different groups, Christians killed as guerrillas, Christians who helped save people, and repressive Christians who believed that they were saving the homeland."

Could Bergoglio have done more for others given his intelligence, his connections, his political instincts?

Who am I to judge?

WHAT IS CLEAR to me, though, is that during this time, when Bergoglio had strong disagreements with his fellow Jesuits over the proper formation process of younger Jesuits and the interplay between faith and political action, those disagreements were compounded by certain traits of Bergoglio—self-certainty, discipline, and impatience. How he made decisions and how he treated people caused a deep division within the Jesuit order in Argentina.

Bergoglio said as much in his 2013 *America* magazine interview:

In my experience as superior in the Society, to be honest . . . I did not always do the necessary consultation. And this was not a good thing. My style of government as a Jesuit at the beginning had many faults. That was a difficult time for the Society: An entire generation of Jesuits had disappeared. Because of this I found myself provincial when I was still very young. I was only thirty-six years old. That was crazy. I had to deal with difficult situations, and I made my decisions abruptly and by myself. Yes, but I must add one thing: When I entrust something to someone, I totally trust that person. He or she must make a really big mistake before I rebuke that person. But despite this, eventually people get tired of authoritarianism.

My authoritarian and quick manner of making decisions led me to have serious problems and to be accused of being ultra-conservative. I lived a time of great interior crisis when I was in Córdoba. To be sure, I have never been like Blessed Imelda [a goody-goody], but I have never been a right-winger. It was my authoritarian way of making decisions that created problems.

I say these things from life experience and because I want to make clear what the dangers are. Over time I learned many things. The Lord has allowed this growth in knowledge of government through my faults and my sins.

Those faults—and sins—would follow Bergoglio to his next two jobs, as rector of Colegio Máximo and then as the confessor of the Jesuit community in Buenos Aires. They would become as defining for him as his intelligence and charisma. Indeed, his "interior crisis" in Córdoba—in that small room overlooking a street filled with drunken students—would not occur until more than ten years later.

17 Rector

I GOT THE deepest sense yet of Bergoglio's power and effectiveness as a mentor in an Argentine steak house near the Recoleta cemetery where Evita is buried. I was eating lunch with three jovial, easygoing Argentines, so I felt at moments more like a local than an American tourist. I had met Father Petty a few days earlier, and at the end of our first meal together, he said, "I have a knee operation tomorrow and then a day to recuperate. Would you like to have lunch with Father Gauffin, Father Nardin, and me afterward? They are coming to pick me up and bring me back to Santa Fe. They both were scholastics at Colegio Máximo when Bergoglio was rector. They are good men— smart and fun. You will enjoy their company."

Petty could not have described the two men better. Fr. Leonardo Nardin, in his early fifties with closely cropped hair, was born and raised in Santa Fe. An artist and a musician, he has a degree in sacred liturgy from the Benedictine College of St. Anselm in Rome. He was the director of the choir when Bergoglio was rector of Colegio Máximo. Fr. Alejandro Gauffin, in his early sixties with gray hair, is from Salta in the mountains of northwestern Argentina, close to the border with Bolivia. He has a degree in theology from the Universidad del Salvador. Both men studied at Colegio Máximo in the late 1970s and early 1980s under Bergoglio, who became rector of Colegio Máximo in 1979 after his tumultuous six-year term as provincial came to an end. "The rector of Colegio Máximo runs the institution. He is the superior of the Jesuit community there, and there were a lot of Jesuits at Colegio Máximo at that time. It was a very, very important job," Father Morello of Boston College told me later.

We sat down and ordered steaks and red wine. It didn't take much prodding to get Nardin to talk.

"One of the first things [Bergoglio] did was say that the neighborhood, San Miguel, needed its own church," Nardin said. "So on March 19, 1980, the parish of the San José Patriarch was inaugurated. He wanted to give it that name. It was a shed, a vegetable shed that had been converted to a church."

Gauffin added, "One day Bergoglio asked, 'Who wants to be in charge of the administrative office?' I raised my hand—and he named me secretary of the parish. I was to attend to the people's needs. I was twenty-four, twenty-five years old." Gauffin was not yet a priest when Bergoglio gave him the assignment.

"There were about fifteen or twenty young Jesuits," Gauffin continued, "and he told me, 'Give work to all of them.' So I drew a map, a map of the neighborhood, and put numbers on it, each block a number. I said, 'Leonardo, thirty-four and thirty-five. Juan, twenty-seven and twenty-eight,' and so forth. I assigned blocks for each of them to be in charge of—"

"Like your campaigns," Petty said, and all three of them laughed.

"You're right. It sounds like a political operation," I said.

"Bergoglio also told me, 'Give each of them an image of the Virgin,'" Gauffin continued. "So they would arrive, I would give them an image of the Virgin, and Bergoglio would tell them, 'Go to the homes, go to all the homes.'"

"Except those of the evangelicals," Nardin interjected.

"He said that? Not to the evangelicals' homes?" Petty asked. I was surprised he had not heard that part of the story.

"Yes," Nardin replied. "He said, 'Don't go over there to have arguments with people of other religions.'"

"Very much like Ignatius, who said don't get into fights," Petty observed. "[People] love a fight, especially against a young priest."

There was a pause in the conversation as the wine arrived and was poured.

"Alejandro is a very capable organizer," Nardin said, returning to Gauffin's appointment as parish secretary. "So yes, he was put in that position—of course, under Bergoglio's wing."

"Under his wing?" Gauffin said, laughing. They looked at each other and smiled. "More or less, because he didn't let me go out! I had to make sure everything was working. But he was also there. I was the organizer, but he was directing everything."

"When talking about Bergoglio, one could say that even when he is not present, he is there, so you can imagine what it's like when he is actually present!" Nardin said, and all three priests laughed again.

The steak arrived and the waiter topped off everyone's wineglass. Nardin said something that my translator didn't pick up, but Petty did. His eyes smiled. He coughed. I couldn't tell whether he was about to tell a joke or a story.

"There is a brother in Spain, a lay brother, who was grumpy, and when someone called to speak to the provincial, the lay brother says, 'He's not here.' So the other fellow says, 'But he must be there.' So the lay brother says, 'Look, when he's here, he's not here. But when he's not here, he's not here!'"

They all laughed again. When the laughter died down, Gauffin said, "Bergoglio is the opposite."

"Bergoglio is the opposite," Petty agreed. "When he's here, he's here. And when he's not here, he's always here, because he's involved in everything."

Gauffin's face became very serious. "Jorge was aware of everything, he didn't miss any details, he always—"

Petty cut him off: "He didn't miss a detail, he had a very broad vision, and he knew exactly what was going on, everywhere."

They were talking fast now. No one had touched the food yet.

"Once I remember when the Jesuits came back from the neighborhood—" Gauffin began, before Nardin interrupted to say, "Provide some context." They were very good storytellers, but they prodded each other to be even better.

Without waiting for his friend, Nardin continued, "The context was that all the Jesuits would go on Saturday afternoons and Sunday mornings to work in the neighborhood, doing all sorts of things. We had a schedule, and we had a time at which we had to be back. We had to be there for dinner at eight thirty, but we could not arrive any earlier than eight twenty, nor later than dinner time. There was a ten-minute window allowed."

"Bergoglio was there, and he would receive us very affectionately," Gauffin said. "But he looked at the shoes of some of the priests and he said, 'Today you haven't done anything.' It had rained and it was muddy, and they had nothing on their shoes, they were shiny."

"He told them they returned without the smell of sheep," Nardin added.

Petty explained, "He wanted priests to be like shepherds tending to their sheep, to their parishioners. If they had muddy shoes, he'd use a saying of his, 'smell of sheep,' *olor a oveja*. I think that is wrong, though, because the sheep, poor dears, don't have any smell. It's the wool that smells!"

We all laughed. They started to eat, but I didn't. I was scribbling notes, afraid that I was going to miss some nugget or insight.

"In the Colegio Máximo, life was very intense," Gauffin said while he chewed his steak. "For some people, the discipline was very normal. For him"—he pointed at Nardin—"it was. But for others, it was hell."

"Yes, but Bergoglio pointed out the reason," Nardin explained. "He would set timetables because he defended time for study, and prayer, and community life and work. Yes, all of us had tasks to perform; I worked in the kitchen for a long time. On Saturdays, we would work four hours in the kitchen in the morning, preparing the Saturday lunch, the Saturday dinner. And then we would work in the neighborhood, our apostleship. We would come back here at eight in the evening to heat the food and have it ready to eat at eight thirty.

"We lived with great austerity. So, not having many resources, it was more work to prepare the meals. On Saturday night, two or three of us volunteers would stay up preparing Sunday lunch. Sometimes we stayed up until one, two, or three in the morning. And many times, Jorge would appear at one A.M., to offer us a beer, which for us was like an elixir, a big gift, a gesture of sensitivity, that he came to share a moment with us. But because we were still working, he would not go to sleep, either."

Not to be outdone, Gauffin said, "I had to work for a long time with the pigs. It was a job for many of us, the pigs, because we had fifty, sixty, seventy animals. So we had to go to the pigsty at a certain time on Saturdays, clean the sties, wash the pigs. We would end up with a stench, even after a bath you still had the smell."

"On our day of rest, Bergoglio would go and feed them in the morning. He would go there with all the pans, empty them out in the pigsty," Gauffin said. "Bergoglio would roll up his sleeves and rummage through the garbage looking for special things for the piglets. He would not have a problem with that. He knew all the pigs. He would tell you stories about, let's say, Francisco, or whoever. He would name them, each pig had a name. There were people who came from Buenos Aires who thought this was a punishment, that it was not dignified, that it was humiliating to have to go and work in the pigsty, but Jorge believed that one has to try all tasks, even the humblest. He said that we should live like the poor people. If they work eight hours a day, why can we not work a few hours to earn our daily bread? He was like that. And that was good."

The conversation then turned to America, to politics both local and international, and then to our meal of steak and red wine. They remembered Bergoglio as a very good cook.

"He would make comments while we were working," Nardin said. "Do this this way or that, or put such and such a filling. He would look in the refrigerator. We would recycle food a lot, because there was not much of it."

"These were times of poverty," Gauffin explained. "There weren't resources for the food, like—"

Nardin interjected, "I believe that if he had wanted to, he could have obtained resources, because he is very good at getting resources, but I think he did not want to. I think his austerity was intentional. He lived his life like this."

"Ah, yes, yes," Gauffin agreed. "And he always made sure that something was left over to give to the poor, always, so much so that he told me, 'I want a soup kitchen in such and such a place, or for the kids in the neighborhood.' So we would bring food, and people in need would come with their pot, we would fill it up, and they would leave with their little pot. . . ."

His voice drifted off. No one spoke for a moment.

These guys knew Bergoglio long before the arc of his life showed any hint of global power and fame; they knew him authentically, intimately, in a way only people who live together could. And their energy and admiration were sincere; they spoke about this man the same way Yayo Grassi and Jorge Milia spoke about him.

"Can I tell a story?" Nardin asked, breaking the silence. "One day Jorge called me and he said, 'Look'—because he would talk like that—'I'd like the kids from the parish to go on vacation to Mar del Plata, to the seaside.' And I said, 'Okay, sounds great,' and he said, 'Okay, but two things, I want you to take two hundred or more kids, and secondly, I have no money.' So he said, 'Do you think you can do that?'

"I looked at him as if to say, 'Impossible.' So he said, 'Well, if you don't want to try, let's not do it,' so I said to him, 'Okay, let's try.'

"After that, we were very lucky, because we had met, when John Paul II came to Argentina, the owners of a big bus company, and we went there and told them, 'Look, we need to take two hundred kids to Mar del Plata, which is about five hundred kilometers away,' and they said, 'Okay, that's not a problem.' Then I said, 'Well, we don't have any money,' and they asked why, and we said, 'Well, Father Jorge asked us to make this happen.'"

They all laughed and Nardin continued. "They had no idea who we were, they knew nothing about us! But we told them that these were poor children, which was true, so they said, 'We'll think about it. Wait here.' So they went inside, they talked it over, they returned and said, 'Yes, okay, if it's for the poor, we will do that.'

"So shortly after that we started the first camp with three hundred kids. Almost none of whom had ever seen the ocean before. It was for two weeks. We would take a lot of food from here, but there, in Mar del Plata, we would ask for donations of meat, fish, everything that was needed. All donations. We would celebrate mass on the beach with the wealthy people. We would take all our kids, and we would tell them, 'Okay, ask God to give us food.' And in one of the masses, one of the kids made a request for bread during the prayers of the faithful, and that moved the congregation."

"And this was all Bergoglio's idea?" I asked.

"Yes, he wanted the kids to enjoy the camp, to have a good time, vacations, opportunities, but on the other hand, one has to think that this did us good as well."

As I reflected on the conversation, I couldn't help but think that Bergoglio was, in some ways, re-creating his experience as a sixth grader at Colegio Wilfrid Barón de los Santos Ángeles. As the Salesian priests had done for him, he structured a full day for the scholastics at Colegio Máximo, filled with studies, hard work, and discipline, but there were also fun activities and an air of excitement. Now he was the teacher and mentor, not the student.

I asked the priests whether they knew where that impulse to help the poor, the needy, those kids, came from. Was it from his childhood? From his neighborhood? Was it from his time studying to be a diocesan priest? Jesuits have traditionally taught wealthy students, while diocesan priests run poor parishes.

Petty replied first: "The Councils of Medellín and San Miguel."

"I think he brings it from his family," Nardin said, "that special sensitivity toward the poor. They told me that when he was a scholastic in the Colegio in Santa Fe, every day, he would pass by a place where the employees would gather on their break to drink maté, and he would drink maté with them."

Petty explained, "I think what Leonardo is saying is that, rather than diocesan versus Jesuit, it was more a family trait. Because the diocesans would be very keen on parish work, but not necessarily the poor parishes. They would be happy to go to all the rich parishes, of which there are plenty."

Fr. James Kelly, a Jesuit priest from Ireland who taught and lived at Colegio Máximo for four years while Bergoglio was rector, told me that he believed Bergoglio "received his deep, deep faith from his family. That is where he learned his faith. Jesuits in Rome were focused on both faith and justice. Bergoglio never accepted that faith and justice were equal. He was always interested primarily in faith. He was interested in justice as well, but it was never equal to faith. And that stemmed from his family."

Here, then, was a man grounded in the theology of the people— the theology discussed and refined in 1968 in Medellín and in 1969 in San Miguel. And here, too, was a man grounded in his grandma Rosa's earthy vision of Catholicism. His was a Catholic path filled with discipline, self-sacrifice, and faith, yet with a devotion to the *pueblo*. He was creating a world at Colegio Máximo that reflected his own formation and these paradoxes.

Nardin looked at me with a serious gaze. "I would like to add something. My time in the novitiate at Colegio Máximo when Bergoglio was there was the happiest time of my life. I have not known another time that was so nice, so full."

"And why is that?" I asked.

"Because he loved pigs!" Petty exclaimed, needling his compatriot.

After another outburst of laughter, Nardin looked back at me. "Because we lived the same consolation that the Church is living now. He's a person that makes one work hard, is very strict, sets goals, encourages. There was a broad horizon. We could be very creative. We were not tied to control. He was very open in his way of thinking. But he demanded that we examine ourselves and grow. I think he has made all of us Catholics question personal attitudes, right?"

When asked whether others would have preferred a more intellectual style, Nardin replied, "Not more intellectual. Less demanding. We were very happy, but he was very demanding. His gestures made us question our attitudes, so if someone does not like to be questioned, clearly, they will feel upset. But for me, the Máximo is my paternal home."

WAS THIS STRONG discipline part of the authoritarianism to which Bergoglio himself alluded? Was it one of the sins of his past? I remembered that Miguel Mom Debussy, the former Jesuit who served for a time as Bergoglio's driver and is now an outspoken critic, told me how tough Bergoglio had been on him and others, how one scholastic who was badly berated by Bergoglio went into the bathroom and collapsed. Mom Debussy told me another story to illustrate his point.

"One of the things that Bergoglio took a liking to was to bring back old elements of the pre–Vatican Council liturgy," Mom Debussy said. "He returned to a lot of incense, old church ornaments, and rituals that had been done away with. One of the discussions I had with him was regarding those matters. I would argue with him and say, 'Why do you give so much importance to liturgy? It's a matter of formalities. Here, we have to fight for the poor; change the structures that lead to poverty; not give them charity, a package and a little bread, but rather, change the structures.'

"Because he knew that it really infuriated me, what did he do?" Mom Debussy asked, and then answered his own question with a wry smile. "He named me master of ceremonies. Every morning at seven, the students and very frequently Bergoglio would celebrate mass, and I would have to prepare the ornaments for him before mass. He would set out a Gothic vestment, or he would send me to fetch what is called the guitar vestment, the old one, with velvet and embroidered gold, something extravagant. He would do this on purpose. He also insulted me, even said I was a fool, useless, in front of people who were not even Jesuits. I was not the only one. I recall at least two more. All of us who in one way or another opposed Bergoglio, all of us ended up outside the Society."

Fr. Rafael Velasco, a Jesuit who is now pastor of San José Patriarch, the church Bergoglio built out of a vegetable shed, studied at Colegio

Máximo when Bergoglio was rector. He told me one sunny afternoon, as we sat inside the church, that "Bergoglio was very strict. He
could get mad at students. He yelled at a scholastic once who had not
set the table with the correct number of plates. Everyone feared him
a little bit, but at the same time, he could be very intimate with the
scholastics. He went to sleep early, but he woke up early. That was
part of his mystique. He was in everything. He was always there."

Velasco's two dogs wandered about as we sat in the church pews
chatting. A puddle of water had collected in front of the altar, the result of a leak in the roof. One of the dogs trotted over and started to
lick the water. In the corner, two older ladies swept the floor with
handmade straw brooms.

*This doesn't look like the Catholic church I attend in Potomac, Maryland.
Actually, it doesn't look like the inside of any Catholic church I have been to
in the United States. I can't decide whether the scene is beautiful or appall-
ing. But it is most definitely a Bergoglio-type church—earthy, colorful, active.*

OVER LEMON ICE cream with Nardin, Gauffin, and Petty, I asked
them a question that had been gnawing at me. I had started to wonder
whether Bergoglio was really just a political animal, so I asked, "Do
you think this is an act, or is he for real?"

Nardin answered immediately, "Completely authentic."

"Yes, completely authentic," Gauffin agreed. "When he got mad,
though, it was best to get away from him. He was strong, very strong."

"But we have never known him to get mad for capricious reasons,"
Nardin added.

"He could send someone to hell, easily," Petty said.

"Yes, easily," agreed Nardin. "But I have never seen him do that."

"Leonardo has never seen him do that because he was very favorable to Bergoglio," Petty observed.

"What?" Nardin asked.

"You had a very favorable view of Bergoglio," Petty replied. "There
are others with other views."

"Yes, of course, there are. There are many," Nardin acknowledged.

"Because they were a bunch of undisciplined guys and Bergoglio imposed discipline," Petty continued.

"Well, that's what they say," Nardin replied. "But let me tell you something that happened to me. In one of the camps, a kid got sick. He got appendicitis. They went to wake me up and I told them, 'He'll get over it.' They called me again and I again said, 'He'll get better.' I was so tired. When I woke up in the morning, at eight or nine o'clock, the kid had been hospitalized in a clinic. So I called Bergoglio and said, 'Jorge, you know what has happened, there is a kid in the hospital with acute appendicitis. He's seriously ill. I didn't realize. I fell back to sleep and, well . . .'

"And he said, 'Okay, you are not to leave Mar del Plata until the kid is fully recovered.' So I stayed in Mar del Plata for twenty days until finally the mother arrived. That was Jorge. He would trust you a lot, but if you messed up, he would correct you."

Nardin started to laugh.

"Why are you laughing?" I asked.

"I'm laughing," Nardin answered, "because Jorge had many of those ways of pointing out our pettiness. I remember a story from when we received some Peruvian and Ecuadoran Jesuits for the formation. We Argentines dressed somewhat more conservatively at the time than we do now. And this colleague, Tarcisio Vallejo from Ecuador, came with a sweater full of colors, shapes, who knows what. So I laughed at him. The following day I had to wear the sweater all day."

"Bergoglio made you wear the sweater?" I asked.

"Yes. I'm not sure if inside out or what, but yes," Nardin said, turning to Gauffin. "Do you remember?"

They both laughed.

"What did that teach you?" I asked.

"Not to laugh at others," Nardin told me. "It was a blessing, really. I never felt humiliated or anything of that sort, but Bergoglio would put you in situations that would lower your pride."

. . .

On Holy Thursday 2013, just over two weeks after being named pope, Pope Francis visits the Casal del Marmo youth prison in Rome, where he washes and kisses the feet of juvenile offenders, including two young women. REUTERS / Osservatore Romano

During a public audience in St. Peter's Square in November 2013, Pope Francis embraces Vinicio Riva, who suffers from a non-infectious genetic disease that has left him covered in sores. EPA / CLAUDIO PERI

A young Jorge Mario Bergoglio.
COURTESY OF THE GENERAL CURIA
OF THE SOCIETY OF JESUS

Bergoglio was raised in this modest home in the Flores barrio of Buenos Aires. Today, the house bears a sign that reads: IN THIS HOUSE LIVED POPE FRANCIS.
LEGISLATURE OF THE AUTONOMOUS CITY OF BUENOS AIRES, MARCH 2013. MARK K. SHRIVER

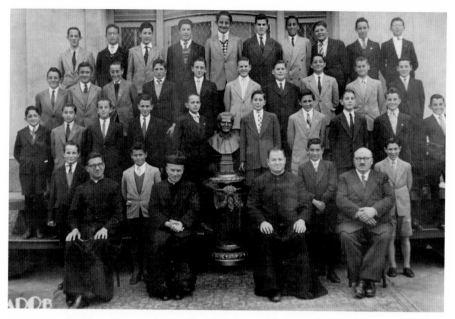

Bergoglio (second row from the top, sixth from the left) spent a year at boarding school, where the Salesian priests inculcated within him a "Catholic culture."
COURTESY OF THE GENERAL CURIA OF THE SOCIETY OF JESUS

A portrait of the Bergoglio family. From left to right, standing: Alberto, Jorge, Oscar, Marta. From left to right, seated: Maria Elena, Regina, Giovanni, Rose, Mario, and Marta's husband, Enrique. COURTESY OF THE GENERAL CURIA OF THE SOCIETY OF JESUS

The Basilica of San José de Flores where Bergoglio, a budding young scientist, stopped for confession one day and made a decision that changed his life. MARK K. SHRIVER

The confessional in the Basilica of San José de Flores where Bergoglio felt "totally certain" that he was to become a priest. MARK K. SHRIVER

The Calling of St. Matthew by Caravaggio.
Bergoglio has compared his own call to the
priesthood to Matthew's call to become one
of Jesus's disciples.

Bergoglio as a young priest.

Bergoglio celebrates mass with the revered Pedro Arrupe, who served as Superior General of the Jesuit order for eighteen years.

Colegio Máximo de San José in San Miguel, which Bergoglio called home for some thirty years.

Bergoglio's simple bedroom in Colegio Máximo included a single bed . . .

. . . a small kneeler to pray . . .

. . . and an altar and a few chairs.

Bergoglio baptizing Ariel Leal, age five, on March 19, 1980, at the parish of San José Patriarch in San Miguel. Bergoglio had asked Father Alejandro Gauffin to serve as the child's godfather. COURTESY OF ALEJANDRO GAUFFIN, S.J.

Bergoglio distributing first communion to a group of girls at San José Patriarch in 1986. COURTESY OF ALEJANDRO GAUFFIN, S.J.

Bergoglio's austere bed-
room in Córdoba, where
he spent two years in exile.

After reportedly turning down the position of auxiliary bishop of Buenos Aires
twice, Bergoglio finally accepted. He is pictured here at his episcopal ordination on
June 27, 1992, kneeling in front of Cardinal Quarracino as he receives his ring.

Bergoglio presents Rabbi Abraham Skorka with an honorary degree from the Pontifical Argentine Catholic University. Skorka called the act—the first time the university had given an honorary degree to a Jew—a "revolution." Courtesy of León Muicey

Bergoglio signs the Manifesto calling for the bombing at the Asociación Mutual Israelita Argentina to be resolved. Fernando Massobrio / La Nación

With Father Pepe holding the book, Bergoglio speaks at the inauguration of a chapel in Villa 21-24 on September 13, 1997. Pepe built a number of small satellite chapels to reach people in the *villa* who could not go to the main church.

Bergoglio, wearing purple and his bishop's mitre, looks on while Pepe speaks during a mass and procession in the *villa* on February 21, 1999. The mass and procession, held in the streets of the *villa*, asked for peace and love in response to several violent deaths.

Bergoglio and Pepe attend a youth group meeting on April 2, 2005, at the trade school in Villa 21-24. There, he received the news that John Paul II had died, and offered mass in his memory. (The photo below was taken on the same day at the same location.)

Bergoglio offers the mass for John Paul II at the trade school.

Bergoglio washes the feet of drug addicts on Holy Thursday 2008. That day, Pepe decided to create *Hogar de Cristo* to care for addicts living in the *villas*.

Pepe's multifunctional church in Villa La Cárcova. It's part sanctuary, part dining room, part study hall. MARK K. SHRIVER

Magui Alonso, left, and Paz Alonso, right, with Father Toto at the Virgen de los Milagros de Caacupé church in Villa 21-24.
COURTESY OF MAGUI ALONSO AND PAZ ALONSO

The modest but colorful interior of the Virgen de los Milagros de Caacupé church in Villa 21-24. COURTESY OF MAGUI ALONSO AND PAZ ALONSO

Cardinal Bergoglio often laughed and joked in private, but in public, he appeared solemn and unsmiling. STR / Stringer

Bergoglio eschewed a chauffeured car in favor of taking the subway. In this photograph, he is on his way to celebrate the Te Deum at the cathedral on May 25, 2008.

EMILIANO LASALVIA / STR / CONTRIBUTOR

Nilda Gomez in front of the ruins of
the República Cromañón nightclub.

A memorial to the victims of the fire at
the República Cromañón nightclub.

Our Lady of the Car-
toneros watches over
the workers at the
Centro Verde Barracas
plant in Buenos
Aires.

Sergio Sanchez stands amidst recyclables
and other materials at the Centro Verde
Barracas plant in Buenos Aires.

My daughter Molly was among the students who greeted Pope Francis when he arrived at Andrews Air Force Base just outside of Washington, D.C., on September 22, 2015. She took this photograph of the pope walking with President Obama and his family.

MOLLY SHRIVER

My family and I standing in front of the Basilica of the National Shrine of the Immaculate Conception on September 23, 2015, where Pope Francis celebrated mass before 25,000 people. Tommy and I are in the back row; Emma, Molly, and Jeanne are in the front row (L-R).

MARK K. SHRIVER

A FEW DAYS later, I met Maria del Carmen, a woman who had volunteered at San José Patriarch Church when Bergoglio was the parish priest. Father Paredes, who had studied at Colegio Máximo when Bergoglio was rector, had given me Maria's phone number and told me to call her when I arrived in Buenos Aires. "Maria knows Bergoglio well. She volunteered at his parish. She's a wonderful woman."

Maria didn't offer me maté that morning, but rather a very warm glass of Coca-Cola and a big happy smile. Born in 1947 and raised in the Chaco province of Argentina, near the border with Paraguay, she moved to Buenos Aires when she was nineteen years old and to San Miguel twelve years later, in 1978.

Maria was involved from the outset in the creation of San José Patriarch parish. "The streets at that time were full of potholes. When it rained, there was mud to walk through. Bergoglio could just as well be wearing a boot on one foot and a sneaker on the other because he was not concerned about his shoes. What concerned him were the people, above all, the children, the elderly, the poor. He was a pastor. One could say that it was the golden era because at that time there were many seminarians, many novices, and they would go out on Saturdays and Sundays to work in the neighborhood visiting homes, ministering to needs."

She teared up at the memory, then wiped her eyes and continued: "We would make empanadas and sell them. Father Bergoglio would knead and bake *pastafrola* [a typical quince jam pie]. Because the parish progressed, other chapels were built. Father Bergoglio had such a broad and loving vision. He tried to cover all the needs that the families might have. Caritas [a Catholic organization that serves the poor and vulnerable around the world] brought clothes, medicine, supplies, food. He saw the needs of the people as his primary concern."

I don't think I could have stopped her if I'd wanted to.

"He was involved in everything, everything, a mystical man. He was like a great patriarch with eagle eyes. He would cover everything with his gaze." Maria pointed at the ground and said, "He would stand here, but he was seeing what happened, I don't know how far away. He was always looking. I say he had eyes everywhere!"

She went on, "He was serious, pensive, but he would surprise one with a greeting and a joke. He would call me plump old lady and I would tell him, 'Yes, it's good to get old because we leave a track behind us,' and he would laugh.

"Sometimes he would say to me that he was a little concerned because I had an outside job, I took care of my children, I did the housework, and on weekends, I would go to the parish to do things and sometimes to visit people who were sick. He would say, 'Well, but we always have strength. Strength is always there, right?' He always kept a low profile, he never drew attention to himself. When I was cleaning or fixing something, he would approach me and say, 'Don't draw attention to yourself at all, the less that they notice, the better. Work is for God.' He always taught us to keep quiet and work for God."

The room went quiet. Maria's eyes welled up again.

"In 1983, my son got sick and he was hospitalized in the capital city. At about seven in the morning, Bergoglio arrived at the hospital to visit him. By the time I arrived, Bergoglio had left. The nurse told me, 'A priest came to see him.' 'Who?' I asked her, and she said, 'I don't know. I'm still upset. He gave me such a deep, deep gaze. I felt a shudder. Who is this priest?'

"Well, I went in and my son told me that Father Jorge had dropped by to visit. That night, Bergoglio sent a seminarian here to the house, because at that time there were no phones here, to tell me that I should not worry, that he had dropped by and seen my son and that he would be home in two or three more days. Bergoglio touched him and blessed him and said, 'Now the worst is over. You'll be going home.' He would always surprise us with such gestures."

Maria then told me a story that illustrated the commitment to popular religiosity that Bergoglio surely first experienced, and cherished, at the side of his grandma Rosa.

"The son of one of the people I knew traveled to Jerusalem. He brought me a little bag with soil from Jerusalem and I was very happy. So on Saturday, I took the bag to Bergoglio and said to him, 'Father Jorge, look, I have this. Do you want to bless it for me?' And he took the bag and said, 'I cannot bless this soil. This is already blessed. That is where our Master walked, that is where Jesus walked.'"

She had the bag on a table in the corner of her small but tidy living room.

"Bergoglio always gave preference to the most needy, the people who had less, and if the seminarians had to give up eating one day, to take their food to someone who needed food, they would do so. The students and seminarians themselves said that more than once they went without a meal because it was given to someone else who needed it. Bergoglio would say, 'You have everything here, you are comfortable, and this person has nothing. We have to get him our food or our money. The money that we have to buy food, we have to use to buy medicine for such and such a person because he needs it.

"You don't know what he will surprise you with. You treat him seriously and he comes up with something that makes you laugh. A few months before he was named pope, it was terribly hot that day, I had gone to Buenos Aires to pick up a legal document that I needed. He was not at his office, so I left a note for him, 'Padre Bergoglio, my best wishes, 'bye.'

"When I got back home, five or ten minutes after I arrived, the phone rang. I don't know why, but Bergoglio came to mind. I answered the phone and said hello and I heard, 'Mrs. Maria del Carmen,' and I said, 'Father Bergoglio, how come you're calling me?' And he said to me, 'I'm calling to say hello, to see how the kids are doing'—because for him, my children are still the kids. So then I told him what the slacker was doing, because that's what he would call my son, the youngest. He would say, 'What a slacker.' That means he is lazy, so I told him, 'He is in Spain. He's in Madrid,' and we talked. Then he said, 'I want you to pray for me.' And I said, 'Okay, Father, but you pray for me, too,' and he laughed and replied, 'Do you think that I ever stopped doing so?' and I said, 'Okay, Father, okay.'"

She smiled one of the biggest smiles I have ever seen and shook her head.

Maria showed me some notes that Bergoglio had signed. She

proudly displayed them on the small kitchen table. Some were thank-yous to merchants who had donated food or goods to San José Patri-arch in the "golden years." Maria said, "We didn't have chairs in the parish. We had one little old broken chair. Someone must have left it. Bergoglio would say, 'Don't worry. The day will come when we will get some chairs. The day will come.'

"Well, so one day going to work, I ran into a man that owns an important furniture shop in the city, and he said, 'I can donate some benches. I can donate everything.' And I returned happy to tell Father Bergoglio that we had benches. Then the floor donation appeared, all the ceramic tiles, so little by little, the church was completed, without any money, because people there were poor and all they could leave were a few coins.

"Bergoglio always had a smile when he was given something. He was only concerned with moving forward, and he would always say that I should always remember that the best weapon, the best cannon, to which nobody can put up a resistance, are fifty Hail Marys! Yes, the bullets against which there is no protection, right, are fifty Hail Marys. He would say, 'Remember, fifty Hail Marys, fifty Hail Marys, remember the cannon!'"

MARIA INSISTED THAT I meet some of the young people who had been involved in the activities organized by Bergoglio and his stu-dents. So a few days later, I set out for Colegio Máximo again. I met Mario Maidana, forty-three, and Daniel Lemos, forty-four, in front of Colegio Máximo. They suggested that we walk around to a couple of benches in the shade behind the massive building. They clearly knew the grounds well. They still live in the neighborhood and are now fathers and husbands. Mario had met his wife in one of Bergo-glio's youth groups.

We spent an hour talking about the same things that Gauffin, Nar-din, and Petty had been talking about. Both men referred to the time with the same wistfulness and gratitude as the two younger Jesuits who had been reminiscing with me over steaks back in Buenos Aires.

"He was like one of our fathers," said Mario, "but he was always referred to as Jorge, Jorge, Jorge. All the kids referred to him that way, and he preferred to be called that than to be called Father Jorge. He always wanted everyone to be on the same level, that's what it was."

They talked about movie nights that were so jammed with kids that if anyone had to go to the bathroom, he or she had to crawl out through the window; they talked about parish patron saint festivities filled with food and fun; and they talked about the annual picnic where hundreds of kids, Catholics and non-Catholics alike, convened at Colegio Máximo for a day of games.

Daniel described Bergoglio: "I do not remember him being a strict person. No, quite the contrary, he was very soft, calm. I remember, it was for Easter week, the ceremony of the washing of the feet. Well, he would wash the feet of the people, of the kids that were in the area. . . ."

His voice trailed off.

I know people who have had their feet washed on Holy Thursday. They were chosen in advance and every one of them scrubbed their feet clean at home before allowing the priest to "wash" them during the mass.

I had to ask, then, "Did you wash your feet before you went to the service?"

"That was not prepared at all," Mario replied. "People would come to church, and there was a brother at the door of the church and he would ask, 'Would you like the Father to wash your feet? And if you said yes, okay, and if not, okay. It was a decision made at that very moment. Nothing was prearranged."

And then their thoughts turned to the sea.

"Just imagine," Mario said, "our parents would give us permission. We were five or six years old, maybe nine, to go to camps, three hundred kilometers away, without any parents, only with the priests, and that was the first time we ever saw the sea!"

"What happened," Daniel said, "was that we would leave here, and because there were so many kids, we would take only what was essential—water, rice, and noodles. Whatever could be prepared easily. And then, once we were there, the priests would go about asking the larger companies there, the meatpackers, the supermarkets, for donations to supplement what the camp needed. We never lacked anything, and we never felt hungry, on the contrary we had everything. The generosity of the people in this beach town was amazing."

I asked if Bergoglio ever went on these trips.

"Yes, I think he went twice," Mario said. "However, he was always in contact with us, so he knew all the time how things were going. He was always informed of everything."

I recalled Petty's description of Bergoglio as the man who was always there even when he wasn't there. I told these guys the story, and they nodded in agreement. Daniel looked across the field to where the pigsties used to be.

"I remember always seeing him walk here in the park, inside, and on the sidewalk outside," Daniel said. "He would always be walking, meditating, I guess. He was alone, thinking."

"He would walk through the neighborhood a lot, too," Mario said. "He would always know what was happening with the families. If he said the nine o'clock mass for the adults, he would go to walk in the neighborhood afterward. Somehow, he always knew who was sick. He would take them communion. He was always everywhere."

THE DIVISIONS THAT Mom Debussy spoke of—that Nardin and Gauffin had mentioned as well—continued to deepen. The man who knew everything—who was there even when he wasn't—would serve as rector of Colegio Máximo until 1986. He would then be sent to finish his doctorate in Germany, but he would soon return. He missed his beloved Buenos Aires; he never did finish his doctorate.

Back in Argentina, Bergoglio was assigned a part-time teaching job at Colegio del Salvador in Buenos Aires and was named confessor of the Jesuit community. The man who had been in charge of something since the day he had completed his training was now, while not powerless, certainly less than powerful.

He would take the train to Colegio Máximo on Sundays, eat with the scholastics that evening, and teach on Mondays. "The rector asked him to teach," Velasco told me. "But he wanted to keep control of the students and how they were trained. This was the late 1980s. He was still very focused on a strict curriculum. He did not want us to read any liberation theology."

I had coffee with Leandro Manuel Calle, who entered the Jesuits in 1987, was ordained in 1999, and left the priesthood in 2007. He studied at Colegio Máximo in the late 1980s. When asked about his experiences there, he answered pensively, "When I entered the Colegio Máximo, Bergoglio would only go there to teach. He would go there on Sundays, and on Mondays he would teach. But I remember very well because he had a room there."

Calle paused. "I can talk to you about the post-Bergoglio times, what he created."

He paused again. "I knew all the guys that passed through there, and what one can see is something very complex. Something very complex."

I remembered the hesitation in Gauffin's and Nardin's voices when this time period—the late 1970s to the late 1980s—came up. Nardin had told me, "Well, there was a split when Jorge stopped being rector of the Máximo. There was a split within the province, an internal fight, an internal crisis. It's very complicated to explain, very complicated to understand."

Gauffin had said to me, "There was a crisis within the Jesuit order when he stopped being rector and it's too difficult to explain. You have to have lived it."

Calle said, "There is an expression that is used here in Argentina, 'The dirty laundry is washed in the home.' In other words, family problems are dealt with within the family."

This time was, obviously, a painful period for all involved, a time no one really wanted to discuss, one that was filled with hurt and ambiguity. I hesitated to ask Calle to relive that past, but he volunteered, "When we talk about left and right, it is not a problem of left and right. In Argentina, we tend to put Bergoglio to the left or to the right. It is much more complex. Much more complex. It falls within a spiritual, emotional level, of domination, power. For me the big theme for Bergoglio is the issue of power. Because, in those years, in my opinion, the issue was that of paternity—spiritual paternity. And I think that it is a great mistake—for everyone!—to exercise spiritual paternity, to be sons and fathers, when the Gospels talk about being brothers. That is something Bergoglio doesn't like much, because the concept of brother generates a horizontal line, not a vertical line."

Spiritual paternity? I remember that Nardin had referred to his time with Bergoglio so fondly that he called Colegio Máximo his "paternal home." Mario and Daniel said he was like a father to them, and Maria had used a phrase to describe Bergoglio that was unforgettable: "He was like a great patriarch with eagle eyes."

"Do you understand?" Calle asked. "So the relationship is always, I'm above the other or another is above me, but it is never like this." He waved his hands horizontally. "And if one reads the Gospels, which is what a man of the Church should do, Jesus, what he emphasizes is fraternity."

Calle was upset at reliving the past, but he was not yet done.

"In the years 1989 and 1990, the Society was splitting in two, right there at Colegio Máximo. In other words, the problem of those higher up reached us, and there was a crisis, a crisis that all Jesuits will deny, pro-Bergoglio, anti-Bergoglio. I clearly was in the anti-Bergoglio camp."

When asked whether all the young Jesuits were in that camp, he replied, "No, no, no. Because, as I say, it is not a matter of right or left, young or old. It's a spiritual, emotional, and ideological question into which the left and the right slipped . . . it is complex, complex. The subject of power is complex. Because when you seek power you are not concerned very much with ideology. That is my view. But I will insist once more that it is complex."

Before I could ask a question, Calle said, "You cannot put labels on Bergoglio. Labels don't serve with Bergoglio. It's very complex. Because, for example, when it comes to the poor, he is a person who is extremely sensitive. He is sensitive. And he is an austere person."

"It's very complex." How many times had I heard that now?

The accusations spun around in my head. Authoritarianism. Sins and errors. Excessive discipline.

And the differing opinions: What some called a time of dictatorial paternalism and others called the happiest days of their lives. What some saw as mentoring and others saw as manipulation and power plays. There were the idyllic scenes of children playing and learning their faith, of priests working around the clock but loving the routine. But there was also the acknowledgment by seemingly all that there was a divide, there was tension—dirty laundry, if you will, that should be cleaned only in-house.

What do I, a fifty-two-year-old American, make of Bergoglio at fifty-three? A man who, some twenty-five years after interacting with these men and women, can make some of them weepy with admiration, can make others shake their heads in wonder, and yet make other grown men visibly upset?

One could describe Bergoglio, exaggerating only slightly, by paraphrasing his own words when he described the Catholic Church during the Dirty War: part sinner, part saint. I prefer the image that Father Scannone, the Argentine Jesuit theologian and one of Bergoglio's teachers, painted when he told me, "I have seen him grow through every stage of his life. He was like a flower that was growing and growing and is now blooming."

But before the flower could bloom, it would have to be repotted, not in Buenos Aires but in the interior of Argentina, in Córdoba.

What happened in Córdoba—and what happened afterward—that makes old friends and foes alike shake their heads in amazement? Why and how did the pious, disciplined, focused patriarch blossom into the smiling, big-hearted, gregarious shepherd?

18 Córdoba

HAVE YOU EVER been so low, felt so defeated, that you questioned your very reason for being on this earth? I have. It was September 2002 and I had lost my race for the Democratic nomination for Congress in Maryland's eighth congressional district. I declared for the seat in April 2001 and spent months before that announcement preparing for the campaign. I had hired the best-paid political advisers in the country. I had spent at least two years running—and lost by less than twenty-five hundred votes.

But I could say that I had been running for the seat for years and years. I had been a state representative—in Maryland, we called them delegates—for eight years, but it was more than that. Elected office had been the topic of innumerable dinner conversations throughout my youth. No, we were never told that we had to run for office, but I definitely got the sense that it was the most honorable—and expected—profession there was. And that feeling, that expectation, had had a profound influence on me as I grew up.

The Washington Post chose my primary race as its congressional race of the year. Two other strong candidates were vying to challenge the beloved but vulnerable incumbent Republican representative, Connie Morella, in the November general election.

The pressure was on, and the press was on the case.

Our internal polls showed my lead slipping with each passing week. With just a few weeks to go before the election, I fell behind. I had raised a ton of money; I also put a lot of our own cash into one final push. My mother, eighty-one, and my father, almost eighty-seven and in the throes of early Alzheimer's disease, had even gone door-to-door for me, on rainy days and searing hot days, during the campaign.

On election night, the results dribbled in. It was close, way too close to call, even though I was trailing throughout much of the evening. I had a crowd of supporters in the hotel. I went down and thanked them. Everyone cheered, but the election had yet to be decided.

The night dragged on. The TV cameras left because the late news had come and gone. My wife, Jeanne, and I decided to leave, thinking the result would not be official until the next day. But on the drive home, my campaign manager called and made it official.

I had lost.

I pulled into the driveway, got out of the car, and called to congratulate Chris Van Hollen (who went on to defeat Representative Morella in the general election). I offered to do a joint event with him later that week.

Thank God I didn't have to give a concession speech, I thought as I flopped into bed, exhausted and crestfallen.

The next day, after a rejuvenating breakfast with Jeanne and our two children, Molly and Tommy (Emma was born in 2005), feelings of humiliation and defeat soon surfaced. I felt as if I had tarnished my family's legacy, my parents' hopes for me, and my supposed calling.

I looked at my dad, a man who had suffered one of the most lopsided losses in the history of American presidential campaigns when he ran with George McGovern in 1972. He had lost, massively, and suffered, I now understood, massively. But he was a Shriver, not a Kennedy. I was half and half, and I had clearly dishonored the more famous family's tradition.

We don't lose, we Kennedys. I had always, deep down, believed that, despite plenty of losses. I remember the sensation of just wanting to go away, to go somewhere else, far from my family and friends. Into, you might say, exile.

Several years later, as my father was slowly succumbing to Alzheimer's, I finally began to come to terms with my electoral defeat. The disease has a way of stripping away all the pretenses, all the fronts. What I saw as I cared for him was a man who loved me purely, who loved me for who I was, not because I had won two elections and lost one, not because I had a big job at Save the Children. No, I realized at last that love, not power or fame, is the real success.

For several weeks after his passing, I felt physically stuck in grief. I have come to see that time as what Ignatius called desolation. But then one day, at the urging of a friend, I decided to try to write about my father's life and my relationship with him. As I sat in my basement making a list of the lessons my dad had taught me, I wrote that an important one was that my electoral loss in no way affected his love for me. As I wrote, I felt a sense of peace. It was almost a physical sensation, as though goodness were enveloping me. This man was my father! What an amazing privilege. This man had brought me closer to God! What an amazing fact. This man's love for me, like God's love, was the same whether I went to Capitol Hill as a U.S. representative or not, whether I worked for Save the Children helping poor kids all across America or did something else. What I did didn't matter—he just loved me.

Having eventually turned that night in my basement into a book about my dad, I now realize that our darkest hours can transform into our most enriching times on earth. Desolation can turn to consolation if the right guide is there to teach us to discern the messages hidden in our fear, in our hopelessness and despair. For me, my dad was a proxy for God—through my father, I slowly started to hear God's message about worldly priorities, love, generosity, and mercy. I believe that that experience was what Ignatius called consolation.

And so, when I researched the circumstances of Bergoglio's own massive "defeat"—his exile from his beloved Buenos Aires—I wanted to focus on the growth of the man as much as the facts of his banishment. How a person changes has always been the narrative that most interests me.

We know that his approach to the formation of Jesuits caused deep divisions in the order, as did the manner in which he went about that task. As the 1980s went by, many Jesuits still believed that Bergoglio was too rigid in his demands of young Jesuits, and that even though he was not provincial anymore, he was still trying to shape and manage every dimension of Jesuit life in the province. Even his admirers said it was a complex time that they wouldn't—or couldn't—describe. It was just too painful. In 1983, Pedro Arrupe, Bergoglio's mentor and inspiration, was replaced by Peter-Hans Kolvenbach as superior general in Rome. Bergoglio's critics and antagonists in Argentina had the new boss's ear. The tension and division persisted, and worsened.

Externally, in terms of Argentine and Catholic culture and politics, the damage of simply having any role of power during Argentina's Dirty War had tainted Bergoglio. He had saved many lives and tried to bring peace and reason to his convulsing homeland, but in so doing he had made enemies. In particular, his role in the Jalics and Yorio saga had caused some powerful Jesuits to split with him, and they were working behind the scenes to undermine him.

But the more people I spoke with, the clearer it became to me that Bergoglio, as much as he wanted power, wanted most of all to keep mentoring. He had stated, during his juniorate in Chile in 1960, that his professional dream was to be novice master. But when you get your dream job as your first job, there is the risk that you will never want to leave it, or, in Bergoglio's case, never want to leave behind the responsibility and pleasure that come with it, nor the habits, skills, and authorities that accrue.

For all these reasons, the Jesuit provincial at the time, no doubt with the blessing of Kolvenbach, decided to move Bergoglio from the capital city, his beloved Buenos Aires, to the interior, to Córdoba. He was not given a big title or a position filled with responsibility. He heard confessions, read, wrote, and took care of the elderly Jesuits.

Some Jesuits have told me that there is no such thing as a demotion within the order. They told me that the provincial talks to each Jesuit in the province and prays—tries to discern—what the best role is for that man. What an outsider like me sees as a demotion or exile is, to these men, just a new role in which to find and serve God, a new role in which to grow spiritually.

But in this case I believe the divisions Bergoglio created in the 1970s and 1980s were so deep and divisive—grown men who lived through that period still can't even describe it, they just shake their heads and want to change the subject—that Bergoglio's superiors decided that he had violated a key principle that Saint Ignatius himself had written into the Jesuit constitutions: "Anyone seen to be a cause of division among those who live together, estranging them either among themselves or from their head, ought with great diligence to be separated from that community, as a pestilence which can infect it seriously if a remedy is not quickly applied."

Father Petty, who was then teaching at the Catholic University of Córdoba, remembers seeing a Bergoglio in exile whom he could barely recognize. "I was worried about him," Petty said. "He was going through a very rough period. You could tell that all he had built might have come crashing down around him. It was obvious he was in the midst of a big internal struggle in Córdoba. He would go visit sick and retired priests in the infirmary, care for them, cook their meals, but he didn't speak with other Jesuits very much at all. His work was that of a free-floating assistant priest. And he wore the struggle in his face."

Father Velasco, who would later serve as president of the Catholic University of Córdoba, knew Bergoglio even better than Petty did, and witnessed the internal strife firsthand. "The simple fact is that they gave him little to do," Velasco told me. "He was reduced. He was so capable, so active, but was given little to do there. He was very sad in Córdoba. We knew it; he didn't have to say it, we could tell. But he never complained. He simply did not complain."

It is shocking to read Bergoglio's own writing from his Córdoba time. In an essay entitled "The Exile of All Flesh," he writes, "The man or woman who consciously takes charge of his exile suffers a double loneliness. They are lonely amid the crowd, strangers in a strange land. But they also taste a spiritual loneliness, 'the bitterness of solitude before God.'"

He then brings up the Hebrew prophet Jeremiah, a leader who succumbed to internecine struggles and backbiting among his people. Jeremiah had been placed in stocks for all the public to see, threatened, ridiculed, and finally banished. But because his urging for reform and his criticism of his people for heeding false prophets were not heeded, Jerusalem was eventually conquered by the Babylonian army.

Jeremiah became known as "the Weeping Prophet," for, in one part of the Bible, he weeps over the fate of his people:

> *If you do not listen to this in your pride,*
> *I will weep many tears in secret;*
> *My eyes will run with tears*
> *for the* LORD's *flock, led away to exile.*

"It's the prayer of a man who gave everything and would like—at least—that God would be on his side," Bergoglio wrote. "But in life, sometimes it seems as though God puts himself on the other side."

That last sentence sounds like a man in a state of Ignatian desolation.

Saint Ignatius believed that our feelings of peace, or alternatively of despair, are stirred up by spirits, some good and some evil. The feelings fit into two categories: "consolation" and "desolation" in the language of Ignatian spirituality. These were discussed in chapter 10, so here let me simply quote from the publication *Ignatian Spirituality* to refresh the concepts:

> Spiritual consolation is an experience of being so on fire with God's love that we feel impelled to praise, love, and serve God and help others as best as we can. Spiritual consolation encourages and facilitates a deep sense of gratitude for God's faithfulness, mercy, and companionship in our life. In consolation, we feel more alive and connected to others.

Spiritual desolation, in contrast, is an experience of the soul in heavy darkness or turmoil. We are assaulted by all sorts of doubts, bombarded by temptations, and mired in self-preoccupations. We are excessively restless and anxious and feel cut off from others. Such feelings, in Ignatius's words, "move one toward lack of faith and leave one without hope and without love."

The key question in interpreting consolation and desolation centers on where the movement is coming from and where it is leading. Spiritual consolation does not always mean happiness, nor does spiritual desolation always mean sadness. Sometimes an experience of sadness can be a moment of conversion and intimacy with God. Times of human suffering can be moments of great grace. Similarly, peace or happiness can be illusory if these feelings are helping us avoid changes we need to make.

Father Scannone puts this time clearly in Ignatian terms: "When he was in Córdoba, well, they talk about his exile, or whatever they call it. I remember having seen him there, very serious and very dour. I think he was going through a sort of dark night. A spiritual purification. And shortly after, they made him a bishop, so I think God's providence was preparing him, but that is my interpretation, from the outside, of course. But there I did see him with an expression of desolation."

Scannone's reference to Bergoglio's having been named a bishop, of course, reveals the ending of Bergoglio's desolation in Córdoba and the beginning of his return to a state of consolation. Bergoglio kept praying, and perhaps God did intervene. I was told by multiple sources that Bergoglio was offered the role of auxiliary bishop twice and turned it down twice. It is startling to an outsider that a man in such a state of desolation would refuse what I see as a promotion and a return to Buenos Aires, but remember that Bergoglio was a Jesuit and as such had taken a vow not to seek higher ecclesiastical office. Furthermore, a bishop is in charge of all the priests in a diocese—not just Jesuits, but Franciscans, Salesians, diocesan priests, and more. Finally, if he became a bishop, he would no longer live with his Jesuit brothers, and community is a critical part of a Jesuit's life. Bergoglio would, in essence, be leaving his beloved Jesuit structure and companions forever.

His vow of obedience to the pope eventually led him to accept the role.

A former Jesuit who remains very close to Bergoglio and asked to remain anonymous told me that he said to Bergoglio at the time, "You can either be a dead Jesuit or a live bishop."

Two YEARS AFTER his exile, in June 1992, Bergoglio was named auxiliary bishop and episcopal vicar of the Flores district in Buenos Aires. He was about to commence another startling rise to power and prominence. The following year, he would be named vicar general of the Archdiocese of Buenos Aires; in 1997, Pope John Paul II appointed him coadjutor archbishop, which meant that when the incumbent cardinal, Antonio Quarracino, resigned or died, Bergoglio would succeed him. Such an appointment is rare, and his ascension to it in just five years is stunning. Less than a year later, following the death of Quarracino, he became archbishop, and in 2001, he rose through the ranks yet again to become a cardinal.

But this ascension would be different. His time in Córdoba—the time of his "great interior crisis"—had changed him. Listening to countless confessions surely must have given him new insights into human suffering and the primacy of mercy. Back in Buenos Aires in June 1992, he would continue to learn, slowly and surely, a lesson that he is teaching us all today: Neither power nor position brings God's consolation. He would learn that true consolation would come from supporting the families of murdered Jewish children and adults; from engaging in meaningful interfaith dialogue; from providing pastoral support to the families of the victims of a deadly nightclub fire and fighting for justice in the wake of that tragedy; from helping organize and support laborers in the poorest barrios of Buenos Aires; and from living according to the Ignatian way—discernment, serving the poor and most marginalized, and ministering to souls—even if he wasn't doing so within the framework and hierarchy of his beloved Jesuit order.

19 Sons of Abraham

I DON'T KNOW about you, but it was always pretty easy for me to hang out with people from the same religious background. I went to Catholic grade school, Catholic high school, and Catholic college, so I knew a lot of Catholics. Although I went to a couple of other schools, one Protestant, one secular, most of my best friends were Catholic.

I knew that some of my mom's best friends and closest colleagues were Jews; I knew that my dad worked at a predominantly Jewish law firm; I also knew that both of them had colleagues and friends who were Protestants and Muslims and atheists.

I had been exposed to all of these groups, but my exposure to people my own age of different faiths had been limited until I entered politics in 1994 at the age of thirty.

The Maryland House of Delegates district in which I ran had a large percentage of Jewish voters, so in order to win the primary and then the general election, I had to reach out to the Jewish population. Through a friend of a friend, I was introduced to Rabbi Joseph Weinberg, the head rabbi of the Washington Hebrew Congregation, perhaps the most influential Jewish congregation in the D.C. area and home to many potential constituents.

I had never visited Washington Hebrew—I had not gone to a bar or bat mitzvah as a kid, nor had I attended a wedding or funeral or any type of service there at all. I didn't know any rabbis, either, but I knew that Weinberg was an influential member of the Jewish community and a critical person for my political future. So I asked for a meeting.

Weinberg came out to the reception area to greet me and walked me back to his office. It was a small space filled with books and pictures of his wife and children. He was six feet tall and razor thin; he had a warm smile and a soft, calm voice. We talked about growing up in Montgomery County, Maryland, about schools, about God, about social justice, about marriage, about our families.

Toward the end, we talked about my political aspirations.

As I got up to leave, he offered to introduce me to his son Jonathan, who was a couple of years younger than I, a lawyer by training and a lifelong Montgomery County resident. I thanked him for the introduction and left.

Jonathan was just as thoughtful and warm as his dad and just as committed to improving the common good. He would become the chair of each of my three political campaigns, and he and his wife, Jennifer, have remained great friends with Jeanne and me ever since, even though my political career ended some fourteen years ago.

Despite my own sheltered existence, I was amazed when I recently found myself in the position of introducing a rabbi and a priest who worked within miles of each other, yet neither man had any idea who the other was, nor did they know much about the other's institution.

Maybe I should not have been so amazed. In my thirties and forties, I saw that many of my Catholic and Jewish friends tended to hang around people just like themselves. Yes, people worked in diverse workplaces, but it seemed to me that people's friends—their closest friends—tended to be people with the same religious background; Catholics hung around with Catholics, and Jews with Jews.

So as I embarked on my journey to understand Pope Francis, I was surprised to find that he had written a book in collaboration with a rabbi. And I was even more surprised when I opened *Pope Francis: Conversations with Jorge Bergoglio*—Bergoglio's only authorized biography—and saw that the foreword was written by that same rabbi, Abraham Skorka.

Skorka's first line caught my attention: "As far as I know, this has to be the first time in two thousand years that a rabbi has written the foreword for a book about the thoughts of a Catholic priest."

That is a pretty amazing claim—and it is particularly amazing that a rabbi wrote the foreword to the authorized biography of the sitting cardinal of a very important city in a very Catholic country. And given the history of anti-Semitism in Argentina, the relationship between the two men—and Bergoglio's relationship with the Jewish community in general—struck me as that much more unusual.

Nearly a quarter of a million Jews live in Argentina—the vast majority in Buenos Aires—the largest population of Jews in Latin America and second only to the United States for Jewish population in the Americas. Yet their experience in Argentina has been anything but smooth. Jews have immigrated to Argentina for more than one hundred and twenty years, fleeing the czarist Russian Empire in the 1800s and Nazi Germany in the 1930s. Jews have felt the brunt of anti-Semitism in Argentina, starting with the death of dozens of Jewish children in the winter of 1889 after they were abandoned at an unfinished train station. In 1938, an Argentine foreign ministry circular effectively closed Argentina to Jewish refugees seeking to flee Germany. This embedded anti-Semitism continued with President Juan Perón's effort to bring Nazis and other war criminals to Argentina from 1946 on.

These acts of anti-Semitism are not confined to the nineteenth century and the first half of the twentieth. On March 17, 1992—a few months before Bergoglio was named auxiliary bishop of Buenos Aires—twenty-nine people were killed and more than two hundred forty were wounded when a car bomb exploded in the front entrance of the Israeli embassy in downtown Buenos Aires. A group called Islam Jihad claimed responsibility immediately after the bombing, but no arrests have ever been made.

Then, a little over two years later, on July 18, 1994, a car bomb exploded outside the Asociación Mutual Israelita Argentina (AMIA) in downtown Buenos Aires, killing eighty-five people and injuring more than three hundred. No arrests have been made in that attack, either.

"These two bombings were not just an attack on Jews," Dr. Sergio Berensztein, a leading political analyst in Argentina, told me, "but an attack on Argentina. Jews had been discriminated against and been victims of violence before, in the 1920s, 1930s, and 1940s. And the Catholic Church as an institution was not open to Jews, even though there were individual Catholics who were very supportive and helpful to Jews. But these two events stunned the entire country."

I have to meet Rabbi Skorka, I thought as I studied this perplexing history. *This man will have insights into how Bergoglio, as a Catholic leader, addressed these attacks and the Jewish-Catholic relationship.*

THE SECURITY WAS very tight at Skorka's building in downtown Buenos Aires—I passed by a guard station and through a locked gate and a buzzer system on my way in. The interior of the building and the rabbi's office were very austere. A few pictures of his family stood on his desk, his bookshelves were crammed with books, and the chairs were solid wood with no cushions. His degrees hung in simple frames on the wall.

Skorka is about five feet four inches tall with thick salt-and-pepper hair. He has a warm face and kind eyes. He was wearing a yarmulke and a long-sleeve shirt but no tie.

"You're writing a book about Bergoglio, yes?" He smiled. "Let's talk."

He had been kind to take the meeting, but I got the very strong sense that he was a serious man with a lot on his plate. We didn't exchange pleasantries, and there was no offer of coffee or maté. He was all business.

"I first met Bergoglio in 1997," he said. "He was not yet a cardinal. He was an auxiliary bishop in Buenos Aires. He paid special attention to several points—first and foremost was the suffering of poor people, the exploited people, people who are living in slavelike conditions. He was very sensitive to people's lives, especially those that are filled with misery. He is very sensitive to the great drama of humanity."

He spoke English with a heavy accent. "Do you mind if I speak in English?" he asked. "It is good practice for me."

"Of course," I said. "You speak well."

He nodded and continued.

"Bergoglio understood that the relationship between Jews and Christians had to be a real relationship—not just a dialogue, but a special relationship.

"Why?" Skorka asked himself, and then he answered his own question. "Christians were formed from a very special moment in the history of the Jewish people. All Christian churches grow out of the Jewish experience. We have had divergences and clashes, but what Bergoglio understands and fights for is that we need to enter into a close dialogue, not to convince or to change the other, but to better understand each other. Bergoglio has said to me many times that Catholics can learn from the Jewish masters about the Holy Scriptures. He believes that the Bible has power, real power. And that to better understand each other, valid dialogue is necessary.

"Bergoglio," he said, "in his way of thinking, is a very coherent person."

"What do you mean?" I asked.

"In 2012," Skorka explained, "he was the chancellor of the Pontificia Universidad Catolica Argentina—Pontifical Argentine Catholic University—and he bestowed upon me an honorary degree. His intent was to say to all the Christians, 'Look, we can learn from a rabbi,' and this is a very, very deep point. It was the first time that a pontifical university had bestowed such a title on a rabbi, a Jew, here in Argentina, in Latin America. Bergoglio made a revolution by this action!

"In our past, of course, there were anti-Semitic expressions from the Church against Jews, especially in the thirties, in the forties, in the fifties, and of course there were expressions in the seventies. But through the work of people who were very, very engaged on the Catholic side, a whole effort developed here to uproot anti-Semitic expressions from the Church."

I asked Skorka if there was a special moment during the ceremony that he remembered. "It was when no microphone was close to us, and Bergoglio told me, 'You cannot imagine how much I have dreamed of this moment.'" Then Skorka repeated Bergoglio's words in Spanish: *"Usted no puede imaginarse cuánto soñé con este momento."*

In Spanish, there are two ways to say "you"—an informal way (*tu*) and a formal way (*usted*). When asked why Bergoglio used the formal *usted* when talking with the rabbi when the two had been friends for so long, the rabbi replied, "It's a manifestation of a great respect we have for each other. Despite a few jokes and whatever, we maintain the formal 'you.'" The rabbi told me that he does the same with Bergoglio.

I had expected that Skorka would spend thirty minutes or so with me and we were now at that point. But he did not give any hint that it was time for me to go. Quite the contrary.

"I will tell you stories about Bergoglio." He smiled. "Interesting moments. This is a very, very interesting story of our friendship and our commitment to the dialogue between Jew and Christian.

"Many years ago, I presented him with a book titled *¿Hacia un mañana sin fé?* [*Toward a Faithless Tomorrow?*]. Bergoglio wrote the foreword to this book. Then one day, the journalist of *Clarín* Sergio Rubin called me by phone and told me, 'Look, we finished Bergoglio's biography with his help, an authorized biography. And when we asked him whom he suggests to write the foreword, he said Skorka.'

"I was totally surprised, astonished, overcome with emotion. Imagine, yourself, the archbishop of a city! A cardinal! A cardinal!"

Skorka's arms were gesticulating, he was almost shouting. "A cardinal!" he said a third time. "It's incredible!"

The shock of it still seemed to stun him.

"You are right," I said meekly.

He didn't acknowledge my comment. He was in his own world.

"When I heard, when I heard . . . Look, you have to analyze what occurred, because you saw the book already, I suppose. And wasn't it something strange before your eyes? What?" he exclaimed. "Skorka is writing the foreword to the book of a cardinal."

"As an American, I think it's surprising. But not *that* surprising," I said.

We discussed whether this would happen in America and the rabbi emphatically replied, "No! No! No! I assure you that no."

"I guess you are right," I said. "I mean, if you ask a cardinal who should write his—"

He interrupted me, "Ask several cardinals in America if they would, years ago, accept the foreword from a rabbi."

"No, it wouldn't happen," I agreed.

Skorka kept talking right through me. "For a book of his biography? Authorized biography. Impossible! Impossible!" he said emphatically.

With barely a pause, the rabbi started to tell another story.

"One day, it appeared in the newspaper that the brother of Bergoglio had passed away, so I went to be with him at the funeral home and we spoke about life and about all the themes you can imagine that two people of faith can speak, one with one at such a moment, in such a place, and we spoke from the heart one with the other.

"At a certain moment, I asked Bergoglio, 'May I ask you a question?'

" 'Yes, yes, ask me,' Bergoglio said.

" 'How was it that you selected me to be the person to write the foreword of your book?' and he immediately without thinking, spontaneously, he told me, he looked at my eyes and said, 'So it came out from my heart.' " Skorka's voice became soft and he repeated in Spanish, *"Así salió de mi corazón . . . Así salió de mi corazón . . ."*

I asked, "When you say it was spontaneous, he had clearly thought about this beforehand, right? I mean, he must have thought—"

He cut me off. "You have to understand his answer as I told you, spontaneously, without thinking," Skorka replied. " 'So it came out from my heart.' When you are going to write this story—don't give an interpretation of these words."

"Yes," I said. "Don't worry."

"No! No! No!" He was not yelling at me; he just wanted to make his point clear. "I tell you why, because the beauty of this story is to give each one of the readers the possibility to interpret the sentence as each one understands the sentence. You cannot interpret the sentence, because you don't know. I myself cannot tell you that what he tried to tell me. I don't know. The only thing is a description of a very deep sentiment that caught *my* heart when I heard that. That's clear? You know what I mean?"

"Yes, sir, yes. A deep sentiment that caught your heart," I said.

"He caught my heart at that moment in a very special way. It's not a rational thing—it spontaneously came out from his heart."

He became quiet. I didn't say anything. All I could think of was Saint Ignatius and the Spiritual Exercises and the desire to balance intellect and movements of the heart. Bergoglio's heart had clearly touched Skorka's heart, and it does to this day.

Skorka broke the silence. "Okay, what else?" he asked.

When asked what Bergoglio's favorite story from the Old Testament was, Skorka replied immediately, "Abraham! Because Bergoglio likes the idea of walking. The whole history of Abraham is continuously moving, from Babylon to Canaan and from Canaan to Egypt because there was a great hunger in Canaan. Afterward, he came back to Canaan, and there he went from one place to another, up to the end when he settled in one place. But it wasn't only a corporal moving, a moving of his body, a material moving; he moved in history, he went ahead constantly with the idea to develop the concept of faith, of faith in one God, in a spiritual God, in a transcendental God.

"This is a favorite story for him because he understands his mission as a priest. In this attitude of Abraham, faith cannot be petrified; faith requires constantly moving, developing."

ABOUT A WEEK after that remarkable meeting with Skorka, I found myself a good thirty minutes late to meet Luis Czyzewski.

He was not happy. On my way to his office, I received two texts asking if the meeting was still on. The traffic was horrible, as usual in Buenos Aires, and I was running well behind.

When I arrived at Luis's office, he was brisk: "Come on. We will meet in my conference room. I don't have a lot of time—you are very late."

Luis is about five feet ten, balding, and a bit chunky. He is an accountant, and his office was filled with six or seven employees all at their desks, all with their heads down, working away. No one lifted his head when we walked through the tight quarters toward the small conference room. I got the very strong sense that Luis was a serious, focused businessman who ran a tight operation.

Luis's twenty-one-year-old daughter, Paola, was one of the victims of the bombing at the Asociación Mutual Israelita Argentina in Buenos Aires on July 18, 1994. A third-year law student, she was at AMIA that morning when a van containing two hundred seventy-five kilograms of explosives detonated on the street in front of the building, killing Paola and eighty-four other people and wounding hundreds more. This deadliest terrorist attack in Argentine history spurred national and international outrage. Three days later, an estimated one hundred fifty thousand people gathered in the rain in Buenos Aires in protest.

I thanked Luis for meeting with me, but I stumbled trying to my express my sympathy about Paola. I didn't know quite what to say twenty years after a tragic event, but whatever I said did not come out well.

He waved off my comments and went right into how he knew Bergoglio.

"The contact we had with Bergoglio was not at the time the attack occurred, but quite a while later," Luis said.

"On each anniversary of the AMIA attack, we organize certain activities. On the eleventh anniversary, in 2005, we developed what we called a Manifesto and asked renowned Argentines to sign it. The only condition was that no official, no politician, nobody holding political office was to sign, we didn't want anyone from the government, nobody from the opposition, and nobody from the judicial branch.

We wanted well-known people to sign, as long as they were not government officials, because the Manifesto was directed at the president at that time, the parliament, and the judiciary. The Manifesto said that we wanted them to resolve this matter. So, if you are asking the political power to resolve a matter, those who cannot sign are those who have to resolve the matter, because it is a request made of them. And we started to call prominent people. And at a certain point, we said, we haven't called anyone from any of the religions. Neither a rabbi, nor a priest, nor an imam. And whom shall we call from the Catholic Church? So we decided to pick up the phone and call the Curia. The person we asked to do that was a person who lost his wife in the AMIA attack and who has now also passed away, but he was a rabbi. So the rabbi calls and asks to speak to Bergoglio. Bergoglio at that time was the cardinal. He was the primate cardinal, the most important cardinal of Argentina. Two minutes later, Bergoglio picks up the phone, and the rabbi explains, and Bergoglio says, 'Can you read to me what it is that I have to sign?'

"It is read to him. And he says, 'Okay, I will sign it.' And the rabbi that made the call asks him when he would sign it and he said, 'Come whenever you like.' We took the paper and went to the Curia, two family members and a journalist and a photographer.

"Bergoglio appears and says, 'What is there to sign?' The paper was as big as this table. They open the paper, he reads it and it says sign here, and he signs. And the rabbi then says, 'Cardinal, I want to say something to you.' Bergoglio imagined that what he was about to hear was, 'Well, thank you very much.' And Bergoglio said, 'No, I will not let you say anything to me, I will say something.' And the rabbi said, 'And what is it you have to say to us?' and Bergoglio said, 'I will not let you thank me, the one who has to say thank you is I.'

"It was a gesture that for us was very important," Luis continued. "And what happened with Bergoglio when he became pope? Bergoglio is known for receiving many Argentines. It's not that he wants to receive many, but rather because many want to see him!" He chuckled.

"And during one of these visits, the director of the Latin American

Jewish Congress went together with other people. That was in March or April of this year [2014]. And when the interview was about to end, this person says to Bergoglio—to Francis, he was already Francis—he said, 'We would like you to send a greeting to the relatives of the victims of the AMIA on the twentieth anniversary.' Bergoglio answers, 'Do you have a phone?'

" 'Yes.'

" 'Okay, film me.'

"They started to film with the phone, and Bergoglio recorded a greeting to the relatives of the victims. What he said was very strong. He spoke for a minute or two. . . ."

Luis's voice trailed off. He shook his head and smiled at me, still amazed that the pope had recorded a message spontaneously. Just thinking about Bergoglio had turned him into a warm, smiling man. I knew that this was even better proof than what Skorka had given me of a man who was dedicated to bringing both faiths and all the people of his beloved city together. Luis was not a rabbi or a famous civic leader; he was a grieving father. Bergoglio had tried, while respecting Luis's own faith, to help move him from desolation to consolation. Bergoglio, the wandering Jesuit now on a whole different life course, was still putting his cherished Ignatian principles to work as a pastoral leader.

20 Toto, Pepe, and the Rabbi

FROM AGE TWENTY-THREE to twenty-eight, I ran a nonprofit I had created in Baltimore that monitored juvenile delinquents seven days a week, every day of the year. Our caseworkers would check in with them three to five times a day, waking them up in the morning, making sure they were at school, making sure they were at an after-school job or in bed at night. It was an intensive outreach program designed to steer troubled youths down the right path. We worked out of a public school, PS 180, in the Cherry Hill neighborhood of Baltimore for a couple of years, and then I persuaded the city of Baltimore to rent us an abandoned basketball court for a dollar a year just down the street. I cobbled together enough donations to buy a couple of mobile office trailers, and voilà, we had an office of our own.

Cherry Hill was then, and to a large degree still is, one of the most dangerous neighborhoods in Baltimore. PS 180—later named after the principal of the school, Arnett Brown, a man I worked with, a man who didn't need the public address system because his voice was so powerful—was struggling to keep the kids engaged, motivated, and in school.

The neighborhood had a lot of abandoned school buses that had been converted into cheap, convenient stores. The buses were powered by extension cords illegally wired into the power company's electricity poles. One could buy snacks and soda—and whatever drugs you needed—from those buses.

Yet I never felt scared driving through the neighborhood. Maybe it was because I had driven through it so often that no one bothered me, or maybe it was because I was young and naive. I am proud to say, though, that not one member of our staff was ever attacked in that neighborhood.

The same cannot be said for what happened inside the school. I had a run-in with a caseworker I will call James. James was about six feet tall and appeared to weigh well over two hundred pounds. He was the starting fullback on his football team, and those two hundred pounds looked rock-solid to me. I suspected that he was not checking in with the kids—as they themselves had told me—so I asked him if he was doing his job. He was not pleased by the question, but he assured me that he was.

A few days later, more students told me that James had not visited them. I asked him again if he had checked on them. This time, he grabbed me by the throat, lifted me up, and slammed me against a row of lockers in the school hallway. He put me down a few seconds later, and quit. I stood in the hallway shaking for quite some time.

But apart from that experience, I never felt afraid, never felt that I was going to be hurt.

I was excited at the prospect of visiting Villa 21-24, one of the so-called *villas miseria* (misery housing, or slums), where Bergoglio had spent much time when he returned to Buenos Aires. When I told an Argentine pal of mine that I was going, he said, "Are you crazy? I lived in Buenos Aires until I was eighteen and I go back a couple of times a year. I have never been over there. No one goes there. It's dangerous as hell."

Well, it couldn't be worse than Baltimore, could it?

THE CONCEPT OF priests working in the slums—in places as dangerous as Villa 21-24—did not begin when Bergoglio was named auxiliary bishop in 1992; priests worked and lived in the *villas* in the late 1960s and early 1970s. Father Yorio and his Jesuit colleagues lived with the poor then, but perhaps the best-known priest working with the poor was Fr. Carlos Mugica, a diocesan priest. Mugica was from a wealthy family and had movie star looks. Some thought that he supported the Montoneros in their fight to overthrow the government; others saw him as the embodiment of the Church's commitment to the poor. He was a colleague and friend of Yorio and, though Mugica never supported the use of violence, he became even better known—and more controversial—when he celebrated the funeral mass for the first members of the Montonero movement killed in 1970.

Mugica would be gunned down outside his church in Buenos Aires in 1974 by the Argentine Anticommunist Alliance, a paramilitary squad that was created by a member of Perón's cabinet in 1973. The AAA killed hundreds of people between 1973 and 1975. Mugica's death turned him into a revered martyr by those who believed the Church should fight for the poor.

Bergoglio continued and deepened this outreach to the poor, particularly in Villa 21-24, which would come to have a special place in his heart. In 1993, he met Fr. José Maria Di Paola, often called Father Pepe, who would eventually become the *cura villero*—the pastor of Villa 21-24. Before that happened, though, Pepe had a vocational crisis.

Shortly after he met Bergoglio, and almost seven years after being ordained a priest, Pepe thought about leaving the priesthood to start a family. In an interview with *Avvenire* newspaper in Rome, Pepe explained that he went to work in a shoe factory for a year, and during that time, he formed a very deep bond with Bergoglio:

> When I told [Bergoglio] I was going through this crisis he did not force the hand of fate. He just said: "Whenever you would like, please come and see me." He inspired much confidence in me, and I began to see him once a month. I remember it took me roughly two to three hours to arrive at the cathedral from where I was working. He always waited for me, I knew he would wait for me. He used to come to open the door for me. He accompanied me during that period of deep crisis as a father would—with great pride of the soul. He never told me what I was supposed to do, or not supposed to do. He listened, he was in-

terested, and he spoke with clarity of thought. But always with a freedom of thought. He accompanied me on this road of doubt and crisis with full freedom, and with this, I was able to recognize through his counsel that my vocation was indeed to be a priest, much like the story of the prodigal son.

In April 1994, Pepe was ready to return. He approached Bergoglio and said, "Father, here I am. I would like very much to celebrate the mass. Bergoglio hugged me, and he was very happy. He said to me, 'Shall we celebrate mass on the Day of Friendship, the twentieth of July? If so, let's celebrate mass at Saint Ignatius. I will be saying mass there because a woman has asked me to offer her a confession.'

"I did not know at the time that this woman was an ex-prostitute and that her friends also were prostitutes, but it was in this mass that I resumed my role as priest, united with Bergoglio—and saying that mass together with Bergoglio was incredibly significant."

A few years later, in 1997, Bergoglio sent Pepe to Villa 21-24, where roughly 90 percent of the population is from Paraguay. Later that year, Pepe brought a statue of the Virgin of Caacupé, who is venerated by Paraguayans, to the *villa*. The statue was first welcomed at a mass at the cathedral by then–Archbishop Bergoglio. After mass, the people carried the statue to the *villa*; rather than leading the procession, Bergoglio chose to be at the end, walking and praying with the people.

Pepe worked in Villa 21-24 for nearly fourteen years, building more than ten chapels, a kindergarten, a vocational school, a drug addiction recovery center, a drug prevention center for youth, four small shelters, dining halls, and more. His efforts to prevent youth from becoming drug addicts and to help those struggling with addiction led to conflict with drug dealers. His life was threatened repeatedly, and eventually Bergoglio had to move Pepe out of Villa 21-24. Pepe was succeeded by his friend Fr. Lorenzo de Vedia, better known as Father Toto, who had worked with him in Villa 21-24 previously.

. . .

ON MY THIRD day in Buenos Aires, I was fortunate to meet friends of a friend, two women named Paz Alonso and Magui Alonso, who are not related but are both huge admirers of the pope. They volunteer for Toto in Villa 21-24 and were driving me to meet him and to walk through the *villa*. Magui, age thirty, and Paz, thirty-two, both had a faith and enthusiasm for the Church that is rare in people their age. They spoke rapid-fire, often interrupting each other, about the effect their countryman is having on their convictions.

As we got on the highway, the subject shifted to soccer, and Magui parted ways with her beloved Pope Francis. "He roots for San Lorenzo. I like Boca Juniors, and Boca Juniors is a far better team," she said.

Paz laughed. "I don't know about that, Magui. San Lorenzo beats Boca a lot. You know I love Boca, and my boyfriend is a true Boca Juniors fanatic. He goes every Sunday to the stadium! But San Lorenzo is very good."

"No! No! No!" Magui replied. "Boca is still the best team in Argentina."

We were on the highway and Magui was driving. We started to speed even faster than we were already going.

"Boca is the best and you know it, Paz," she said. "We always beat San Lorenzo. I love the pope, but I can't root for San Lorenzo." She turned around to look at me in the backseat. While she was speeding down the highway. "You must go to a Boca Juniors game, Mark," she said. "Let me check the schedule and—"

"Magui!" I yelled. "Turn around and drive the car! You're about to kill us!"

She turned around and looked ahead. Then she looked at me in the rearview mirror. "I'm sorry, but to understand Buenos Aires, you have to go to a Boca game. Do you want to go to a game, Mark?" she asked. She turned around again and looked at me. "Even the pope knows that Boca is the best and—"

"Turn around, Magui!" I yelled again. "Please focus on the road!"

She shrugged and turned back to face the road. She kept her eyes there for most of the rest of the ride, but every time we hit a red light she would turn around and pitch me on why Boca was better than San Lorenzo.

It was a nerve-racking drive to the *villa*, but both women were fun and easy to be around. As we approached Villa 21-24, though, the conversation turned more somber.

"We are getting close," Magui said. The streets were no longer grand boulevards filled with stores and restaurants; now there were empty storefronts and young men hanging out on the street corners. "Those are gang members selling drugs," she explained. "This is a dangerous area. We need to keep moving."

Maybe it was because I was no longer in my mid-twenties and single, or perhaps I had lost my naïveté, or maybe it was because I was in a foreign country on unfamiliar turf with my friend's words—"Are you crazy? It's dangerous as hell!"—ringing in my head, but for whatever reason, I was scared.

We made a turn and Magui said, "Okay, here we go." The road became bumpy.

What is going on? It was as if I was leaving one country and entering a totally different one.

"Hold tight," Magui said, reading my mind. "We will be at Father Toto's in a minute."

We bumped along until we pulled up in front of a nondescript building.

"This is his church. Let's get out," Magui said.

I looked around for the church but didn't see what I was expecting. There was no big building like the church I attend on Sundays in Potomac, Maryland; there was no grand structure like the Basilica de San José in Flores. I followed Magui and Paz through a door into what looked like a big car repair shop.

"Is this the church?" I asked Magui.

"No, that is next door. This is where people gather. Father Toto's office is over there," she explained, waving her hand.

I couldn't make out any office—just a couple of doors in the corner of this car-repair-like area.

"People gather in here?" I asked, confused.

"Yes, for the big celebrations," Magui said. "We slide open that door over there so that all the people can go to mass. Let's go this way and I will show you."

We walked through a doorway and into a church—actually, it was more like a chapel.

"It's beautiful, right?" Magui said. It wasn't a question as much as a statement. "See that door in the middle? It slides open so all the people can go to mass."

The back wall of the church featured a Garden of Eden–type scene with Guaraní Indians, the native people of Paraguay: A man wearing only a loincloth stood alongside a river shooting a bow and arrow while a woman sat close by, bare-chested and nursing her baby. Another bare-chested man was nearby cleaning out what appeared to be a wooden bassinet for the baby. Under the woman's knee was a painting of Jesus's face; in the middle of the scene was a painting of Mary wearing a crown.

A couple of statues sat on a little ledge in one corner. The ledge, covered by a white cloth, held votive candles in front of the statues. A small painting of Mary hung above them, and above that, a rusty old fan was blowing warm air around the chapel. Chunks of plaster were missing from the wall—it looked like small snowballs in the midst of this idyllic scene.

The handmade wooden pews were rickety. The altar was a simple slab of stone, but behind it was a collection of art and candles and statues and flags and pictures—so many different objects that I had never seen near an altar.

To my immediate left was a framed picture of Mugica.

A few feet away was another statue of Mary dressed in a beautiful blue robe with a golden crown on her head. The statue stood upon another small platform that was also covered with a white cloth. Alongside Mary were candles and a photograph of Pope Francis, a photo of a young man and another of a baby, and yet another image of Mary holding the baby Jesus.

The wall behind the altar was painted with men and women and babies and young children praying together. Another framed photograph of a smiling Pope Francis was nailed to the wall. Chunks of this wall were missing as well. The ceiling was corrugated tin.

A collection of chairs lined the wall, each a different size and shape. If the priest had the fanciest one, I couldn't tell which it was.

Toto walked into the church, smiled, and shook my hand heartily. "Good afternoon," he said in Spanish. "Come this way. I have people that want to talk to you."

Toto was thin, stood about five feet eight, and resembled no other priest I had ever seen. He was balding with a small goatee and an unshaven face; his sparkling eyes darted around the chapel, taking in the scene quickly. He wore a sports jacket with the logo and colors of the Argentine national soccer team, an open-collared shirt underneath. He turned around quickly and led me out of the chapel and toward the back of the garage area.

As he walked, a couple of guys off to the side called out his name. He yelled something back to them and waved. They all laughed.

He opened a door and we headed into the bowels of the structure. A few yards into it, Toto opened a door that led to what must once have been a small storage room. He asked me to sit down in front of his cluttered desk. A rusty old fan bolted into the wall blew warm air around the small space. There were pictures all over the walls and statues of Jesus and various saints in nooks and crannies. "Someone's coming who wants to tell you stories about Bergoglio," he said.

At that moment, there was a knock, and before anyone could answer it, the door opened and in walked a man, whom Toto introduced as Dario.

Toto told me, "Dario knew the pope very well. Both in the good and in the bad, he is like the pope. In what is good, because he is Catholic, a good Christian, and in what is bad because he roots for San Lorenzo. A soccer fan. Sit down, Dario."

They both laughed.

Magui then told them that Paz was a Boca fan.

"This woman roots for Boca?" Dario asked. "Oh, well, my condolences!"

"My boyfriend, my boyfriend roots for Boca," Paz said, smiling.

Everyone laughed.

I could feel the energy in the place. *This is going to be a fun conversation.*

Toto told me that Dario was from Paraguay and was a member of a men's group in the parish. "In Latin America and everywhere it is common to see religion linked to the children and to women, and the elderly. Father Pepe left his mark by promoting the strong participation of men in the church. Dario is one of them." Toto told me that the chapels in Villa 21-24 were "constructed mostly with the manual labor of the members of the men's group."

"I think that in Buenos Aires, maybe in all of Argentina, this parish has the greatest participation of men in the parish activities," Dario told me.

"Of course," Toto said matter-of-factly. "And Bergoglio was often with the men's group. He supported that original idea. Bergoglio was very close to us. Any priest that called, he would answer immediately, and if he was busy at that moment, he would attend to us in five or ten minutes, and for any personal matter, too. He represents a way of being of the Church that many of us had been wanting here in Latin America for quite a long time. A church closer to the people, a missionary church, simpler, more austere. He represents that."

"He's very humble," Dario added.

There was another knock. Toto got up, opened the door, and came back into his office carrying a tray with a thermos and a couple of maté gourds on it. Magui pushed a bunch of papers aside and he placed the tray on his desk.

"Thanks, Magui," Toto said. He poured hot water over the maté, took a sip, and handed the gourd to her.

Magui sniffed. I had noticed that she had been sniffling during the drive over, but I was so nervous that she was going to kill us that it hadn't registered.

I registered it now.

She took a sip from the straw and handed the gourd to me.

I must have looked shocked or nervous, because Dario and Toto both laughed.

"Take a sip. It's maté. You won't die," Toto said.

Everyone in the room laughed.

I placed my lips on the straw and sipped the hot, sweet liquid.

Dario and Toto smiled. I noticed that Toto's legs were bouncing as he sat in his chair. Was it the maté? Or was it nervous energy? Was he excited by his work? I don't know, but I do know he radiated more positive energy, warmth, and enthusiasm than any other priest I had ever met.

"Bergoglio would come here on the bus; previous archbishops of Buenos Aires would come in a car with a chauffeur," Toto continued. "He, from the start, would come on the bus."

"He really came by bus?" I asked.

"Yes, yes, yes," Toto replied. "On the bus. Like regular people. Always. He would get off at the bus stop and walk the four blocks. He would arrive here and he would drink maté with the people."

"He shared lunch with the people," Dario added, "under the metal roof in the kitchen many times. Not only once, many times."

"He had a very good relationship with the people, and he was very helpful," Toto went on. "He would support all the social projects that we had here in the *villa*. For example, in April of 2012, there was a strong storm in Buenos Aires, and the roofs collapsed in two gymnasiums where the kids played soccer. These are special places in the *villa* because there is very little space for children to play. One was in our *Hogar de Cristo* [House of Christ], where the kids who are recovering from addiction play soccer. That roof collapsed, as did the roof of a building belonging to another group in the neighborhood linked to politics, not the Church. The next day, I called him asking him to help us get the funds to repair it. Before the end of the year, we were able to repair ours, thanks to the quick help from Bergoglio. The other one, to this day [November 2014], has not yet been repaired."

The fan was circulating the warm air and the maté was passed around the group a second time. Toto's eyes twinkled when he told the story, his arms gesticulated, and he poked Dario when he wanted to stress a word or two.

I asked Toto why he wasn't wearing a traditional priest's collar. I had seen plenty of Jesuits without collars, but rarely had I seen a diocesan priest without one, especially in his own church.

"It is very common in the barrios to dress very casually, without so much religious attire," Toto replied.

"Did Bergoglio get upset about that?" I asked.

"That also was a change," Toto replied. "Before, when I was a seminarian or in my first years as a priest, when one had to visit the archbishop, one would have to wear a jacket. With Bergoglio, that was no longer necessary. He respected everyone for what they were. If one preferred to dress more formally, he would respect that, but if one was dressed casually, he would also respect him. He was very respectful of our way of being."

Dario then told me that he was responsible for barbecuing the meat for the big festivities in the parish. More than four hundred people attended, including Cardinal Bergoglio. "I was here in the group, when Bergoglio blessed the meal, and then we served lunch to everyone. That happened many times."

Toto then told another story about one of Cardinal Bergoglio's visits to Villa 21-24.

"He had a very concrete dialogue with the youth. There were a hundred twenty kids in the youth group, and the idea was to ask him questions. The first to ask a question was a girl, and we all started trembling because she was one of the most mischievous ones. She asked him, 'Can a girl who is not a virgin become a nun?'

"Bergoglio said, 'Do you want a long answer or a short answer?' and the girl said that she wanted a short answer. So Bergoglio answered, 'Yes.'"

After the laughter died down, Dario looked at me with a serious expression and said, "The truth is, he revolutionized the parish when he was archbishop. In my country, to approach a priest, to be able to speak to a priest, first you must have money and you have to be in a good social position. If you are poor, the priests keep you at a distance. . . ."

His voice trailed off.

There was a bang on the door. Before anyone could open the door, another man walked in and hugged Dario and Toto.

"This is Juan," Toto said. "He was confirmed by Bergoglio."

Dario started to rib Juan about not visiting him. They were both from Paraguay and both helped Toto at the parish. Clearly, they were good friends.

Then there was another knock at the door and a third man walked in, Beto. I learned later that Beto was born in Argentina but his parents were from Paraguay.

"Ah, well, the full team is here!" Toto said. The tiny room was packed with people. Side conversations were being held, people were laughing, and in the middle of this small office filled with lively people sat the smiling, unshaven Toto.

Beto wanted to tell a story immediately. "I am an art teacher. I do sculpture. I restored a marble statue of Santa Teresita, an image that was abandoned and a priest had bought. I start cleaning it and what had been an ugly gray thing became something that looked like a white cotton ball, beautiful."

He smiled. The room was quiet. Beto had everyone's attention.

"Part of it was broken," he continued, "so we cut that part of the base and when we finished with the restoration, the priest invited me to the inauguration. What I did not know was that Bergoglio would be at the mass to inaugurate the statue. When I unveiled it, he told the congregation that he was a devotee of Santa Teresita and he shared some stories about her. That happened in October.

"In January—at that time, Father Pepe was here—Bergoglio phoned to ask Pepe what he was doing. Father Pepe said, 'Nothing.' Bergoglio had the afternoon off, so he took the bus here and they went out for a walk in the neighborhood and they walked past my house. I went outside to say hi to Pepe, because I know him well, and he said to Bergoglio, 'Let me introduce you to—' And Bergoglio said, 'Ah, I know him. He's the sculptor of Santa Teresita.' He recognized me! I was astonished."

I looked around the room as heads nodded.

Beto continued, "Once a year, Bergoglio organized a meeting with teachers from all the districts. He would get us all together and he would provide guidance as to how we should teach the kids in the neighborhood, how we have to take into consideration their personal problems, because they come with a load of problems. His words were very wise. He would explain to us that each family, each kid, since he was born, has always seen his father not working, but rather his mother. And so there were already two generations that were not acquainted with work.

"One lives here and gets used to things, but he would come give us a different view. That was very enriching."

It was Juan's turn to tell his story.

"He would come here for sure twice a year, on the twenty-fourth of June and the eighth of December," Juan said. "One December eighth, a bus pulls up at the corner of Iriarte and Luna, and Bergoglio gets off, alone, with his briefcase. Father Pepe sees him and tells a seminarian, 'Go and accompany the Father.'

"The seminarian goes but he comes right back and says, 'No, he wants to go alone.' And Bergoglio crossed the street—he was coming to greet us, he talked to everyone."

"He came to pray with us there," Dario added.

"He drinks maté. He eats what people eat here," Juan said.

Beto interjected, "On December eighth, the feast of the Virgin of Caacupé, we had a procession throughout the neighborhood, through all the alleys. And when it rained a lot, there was a lot of mud, and he came with his shoes, his archbishop shoes, and we told him more than once, I'm a witness, 'No, stay here. We'll go because it's all muddy.'

"He would not pay attention to us and he would go through the mud with us, and then he would give his blessing at each house. In each house, there is an image of a saint, so he would walk through the mud in order to bless all the images."

The muddy shoes reminded me of the story that Father Gauffin and Father Nardin told me about Bergoglio looking for mud on the scholastics' shoes at Colegio Máximo to be sure they had actually been working with the people. And the story about him blessing all those images—that is a part of the theology of the people, about as far from the highfalutin world of theologians and philosophers as you can get.

Toto wanted to tell a story.

"In the Plaza de la Constitución, there's a train station. A lot of working-class people go by there, and we celebrate mass there to pray for the victims of human trafficking, slave workers."

Evidently, a lot of people were in the plaza for this mass, including a few drunks.

"Bergoglio was celebrating mass. I was organizing it, and because these masses were celebrated in the street, we always had to be very careful, because things had happened in the street before. In this case, this drunk man wanted to interrupt. He approached me, saying, 'I want Bergoglio to bless my Bible.' And I said, 'No, he can't.' But he kept pestering, so I took the Bible to Bergoglio and said, 'Bergoglio, please bless this Bible,' and he blessed it in a jiffy, right away, in two seconds."

This Catholic experience doesn't remind me of any of my Catholic experiences.

Toto had the floor and he wasn't giving it up just yet.

"When I worked in the Plaza de la Constitución, I came up with the idea of setting up a big tent on the plaza, a missionary tent. I would go to the plaza, take a gigantic statue of the Virgin, and people from the church would hand out holy cards and gather the prayer wishes of the people. So, in other words, the Church in the street.

"So when I came up with that idea, I called Bergoglio and told him, 'Look, I want to set up a missionary tent on the Plaza de la Constitución,' and his answer was, 'I think that's very good because one has to shake things up. The Church is not here to control people's life, but rather to respond to the needs of the people where they live.' He liked the idea of moving the church to the public square."

When Toto was asked whether the government got upset with this approach, he said, "No, but Bergoglio would say very strong things against the city and the nation, and some spheres of the government would feel affected by this. Sometimes he would say things, such as when accusations were made regarding human trafficking. 'This city strips you of your skin. It is like a meat grinder'—this is one of the things he said in one of his homilies."

Juan said, "But the government does nothing to solve the problem."

"It turns a blind eye," Dario added.

"Because the government sees that things are happening," Toto said, "and does not denounce these things."

I saw a picture on the wall of Toto and Pepe. They were standing side by side. Pepe had his arm around a smiling Toto. Two men, two brothers, really, committed to a life of helping others. Toto had a scraggly salt-and-pepper beard and long hair. Pepe's brown hair was even longer, and a full beard covered his handsome face.

Although I had known the man for only forty-five minutes, I felt as if Toto was already a good friend. *This guy is the best kind of Catholic priest.*

I asked what had happened to his beard. Without hesitation, Toto said, "I used to have a beard, and a lot of hair on my head, but the wind blew it away!" The room erupted.

When the laughter died down, Toto had one last story to tell before he went to celebrate mass.

"Bergoglio was also very helpful," Toto continued. "For example, the last time I called him—it was March of 2013—he was just leaving to go to the conclave. I called him and he said, 'Speak to me fast, because in ten minutes, I have to go to Rome.' All of us knew that the pope had died."

Three people exclaimed at once, "Whoa, wait a minute! No, no, no, you killed him off!"

"Sorry, sorry!" Toto corrected himself. "That Benedict had resigned. The reason for my call was very simple, I needed his signature on a document related to the construction of the high school, and when he said, 'I'm going to Rome,' I said, 'Well, I absolutely need this signature for these reasons.' So he said, 'Drop by to pick it up.' So when I sent some kids to pick it up, Bergoglio had signed it at that very moment just before leaving for Rome."

The room became eerily quiet.

"I really thought he was coming back to Argentina," Toto said. "I had him down in my calendar as coming here on Easter Thursday, which was a few weeks away. He was supposed to come on that day to celebrate mass here in the parish.

"The place exploded when he was named pope. What an explosion! People went out on the streets and came to the parish as the obvious place to celebrate. The church bells were rung. People brought with them the photo they might have in their home with Bergoglio. That day the church filled up."

"What do you think of the pope picking the name Francis?" I asked.

Toto replied, "It's a message for all the world of the importance of a poor Church, the same as he said later. That is to say, a very strong and clear message of poverty for everyone, within the Church, outside the Church, upward and downward."

It was getting dark out and Toto had to go celebrate mass. We said goodbye and hugged, but before we left, Dario wanted to show me the barbecue grills that he had used to cook for Bergoglio—and four hundred of his closest friends!

We walked through a hallway and into a sparse kitchen. There was an old industrial stove in one corner and an oven alongside it. A storage cabinet stood in another corner and on a table in the middle of the room sat a bag of sugar and a bag of flour.

Dario led me out back where two large charcoal grills sat next to the neighbor's house. There were tinfoil and cooking utensils on the grills. A small walkway led to another one-story building with a tree taking up most of the path.

It is so cramped—there is barely enough room to walk around, much less cook for four hundred people.

Dario was extremely proud, but before I could say anything, Magui said, "Let's go. It's almost dark and it will be very dangerous soon."

We walked back through the kitchen, past Toto's office and the chapel, and out onto the street.

"Let's go this way," Juan said, "and see a home where we house and feed people."

The potholes were filled with water. The houses in the neighborhood stood shoulder to shoulder, each with a different height and look. The occasional narrow alley, just wide enough for two men walking side by side, led to other homes buried deeper in the interior of the *villa*. I could hear loud music in the distance.

The home Juan led us to was simple, with a small living room and a kitchen with a table around which a handful of people could sit and share a meal. In the corner was a table filled with pictures of Mother Teresa and Saint John Paul II and small votive candles. The home served as a temporary shelter for men and women who needed help.

I had had barely enough time to see the small house and shake hands with the occupants before Magui said, "We have to go now." She had a serious look on her face. As we walked back down the street, a couple of people stared at us, but I never felt threatened—I had my new friends with me, and Toto was just around the corner.

As we said our goodbyes, I took one last look inside the chapel. There was Toto, behind the altar, celebrating mass. The chapel was almost empty; a couple of women sat in the last two pews with babies on their laps, and one guy stood in the corner, his hand on the feet of a statue of Mary, his head bowed.

I made eye contact with Toto. He smiled at me, nodded, and continued with the mass.

This is what Bergoglio meant when he said he wanted a pastor with mud on his shoes, a shepherd who smells like his sheep.

I could not imagine coming here on my vacation days myself—but I was starting to better understand the essence of this new Bergoglio.

I KNEW THAT Pepe was very close to Bergoglio when Bergoglio was bishop, then cardinal, and I knew that Pepe had worked in Villa 21-24. Surely he would have critical insights into the man. But it was hard to connect with him. I had written him a couple of emails before visiting Argentina. I had even asked a couple of his friends who live in Washington, D.C., to reach out to him on my behalf. One friend finally heard via email that Pepe would be willing to see me during my trip, but no time or date was set; I was to call him when I arrived in Buenos Aires.

It was just as hard to connect with Pepe when I was in Buenos Aires. I finally arranged to meet him on a street corner in Villa Cárcova the day before I was scheduled to leave. The meeting was at the end of a very full two-week journey, and the meeting place was a good forty-five minutes outside the city.

I thought about canceling the appointment. I had spent two hours talking with Toto and his parishioners, many of whom had lived with Pepe and had told me stories about him; I had walked the streets of Villa 21-24 where Pepe had worked. I knew that Pepe was perhaps the second-best-known priest from Buenos Aires, but I was tired, and it had been such a process to secure the meeting, and now I had to drive all the way out to see him. There was no way, was there, that Pepe could teach me anything more than Toto had already taught me about Bergoglio and life as a *villa* priest?

I kept the appointment anyway.

Like almost every meeting scheduled, someone was late. Usually it was me; this time, it was Pepe. I was waiting on the street corner when a small four-door car, white under its cake of dirt, rusty in patches and dinged all over, pulled up.

"Mark?"

"Father Pepe?"

"Yes," came the reply.

Pepe's hair was long, his beard was full. The front seat of his car was a mess: papers, soda bottles, and plastic food wrappers everywhere. He told me to get back into my car with Miguel, my driver, and follow him to his church.

Miguel was very nervous. He had asked several times if Magui and Paz could take me, but I told him each time that they were not available. "Villa Cárcova is a very dangerous place," Miguel said. "People are killed there. The roads are terrible." I didn't argue with him. I just told him the plan, but it was the quietest drive we took. Miguel didn't say a word the entire trip.

Potholes and puddles marred the streets, the sidewalks were

cracked, and gravel was scattered all over the place. We passed a three-story building slapped alongside a decrepit one-story structure, with an unfinished two-story structure on the other side, metal bars covering their windows. This random hodgepodge of buildings continued down the street. Weeds grew up through the cracks in the road and in the sidewalks.

We made a couple of turns. This street had trees on it, but with no more rhyme or reason than the buildings. Some were a couple of feet tall, some were ten feet tall; some were no more than sticks in the mud, and where a tree should have been, there was nothing.

Pepe drove up over the curb and parked. Miguel pulled in behind him.

We were in front of a black metal fence that separated the sidewalk from a church. Just like Villa 21-24, the church was simple, another nondescript building, though this one was bigger than the other structures and had a large cross right in the center of it.

Pepe had a key chain with about ten keys on it; he fished around until he found the right one and opened the gate. People were milling about the courtyard, mostly women holding babies. Little kids grasped their mothers' legs. A couple of men sat on benches. Pepe greeted people as he walked by—there was not as much energy as there had been at Villa 21-24. Maybe it was because I was there in the morning rather than the evening?

Pepe stopped at a door and, again, fished around on his key chain until he found the right key. He opened the door.

It was déjà vu: a small, cluttered office with pictures on the wall and a rickety old fan. He turned the light on, then the fan. I sat down on a beat-up old chair.

Pepe sat down and looked at me. He smiled. His big brown eyes were beautiful and sad at the same time. Knowing just a little about his life work, the death threats against him, and his continued presence amongst the poor and the drug dealers, I felt a surge of emotion.

Was I tired? Did I miss Jeanne and our kids? Or was it because I was in the presence of a potential martyr?

How can this guy just sit here peacefully, amid the mess inside his office and the squalor outside, and smile at me, when he knows—he knows—that he could be killed at any moment? I guess Toto could be killed at any moment, too, but his energy and the fact that more people were hanging around him made that possibility seem less probable. But this man, smiling at me with those brown, knowing eyes, feels more vulnerable.

I am going to walk out of here and soon head home to my comfortable house, to my beautiful wife and children, and this guy is going to stay here and work. And one day, I may very well pick up the newspaper and read, buried in the paper, a couple of paragraphs about a priest friend of Pope Francis who was gunned down in his office. And that man is looking right at me.

I couldn't figure out whether to hug him or cry.

His first comments in the small office didn't help much. "I am alone," Pepe said, "and I live in a little house inside Villa Cárcova." He said that he was in charge of eight chapels that were scattered across four *villas*. He had organized the construction of the chapels with the goal of turning them into full-fledged parishes, much as he did in Villa 21-24.

He told me that "in 1996, Bergoglio asked me to work with the youth in Ciudad Oculta, which is another *villa*. And in 1997, he named me parish priest of Villa 21-24."

The phone on his desk rang. He had a quick conversation, then hung up.

"There always were priests in the *villas* in the capital city, but the idea of focusing the work on children and youth is what I started," he said. "This was then extended to other *villas*. I also worked on addiction prevention and recovery. That work was also replicated in the other *villas*, and I'm trying to do the same here, in Villa Cárcova."

Pepe went on to tell me why he left Villa 21-24.

"Well, my focus was on drug dealing. We, the priests from the *villas*, wrote a document entitled 'Drugs in the Villas: Beyond the Reach of the Law.' Because I was the coordinator of all the *villas*, I held a public reading of the document, and because it was I who read it, all the drug dealers started to threaten me. In spite of that, I stayed there for two more years, but the drug dealers started to harass people who were working with me, so that's when I decided to leave, because I didn't want to put other people's lives at risk. And I asked that Toto be the one to replace me."

The phone rang again: another quick conversation. I asked Pepe if he was scared when Bergoglio asked him to be the parish priest at Villa 21-24. He smiled and shook his head. "I liked the idea because in Villa 21, as parish priest, I could develop long-term projects," he told me. "And this was because Bergoglio had seen in me a certain charisma that I had when working with the children and the youth in the *villas*, something that had not been done before. So that was something I liked. Something that I found exciting."

"Were you scared?" I asked again.

"No, no, no," he replied. "I was already used to that. I was already working in a *villa*, in Ciudad Oculta, and so I was already used to those conditions."

But this was Villa 21-24, I thought. Pepe must have sensed my doubt.

"That was a very violent neighborhood, very violent, with many gangs that were fighting each other, so the first program that we did was to generate positive leaders in order to offer an alternative. There was violence on the one hand, but on the other, there was a path of prevention, sports, camps, skills workshops.

"Villa 21 is doing very well," Pepe continued. "It has lots of projects, in spite of its social problems. Today, there are things that it did not have before. For example, when I arrived, the church was closed. Now it has the church, it has the chapels in each sector. Where there were gangs, we put a chapel. It has homes for children, for grandparents; it has adolescent centers for boys; it has programs for street kids; it has a vocational school, which we built in the crisis [in 2001]; it has a high school; it has a radio station; it has centers for the elderly; it has a center for recovery of addicts, the first one, which is the Hogar de Cristo. So the Church has had a transformational role in the neighborhood."

He went on to tell me, proudly, that a number of seminarians who had worked with him and had gone on to become priests were now working in other *villas* in Buenos Aires.

The phone rang a third time. We had been together for less than ten minutes. This time the conversation went on for a few minutes. Pepe wrote a few notes on scratch paper and then hung up.

He looked at me and smiled. It was not the joy-filled smile that Toto had worn when we were drinking maté and telling stories in his office.

I asked about the church across the courtyard.

"This church serves as both a church and a dining room," Pepe explained. "And it's a place where children can come to play. In other words, it's not a church in the strictly ceremonial sense. It is used for religious ceremonies but also for school support, providing meals, plus for whatever the need might be. For us, the sanctuary, even though small, is where everything takes place: mass, then we set the table, they eat, then we clear the table and they study at the table. In other words, everything."

I told Pepe that I wasn't accustomed to having the place where mass is celebrated also be used for other purposes like a study hall or a dining room.

"Here as well. It is only in places like these where the culture is different. But what I am telling you is that what takes place here would not occur in the wealthier neighboring vicinity."

I asked if I could walk around and see what had been built.

"No, I'm sorry," he replied. "They called me right now because I have to go to a wake for someone who was killed. The neighborhood is a little violent right now."

"Around here? In the daytime?"

"They killed him at eleven in the morning. Yesterday," Pepe replied matter-of-factly.

"Do you ever get sad doing this work? Or discouraged?" I asked.

"It means . . . having to accept marginalization," he replied. "That is, marginalization as the overriding factor in life. In this neighborhood, marginalization is what is most visible. So that is where I work."

The phone rang yet again, for the fourth time in less than fifteen minutes. When Pepe finished that call, I pressed him: "Okay, but does it depress you?"

"Well, it is part of this reality," he explained. "In other words, the person who wants to work in these environments knows that this is part of reality. If you go to Africa, you know that you might contract malaria, and if you work in a cancer ward, you know that the patients are likely to die."

Marginalization? Africa? I thought of Bergoglio's desire to go to Japan as a missionary to work with those living on the edge of society, the marginalized. Listening to Pepe, I realized that Bergoglio had fulfilled that desire, but right in his hometown.

No wonder he walked around Villa 21-24 on his days off—that was where he had always wanted to be.

Cancer ward? Pope Francis had said in the *America* magazine interview that he wanted a church that was a field hospital. I was in the presence of a man engaged in that very work, a frontline medic of the Church.

I was on a quest to understand Bergoglio, to get stories that would illuminate his rise, beliefs, and motivations, and I had almost missed the opportunity to see and feel exactly what Bergoglio was trying to teach me.

I sensed that I had overstayed my welcome, even though I had been there less than fifteen minutes. I thanked Pepe and stood up. I asked one last question.

"Did you see Bergoglio smile a lot?"

"No," he replied. "I see him smiling more now."

"Why do you think that is?" I asked.

"Well, I asked him," Pepe said.

I sat back down.

"Because I said he was a changed person. Here, I knew him well. Here, he was a very austere person, very smart, very committed. But many times, we would even say to him in a meeting or at a get-together, 'Let's see if you smile,' whereas now, one sees that he goes out, he greets people, things that he didn't do before. So he told me, regarding this, that I should keep in mind that a seventy-six-year-old person such as himself, the Holy Spirit had given him the strength to face this challenge. Because to be a pope means having to attend to people all day, different people, people he doesn't know, people from different cultures, and I think that in this, the Holy Spirit has helped him a lot. And he said to me, 'Yes, there is a change, I have noticed a change.'"

Pepe at last had a joyful smile on his own handsome face. The room felt brighter. I decided not to leave just yet. "Toto told us that Bergoglio would walk through Villa 21, dressed plainly and carrying his little bag. Do you remember that?" I asked. "Did he really walk around the neighborhood like that?"

"Yes, yes." He smiled broadly again. "And he would get off the bus and he wouldn't want us to go and fetch him. He wanted to wander around alone, and sometimes, in the summer, he would call me on the phone and come over and walk around the neighborhood to get to know it better. And he was on vacation! His vacation was to come out there. So perhaps on one of his days off, he would say, 'I'll go to Villa 21 to drink maté, and I'll use the opportunity to walk around there and get to know it a little more, and see more.'"

Pepe shook his head as if he still couldn't believe what he was saying. His reaction was similar to Gauffin's and Nardin's when they reflected on their own experiences with Bergoglio.

Pepe was more animated now. "Sometimes he brought out-of-town friends with him. He would tell them about the work in the *villas*, the churches in the *villas*. We would go out for walks as well."

"Do you think the pope is going to be successful in moving people to focus on the poor, or is that impossible?" I asked.

"I think that what he does is get people to turn their eyes toward the poor, as he did in Buenos Aires," Pepe replied. "In the city of Buenos Aires, he got the city to look at the *villas*, and at places of suffering, to help out but also to learn from them. To have more solidarity, to share. He is creating a greater awareness in the Western world, and in the entire world. He is showing them what we call the periphery, not only so that they help but also so that they learn from the poor, learn about this human reality, and learn about the difficulties people are facing, and in so doing, seek greater integration. He uses that word a lot, integration."

The phone rang a fifth time.

To learn from the poor? To have integration with the poor? The periphery?

I knew that I should leave, but this man was the living embodiment of the ideas that I had heard so much about: Ignatius's call to go to the "frontiers" to serve the poor; the theology of the people, maintaining that the poor themselves had much to teach; and Pope Francis's call to live a truly mercy-filled life. I wanted to stay, stay with him all day to learn. But he had work to do.

I hesitated. I looked around the small cramped office, desperate to make another connection that could spark another question so I could absorb more of the lesson. A photograph of a handsome priest stared back at me. I thought it might be the revered Father Mugica. I pointed to the picture. "And who is that on the wall?"

"That is Carlos Mugica. He is a priest from the group of founders. Like your Washington, you have your founding fathers?" Pepe said, laughing. "Like in the United States."

Washington was our founding father all right, a physically giant man who, by all accounts, was extremely wealthy. Cities are named after him, and every schoolchild knows his story. Mugica, a humble priest, was assassinated. But to people like Toto and Pepe, he was a founding father of the movement to help—and learn from—the poor.

"Do you ever feel you are going to get killed?"

"Yes," he replied, with no emotion.

"Are you scared about that?" I asked.

"Eh. I got used to it," he told me. "When they threatened me, that's when I thought they would kill me. It was a heavy threat. The drug dealers. So I wrote letters. Now I no longer write letters."

"Who did you write to?" I asked.

"I wrote to some priests, to my family. I also went to speak to Bergoglio and I told him I was not afraid. Bergoglio was worried about what was happening to me, and Bergoglio said to me, 'I prefer that they kill me than one of you.'"

The phone rang again. *Good Lord, a sixth time in just a few minutes.*

The call ended quickly, and I asked whether Bergoglio had helped him.

"When I told Bergoglio that they had threatened me," Pepe continued, "the following day he made a public statement in all the media to protect me. Bergoglio vigorously defended the priests and said, 'What the priests say, I also affirm.' He was very concerned, but I told him, 'We acted according to the gospel, so don't worry. We have acted according to God's will.'"

We have acted according to God's will.

The words hung in the air. Pepe smiled, knowingly, joyfully. His face seemed to glow.

This guy could be killed at any moment, yet he smiles like that? He is this calm, this at peace? He is a medic on the front lines, engaged in healing people, but he is also fighting evil in hand-to-hand combat.

The phone rang again—the seventh time in less than twenty-five minutes. It was another quick call, but it gave me a few seconds to compose myself.

I looked around the room in an effort to make yet another connection. I didn't want to leave, but I didn't have any idea how to follow up on his last comment.

We have acted according to God's will.

I pointed at what appeared to be a young child's artwork.

"Ah, things that the kids do," Pepe said. He chuckled and pointed at another picture on the wall. "The photo is torn, but these are the seminarians who are now priests."

He pointed to another photograph. "That's Villa 21, and these are the kids of the home. This is the oldest from the home." Then to a photo of a young man. "He joined the military. He is an officer of the Argentine army. I went to visit him at his regiment. And this one," he said, pointing at yet another, "is a godson of mine who was killed, from Villa 21."

He had such a close connection with his parishioners that he was asked to be a godfather? This shepherd knows his sheep.

I still didn't want to go. I had never spent time with someone who gave his whole life to God at such risk, someone who could be mar-tyred any day yet still kept doing the work that could very well result in his death.

I blurted out, "Is there anything that I should have asked that I haven't asked?"

If I had overstayed my welcome, Pepe didn't say or show it. He had patience, too.

He smiled and then chuckled. "This is my club," he said, pointing at a framed soccer jersey on the wall. Pinned to it was a picture of the back of Pope Francis as he signed the jersey. "That is the rival of the pope's club, and the pope signed it for a friend of mine. The pope wrote, 'Only for Pepe,' because he would not normally have signed a jersey of the rival team." He laughed.

"I love that picture!" I exclaimed.

"We worked together for a long time." He looked me in the eye. It wasn't a piercing look, but I felt as if he was looking at my soul. Here was a man who entered the priesthood, took a leave of absence to re-consider his decision, and was counseled by Bergoglio throughout that period of uncertainty. That must have been an intense experience in itself. He returned to the priesthood only to face death threats; again, Bergoglio was right beside him. They had a deep, personal re-lationship.

"I was the parish priest and I asked to have Toto work with me. He was there for four years, I think. Then he went to another parish, and later I asked for him to be brought back to replace me when I had to move because he understood what we had done here. And that does not always happen. When I had to go because of the drug dealers, I said to Bergoglio, 'Okay, I'll leave, but I ask that you name Toto, be-cause Toto understands the direction in which we want to take the parish.'"

As Pepe walked me back to Miguel and the car, he pointed inside the church. "Here's where everything happens—mass, lunch, our meetings. Everything."

The church was stark—a plain white table covered with a white tablecloth served as the altar, with a simple wooden chair to the side for Pepe. There was only one candle beside the altar and a simple, small crucifix on the wall behind it. A statue of Mary was on the left and another crucifix on the right; both had bright red cloths hanging behind them. The pews were wooden and very simple—they looked a bit sturdier than the pews in Toto's church, but not much.

Chairs and plastic tables were piled up in one corner of the church. A large crucifix hung on the back wall; the windows had bars on them; pictures of the saints and the holy family were scattered on the walls, which looked water-stained. And there, upon one wall, was a rusty old fan that looked exactly like the one that hung in Toto's church.

"Do people come to mass here every Sunday?" I asked Pepe.

"They come when they can," he replied. "A lot of people work whenever they can, and many grew up in areas where there was no priest, so they couldn't go to mass regularly. But they stop in and pray. They're good Catholics."

That last statement caught me by surprise.

"If they don't go to mass regularly, they're still good Catholics?" I asked.

"Yes, of course," Pepe said. "They pray together. They believe in Jesus. They come to the big festivals. Remember, there are not enough priests in many places. Yes, these people are very good Catholics."

Pepe, Toto, and Bergoglio were challenging my very concept of what it means to be a good Catholic. The church was more than a place for worship or other sacraments—it was the center of the community. Their behavior and views were very different from what I was accustomed to, yet there was a sense of solidarity in their parishes that I had rarely seen or experienced in a Catholic parish in the United States.

Here in the *villa*, Bergoglio and his priests wanted to build parishes and serve the people on a new scale, much like what took place in San Miguel around Colegio Máximo. But I soon learned that they needed help. And in asking for and receiving that help, they built more bridges of mercy and consolation.

. . .

Rabbi Alejandro Avruj welcomed me into his office at Comunidad Amijai, a congregation of Conservative Judaism in Buenos Aires, with a firm handshake, a big smile, and a loud "Welcome" spoken in English with a heavy Argentine accent. I could feel the positive energy—I liked him immediately.

The rabbi was about five feet ten with long black hair parted in the middle. He had a beard and eyes that twinkled when he spoke. He looked like the lead singer of a rock band.

"I am not a historian," I told the rabbi. "I am just an American trying to understand Bergoglio and what I can learn from him. I am in search of stories that tell who the man really is."

The rabbi smiled. "Okay," he said, "I have a couple of stories." He leaned forward. I was accustomed to Irish American raconteurs—I could sense that I was about to meet my first Jewish Argentine raconteur!

"In 2001, when Argentina was in the middle of this huge crisis," he began, "you know, the very hard economic crisis, I was coming back from Israel. I was finishing my rabbinical studies in the States and in Israel, and I had a couple of possibilities to work in the States and other parts of the world, but I felt that if I am a rabbi, and if I am an Argentinian guy, in 2001, I have to be here. I began my career working in a very humble and poor neighborhood, here in Buenos Aires, called the Slaughter House. Social work is very important to my spiritual way of understanding religion, you see?"

"Right," I replied.

"As Rabbi Salanter [the father of the Musar movement in Orthodox Judaism] said, my spiritual needs are the material needs of the other. I was appointed head of the JDC, the Joint Distribution Community. It's a very important Jewish organization that works with Jewish people in need, everywhere in the world. It began in World War II. . . . They opened seventy centers throughout Argentina to give food and shelter and medicines to the Jewish population. But at the same time they got a budget for the non-Jewish population, too. And they asked me to lead the program for the non-Jewish population.

"We helped a lot of hospitals around the country. And we began giving work to people in their homes, but especially we began to work in a lot of shantytowns, in very poor places, especially with Caritas, the Catholic social arm, and I was running thirty-two soup kitchens in a lot of different shantytowns in and around Buenos Aires and in Córdoba. We were feeding around seven to eight thousand kids every day, and there is no Jewish population in the shantytowns.

"Anyway, it was a very busy operation. There I met Father Pepe in the shantytown called 21-24. He was running about six soup kitchens, some for kids, some for adults, and we began helping him feed his kids. And then we sent a lot of young Jewish guys to the shantytowns to help kids with their schoolwork, and we developed different programs for giving the people facilities to work, a lot of things.

"One of the things we did was to open a new soup kitchen inside the shantytown. The shantytown is here in the capital, maybe thirty minutes from here.

"You would get like two blocks inside the shantytown and you would see a mountain. A mountain!" He waved his arms and smiled. "There are no mountains in Buenos Aires—it was garbage! In this place, we built a new soup kitchen, with Pepe, and we called the new soup kitchen Shalom. You know what 'Shalom' means?"

Before I could answer, he said, "In Hebrew, it means peace. We opened this place with a Catholic mass, and we got some Jewish guys from the synagogue to play Hebrew songs . . . it was very, very nice. All the neighborhood came, and I met Bergoglio there, in the shantytown. My first meeting with Bergoglio was there, in 21-24, with Pepe."

Before I could ask a question, Avruj continued.

"It's important for me to say where I met Bergoglio, because those of us who knew him before he was Francisco—Francis—are not surprised. Because I met him for the first time, as I said, with his feet in the middle of the garbage.

"When he talks today, I think he is talking about two big things. He is talking about interreligious dialogue, about talking with and embracing the other, and about a poor church, for the poor. These are his two big issues, I think. And I am lucky to know him in those two things, talking with the other, and talking with poor people. Because he, as bishop of Buenos Aires, he could have sent someone, you know. But he was there himself."

The concept of encounter that Ignatius spoke about and the idea of working on the fringes of society—here were two Ignatian ideals confronting me head-on in a Jewish synagogue in downtown Buenos Aires. The rabbi was describing a Bergoglio who, even as bishop, was thoroughly devoted to the philosophy of Saint Ignatius.

THE RABBI'S RELATIONSHIP with Pepe was not restricted to their work together in Villa 21-24. They traveled together with about a hundred other people to visit the same places Francis was visiting in Jordan and Israel in May 2014, although they were not part of the official papal delegation. The rabbi told me that the trip itself sent "an unbelievable message. An unbelievable message! In two thousand years, the first time a pope went to Israel was with John Paul II, twenty years after he became pope. For Francis, it was one of his first trips. Unbelievable!

"We were in Jordan, it was the first place he went, and in Amman, they held this very impressive mass in the football stadium. There were about thirty or forty thousand people—people crying, people singing, flags—it was unbelievable. And I imagine that the forty thousand people in that stadium were the only forty thousand Catholics in all of Jordan!" He laughed. "Yes, ninety-nine percent of the population is Muslim. It was unbelievable. And when Bergoglio left the stadium, he began to go out in the popemobile, and then he saw me and stopped the car, and the Jordanians and the guards of the Vatican, they were going crazy, and he called to me, 'Hey, hello!'"

The rabbi's voice got louder and he started to gesticulate wildly.

As he was talking, I remembered Pope Francis saying in an interview that he was not accustomed to speaking to so many people: "I manage to look at individual persons, one at a time, to enter into personal contact with whomever I have in front of me. I'm not used to the masses." When I first read those words, I thought there was no way he could focus on an individual person, but listening to this unbelievable story, I thought maybe both men were telling the truth, as hard as it is to believe.

"Then I thought, in a country where ninety-nine percent of the population is Muslim, with the only forty thousand Catholic people there, Bergoglio gets out of the popemobile to hug a rabbi. It's crazy! It's crazy! It's impossible!"

The rabbi jumped up, smiling and laughing.

"Imagine—here's a guard with a gun, and I say to the guy, 'Uh, the pope is calling me.' He's a Jordanian guy, I don't know what language he speaks, and there are the Vatican guards. Somebody took me inside the barricade. I was with this friend of mine, right? Imagine, I have the pope there"—he gestured with his right hand—"and my friend here"—he gestured with his left hand—"with all the guards pushing him to keep him from coming with me. What do you do? What do you do? He's the pope, I mean—"

I interrupted. "So you are being pushed toward the pope, who has gotten out of the popemobile to see you, and you are worried about your pal who is getting crushed by the security guards. Why are you worried about your friend?"

"I went for my friend because he had the camera," the rabbi replied.

He laughed, hard, and so did I. The timing of the punchline was perfect. A seasoned comedian couldn't have delivered it any better.

"Afterward, my friend says, 'All those guys that go to the Vatican, they go and they have a solemn picture taken with the pope, you know, but this picture, with this smile, it was like—we were in the middle of the 21 shantytown.'"

"So what happened then?" I asked.

"He got out. I hadn't seen him for a year and a half, but a lot of things happened during that time with this guy, right?" He shrugged and smiled sheepishly, accentuating the absurdity of the statement. "You have like twenty seconds to say something to the most important person in the world. What do you say to him in those twenty seconds? What do you say?"

"What *did* you say?" I asked.

"Ah, good question." He enjoyed stringing me along. "I was there and I was thinking I needed a theological phrase for the ages, right? The perfect phrase. And before I could say anything he said, 'Hey, Alé, how's the family?' He moved me twice in one minute. Right? Because first he stopped everything to talk to me, and then he asked the last question I would think of: 'Hey, your family, how are they?'"

The room became quiet. Avruj stared at me, dumbfounded by the pope's surprising question. Then he broke the silence. "I thought, what are you talking about? I said, 'Well, good, the children have been asking after you.'"

His voice trailed off. He wasn't smiling or animated now. He just looked at me, again, for a few seconds in silence.

"Maybe this is the big question we have to ask: 'How's the family?' We have to meet and we have to talk and we have to ask, 'How's the family?' Because we are all family. This is the question, right?"

I looked into the rabbi's eyes and I could see that he was tearing up. He was silent again.

"How's the family?" he said again softly.

I understood the rabbi's desire to come up with the most important, memorable thing to say to one of the most influential people in the world. It was a chance to impress the man, to make himself seem intelligent and insightful—that's what I would have wanted to do. But what came out of the pope's mouth was a purely human question: How is your family? There they were, in the Middle East, the Holy Land to the three major religions of the world, and Pope Francis asks him the simplest, yet most important, of questions.

Avruj broke the silence, saying that he hoped that when the pope had a meeting with the head of Israel and the head of Palestine, "maybe he will ask the same question, 'Hey, how is your family?' And maybe if they answer that question—well, maybe peace will come. It depends on how they answer the question about their family."

He went quiet again for a few seconds, then shook his head as though to snap himself back to the present.

"And as a result of this trip, with the hundred people that went with us, we raised the money to open two new soup kitchens."

Then he smiled impishly at me.

"So, I have another nice story about Francis. In 2012, in November, we held our annual ceremony to remember Kristallnacht, the beginning of the Shoah, the Holocaust. Because on November 9, 1938, there was this crazy night in all Germany and Austria when the people broke in to about one thousand synagogues, and they burned all the books, all the sacred books, and it was the beginning of the disaster.

"Bergoglio was the cardinal of Buenos Aires, and he said, 'We will hold the Kristallnacht ceremony of the Jewish community in the cathedral'—the most important church in Argentina—and he asked me to conduct this ceremony with him. So I did, and it was very moving, very moving. Imagine the cathedral, so big, and there was this Jewish choir singing Jewish psalms in Yiddish. It was very, very impressive, and he was talking about a lot of things that the Church and the people didn't do to prevent this disaster.

"And I had written a Jewish prayer book with all the services for all the year and had it printed one month before this service. One month before. And I brought the book there that night, and I said, 'On this night, thousands and thousands of Jewish prayer books were burned, with the intention of extinguishing the Jewish culture. And instead of that, we have now, around seventy years later, the most recent Jewish prayer book published in the world. And I want to give this first copy to you, Cardinal. In this place, on this night.'

"It was very moving. And I remember what he said. He said, 'I will take it with me, it will be in my house, because I will begin to pray with this one.' So I think it is in the Vatican now!"

He smiled proudly. But before I could ask a question, he went on.

"I went twice to the cathedral in November," Avruj said, "because then there was a problem in the Middle East and he called for a peace prayer, and he asked me to represent the Jewish leaders. Just as he invited me, I asked him to come to my synagogue. You know Hanukkah? Two weeks later it was Hanukkah, and he told me, 'Of course, I will be there. Of course—we are friends. Tell me, do I get off the subway at Juramento Station?'

"I thought he was kidding. 'Yes, yes, Juramento Station,' I said to Bergoglio. And he came. December here is very hot, right? He came, and he was soaked with sweat, and I said, 'Father, what happened?' 'The subway,' he said, 'you know, the subway in December . . .'

"It was crazy, because if he had arrived in his black car with his driver, nobody would have said anything, right? But not him . . ."

The rabbi's voice trailed off again.

"That's why I say a lot of people are surprised about him, but we who know him are not surprised. So, when he got there, we were drinking maté in my office. This is the gourd, right here." He pointed to a tray in the corner of his office. "People come here to touch it now. Why? Because three months later he was the pope!"

He laughed again. "And what can I tell you, his last interfaith service was in my synagogue, he wore his yarmulke, and he was praying with me and he lit the candle, and he gave a very nice sermon about the light and about sharing light for the world, and it was a very, very nice night. It was the last time I saw him, until the hug in the stadium, right? Yes, and that moment, when he asked about the family."

The stories were flowing out of the rabbi, each amazing and insightful in its own way. "The afternoon he was elected, I called and talked to his secretary, and I said, 'Listen, I have to tell you, because I think you know what is happening in every church here, in every place, in every Catholic institution, the happiness in Argentina right now, but I have to tell you what is happening in a synagogue in Buenos Aires at this minute. People are coming in and hugging me like I'm the pope. It's unbelievable! All the TVs of the synagogue are on the PA system and people are so happy. I understand if this happens in the shantytown, in the church—but in the Belgrano Synagogue?'"

And then, in case I had not heard enough stories about Pope Francis, Avruj had one more.

"One time I was in the hospital. No rabbi called me. Then one night, somebody called, and I hear, 'Alé?'

" 'Yes?' I said.

" 'It's Jorge.'

"The only Jorge I could think of was my wife's uncle, so I repeated, 'Jorge?'

" 'Jorge Bergoglio. What happened, Alé? What happened to you?'

"I was so touched," Avruj said. "Because *he* called me—not the secretary of the bishop—but 'Jorge.' You understand what kind of guy is this person? It's strange. Usually, if you are the bishop, you don't call somebody in the hospital and say, 'Hey, it's Jorge, how are you?' I am not the bishop, but when I call somebody, I say, 'This is Rabbi Avruj.'

"I don't know, I don't know. In the middle of the night, calling the hospital." His voice trailed off again.

"Some people say that it's fake, like a politician," I said. "That it must be an act. That it can't be real."

"Well, that's what I am telling you," Avruj responded. "We who knew him before he became Francis, we are not surprised. I met him in a place he didn't need to be, in the middle of the shantytown, washing the feet of the people."

"You saw him wash people's feet?" I asked.

"Of course!" the rabbi exclaimed.

"At Holy Thursday mass, or . . . ?" I asked.

"No, it was when Pepe left the shantytown. They had a big party to say goodbye, and they held a mass. I was invited and there was Bergoglio himself. He was kissing and washing the feet of the people. There were no cameras or anything. It was a celebration, yes, mass, songs, and whatnot, and then afterward he went up and he washed the feet of all those that wanted him to. Hundreds of people went."

I REALIZED NOW, having spoken with two Jewish leaders, a grieving Jewish father, two Catholic priests, and poor Paraguayans struggling in the *villas*, that Bergoglio wasn't just giving but receiving. He cherished cross-cultural encounters, whether they were in synagogues or in the *villas*; they energized him and his faith. And he had that Jesuit desire to go to the periphery, to go to the margins of society to serve.

In trying to understand Bergoglio, I came to believe that his new jobs as auxiliary bishop and then bishop had made him more a brother figure than a father figure, now more a fellow citizen among many diverse citizens in the melting pot that is Buenos Aires. He was being called to serve and heal, to bring consolation in a city of much desolation; paradoxically, he was becoming more Ignatian while no longer officially in the Jesuit order.

But the evolution wouldn't be so simple, I soon realized. This was a different Bergoglio, but he had yet to fully blossom. In private, he was laughing and joking, but in public, he was still solemn and unsmiling. And his life would become still more complicated, for just as he did with the Jesuits, he would continue to rise, becoming archbishop and eventually cardinal in 2001. His undeniable talent, charisma, and intellect would continue to propel him upward in his new world just as they had in his previous life.

21 Cardinal

MY SECOND TRIP to the Plaza de Mayo, where the Pink House sits at one end and the cathedral at the other, was eerily similar to my first trip: Traffic was jammed, horns were blaring, pedestrians were walking in and out of the traffic, Miguel's small car didn't have air-conditioning, and it was unusually warm.

I was headed to visit the cathedral, which would become Bergoglio's home church when he became archbishop in 1998 shortly after Cardinal Quarracino died.

As I walked up the steps of the cathedral, perspiring, nudged constantly by passersby, with the sound of horns in my ears, I thought of how much the daily stress must have impacted Bergoglio's life and habits.

In photos from that era, Bergoglio looks thin and weary. He looks preoccupied. He was still rising at 4:30 A.M. to pray in solitude; he was still praying the Jesuit Examen a couple of times a day; he was still, in short, living the rigorous internal spiritual life that Saint Ignatius prescribed.

And with his new role, he had new responsibilities. He was now to preside at the Te Deum mass, an annual mass held on May 25 during which the church and political leadership of Argentina gather at the cathedral to give thanks for the nation's independence.

"Te Deum" is a hymn, the first line of which is "Te Deum, laudamus," meaning "O God, we praise Thee." Bergoglio had surely sung the hymn countless times on various occasions over his lifetime of innumerable masses. But this cathedral was a long way away from the chapel at Colegio Máximo where he was surrounded by admiring neighbors and young Jesuit acolytes.

I had scheduled a meeting with Fr. Alejandro Russo, the rector of the Metropolitan Cathedral of Buenos Aires. I waited for him in a chamber adjacent to the altar where the celebrants change before mass. The room was filled with ornate golden chalices and crucifixes and ornaments. Three chairs were covered in red cushions; one was much larger than the others, presumably for the cardinal. Paintings of previous cardinals adorned the wall, all in golden frames. The lamps on the side tables were ornate; beautiful ten-foot-high dark wood armoires stored the priests' vestments.

This part of the Catholic Church was the opposite of Pepe and Toto's Catholic Church. Bergoglio lived in both worlds, but his words and actions showed where his heart lay.

This is the room where Bergoglio gathered his thoughts before his first Te Deum celebration as archbishop in 1999, an event that made clear that the new head of the Catholic Church in Buenos Aires was not like his predecessors.

In the audience that day was the president of Argentina at the time, Carlos Menem, who had been in office for nearly a decade. Menem had implemented a series of free-market reforms, including privatizing state-owned enterprises and pegging the Argentine peso to the U.S. dollar. He also doubled government spending and had to borrow heavily to pay for it. By 1999, the economy was crumbling. The unemployment rate was at 14 percent, and nearly 40 percent of the population lived in poverty. The Israeli embassy and AMIA bombings, both of which occurred on Menem's watch, remained unsolved, and his administration was widely considered corrupt.

That day, Bergoglio challenged Menem and other political leaders, including Fernando de la Rúa, the mayor of Buenos Aires, to, in the words of Austen Ivereigh, "renounce their individual and partisan interests and hear the call of the people for greater participation in civic life."

De la Rúa was elected president in October 1999 on a promise of economic growth and clean government. Bergoglio again challenged the political leadership of the country at the 2000 Te Deum mass:

> We need to recognize, with humility, that the system has fallen into a broad umbral cone, into the shadow lands of distrust, in which many of the promises and statements sound like a funeral cortege . . . until we face up to the duplicity of our motives there will be neither trust nor peace. Until we are converted, we will not know happiness and joy. Because unchecked ambition, whether for power, money, or popularity, expresses only a great interior emptiness. And those who are empty do not generate peace, joy, and hope, only suspicion. They do not create bonds.

A few months later, the economy collapsed, as did the de la Rúa presidency.

"In 2001, the Argentine economy went into a major, major economic crisis, the biggest crisis in our modern history," Luis Secco, a leading economist in Argentina, told me. He served as an economic adviser to President de la Rúa from 2000 to 2001.

The unemployment rate hit 25 percent. For context, in 1933, the height of the Great Depression, about one-quarter of the U.S. civilian labor force was estimated to be out of work; in more modern times, the unemployment rate topped out at 9.7 percent in 1982.

"The government of President de la Rúa imploded," Secco told me. "Argentina was facing economic pressures brought on by its overvalued currency and low commodity prices. The Argentine peso was pegged to the U.S. dollar one-to-one. While the U.S. inflation rate was about five percent annually, ours was much higher, but we stayed one-to-one. Brazil was also suffering and it devalued its currency by fifty percent—fifty percent! That was like a dead shot to the Argentine peg to the dollar. The expectation of an exit from a peg produced a capital flight and a bank run, which led to riots and street demonstrations. Some turned violent.

"Public confidence in de la Rúa plummeted and he resigned.

Shortly after, we defaulted on our national debt. The economy was in ruins."

"What happened when de la Rúa resigned?" I asked.

"We had five presidents in ten days," Secco said, shrugging.

"Five presidents!" I exclaimed incredulously. "Are you serious?"

"Yes. Finally, Congress appointed the former governor of Buenos Aires Province, Eduardo Duhalde, as president. Ironically, de la Rúa had defeated Duhalde in the 1999 election. Duhalde served until elections were held in April 2003.

"During this time," Secco continued, "there was economic chaos. Duhalde and Bergoglio essentially kept the country together. They worked very, very closely during the economic crisis, leading what was called *el Diálogo Argentino* [the Argentine Dialogue]. It was open to all political parties, unions, the private sector, and nongovernmental organizations. Bergoglio also worked with the government, with the Peronist party, with the unions, and with those who weren't a part of any union—what we call the informal sector. For him, it was the idea of solidarity with those who had nothing."

As I walked around inside the massive cathedral, with Bergoglio's words ringing in my ears, I thought for the first time that there may have been a certain divine—and national—destiny in Bergoglio's moving on from Jesuit life to become auxiliary bishop. The move eventually led him to be cardinal of his hometown; it had also put him in the position to be the pastoral servant of a suffering people. Had he remained with the Jesuits, his role and effect would surely have been significant, but they would inevitably have been smaller, more localized. Secco's statement stuck in my head: *"Duhalde and Bergoglio essentially kept the country together."* Bergoglio was in a position to keep the country together, ironically, only because he had been exiled by his own order.

In April 2003, a new president, Néstor Kirchner, was elected, taking office on May 25. At the Te Deum mass that day, the gospel reading told the story of the Good Samaritan who stopped to help an injured man lying by the side of the road after two other passersby had refused to help.

In his homily, Bergoglio told the audience, including the just-sworn-in Kirchner, that "it becomes increasingly apparent that our social and political apathy is turning this land into a desolate road, in which internal disputes and the looting of opportunities are leaving us all marginalized, strewn by the side of the road."

Citing Argentina's best-loved piece of gaucho literature, Bergoglio said, "The poetic prophecy of Martin Fierro must forewarn us: Our eternal and sterile hatreds and individualism open the door to those that devour from the outside." He went on to criticize those who prefer "the advantages of contraband, the purely financial speculation and the pillaging of our nature, or even worse, our people" and who "benefit from permanent conflict in the midst of our people."

He ended his homily with a call to action:

We have no right to indifference and to disinterest, nor can we look away. We cannot "pass by" as they did in the parable. We have a responsibility regarding the wounded nation and its people. A new stage starts today in our country, marked very deeply by fragility, the fragility of our poorest and excluded brothers, the fragility of our institutions, the fragility of our social ties. . . .

Let us take care of the fragility of our wounded country! Each one of us with our wine, our oil, and our steed.

Let us take care of the fragility of our country. Each one of us paying from their own pocket what is needed so that our country can become true. A shelter for all, without excluding anybody.

Let us take care of the fragility of every man, of every woman, of every child and of every elder, with that caring and attentive attitude of the brotherliness of the Good Samaritan.

Kirchner listened to the homily without reaction. "Kirchner did not support the vision laid out by Bergoglio," Secco told me. "Kirchner wanted to build his base and reward his followers. Bergoglio's vision was built around solidarity—that the people needed to work together to effect change, and that the needs of the poor were paramount. Kirchner wanted to reward his followers and punish his opponents. Conflict was inevitable."

The relationship between Cardinal Bergoglio and President Kirchner became strained, with Bergoglio criticizing the government's austerity measures and failure to sufficiently help the poor, and Kirchner criticizing Bergoglio for meddling in state affairs. If Bergoglio had been accused, during the Dirty War and during the wave of liberation theology in Latin America in the 1980s, of excessively prioritizing faith over politics and structural change, well, faith and politics were now running neck and neck in his head.

At the Te Deum mass the next year, Bergoglio's words were even more pointed:

> Today, as always, Argentines must choose. To do nothing is in itself a choice, but a tragic one. Or we choose the mirage of adhering to the mediocrity that blinds us and enslaves us, or we look at ourselves in the mirror of our history, accepting as well all its darkness and "anti-values," and we adhere from the heart to all the greatness of those that gave everything for the country without seeing the results, of those that walked and walk down the humble path of our people, following the footsteps of that Jesus that walks past the arrogant, leaving them disconcerted in their own contradictions and seeks the road that exalts the humble, a road which leads to the cross, the cross upon which our people are crucified, but which is the road of the certain hope of the resurrection; a hope which no power or ideology has yet been able to take away from us.

Less than a year later, on April 2, 2005, Pope John Paul II died. After paying tribute to him at a mass at the cathedral on April 4, Bergoglio traveled to Rome for the funeral and the conclave to elect a new pope. Bergoglio's name appeared on lists of *papabili*—speculated candidates for pope—in the press, along with cardinals from Germany, Italy, Nigeria, Indonesia, Colombia, Honduras, and more. Shortly before the conclave began, a document about his actions during the Dirty War was sent to Spanish-speaking cardinals. The document revived accusations made by one of President Kirchner's allies, Horacio Verbitsky, that Bergoglio had played a role in the kidnappings of Jalics and Yorio. (In an interesting twist, a 2015 biography of Verbitsky revealed that Verbitsky himself collaborated with the dictatorship from 1978 to 1982, including ghostwriting speeches for the military leadership.)

Bergoglio had had troubles with Rome prior to John Paul II's death—for a number of years, his recommendations for new bishops had been rejected in favor of more conservative choices preferred by Rome—and the document did not help. And after John Paul II's twenty-seven-year reign, it seemed almost natural that his second in command, Cardinal Joseph Ratzinger, would succeed him. Ratzinger was elected pope on April 19 and took the name Benedict XVI.

Bergoglio's only comments about the conclave in his authorized biography were short. When his biographers asked him, "How did it feel to hear your name repeated over and over again in the Sistine Chapel during the counting of the votes for the successor to John Paul II?," they noted that he "became serious and looked somewhat tense. Finally, he broke out into a smile and replied, 'At the beginning of the conclave the cardinals swear an oath to secrecy; we cannot talk about what happened there.'"

Bergoglio clearly thought he was off the hook!

But they followed up by asking, "At least tell us how it felt to see your name among the leading candidates to become pope."

Bergoglio replied that he felt "shame, embarrassment. I thought that the journalists had taken leave of their senses."

"Or had a little inside information," the authors offered.

Bergoglio replied, "They covered all the bases with their predictions. They said, just in case, that there were nine potential popes and picked out two Europeans, Ratzinger included, and two Latin Americans, among others. That way, they reduced their margin for error and boosted their chances of getting it right."

"So, we journalists have very active imaginations?" the authors said.

"Very active," Bergoglio replied.

Regardless of the reason he was not elected pope in 2005, Bergoglio headed back to Argentina to continue his work—and continue to be attacked by the Kirchner government. A few weeks later, Kirchner—who did not attend Pope John Paul II's funeral mass but did attend Pope Benedict XVI's installation mass—decided to skip that year's Te Deum mass at the cathedral in Buenos Aires. Instead, he announced that he would attend Te Deum celebrations in the province of Santiago del Estero, prompting Bergoglio to cancel the celebration at the cathedral—the first time since 1810 that the ceremony was not held there.

FR. GUILLERMO MARCÓ, who served as Bergoglio's spokesperson for eight years, is a tall, handsome man who could pass for a mature leading man in Hollywood with his good looks and warm, welcoming smile.

His office in Buenos Aires was filled with photographs of his former boss. At one point in our conversation, Marcó pointed at a picture of Cardinal Bergoglio in which Bergoglio wore a dour expression, and he said in halting English, "This was his usual expression. His face. He don't smile so much."

"Look at this," he said, pointing from the somber photo to one in which the pope was smiling widely, "and look at this."

The difference was remarkable.

I asked Marcó the same question I had asked Pepe: "Does he smile a lot more than he did when he was in Buenos Aires?"

"In Buenos Aires, he didn't smile publicly," Marcó replied. "When I called him when he was in Buenos Aires in the morning, he was always joking. He likes joking. He was always pulling people's leg, saying things, but only among his friends, not in public."

I asked, "Why does he smile so much more in public now than

he—" Before I could finish, Marcó interrupted and said, "Because he likes being pope. He's happy."

"He didn't like being cardinal?" I asked.

"He was made for this," Marcó replied. "He was made for this."

I tried again. "He wasn't happy as a cardinal?"

"Argentina is . . ." His voice trailed off.

Like a good press secretary, he sidestepped the question and pointed to another picture on the bookshelf. "Look, here he is with Obama." He paused again.

"Argentina is very complicated," Marcó finally said. *How many times have I heard that line?*

I pointed to a picture of Pope Francis with Cristina Fernández de Kirchner, who succeeded her husband as president in 2007 and served until 2015. The two of them were standing side by side; she wore a faint smile, while he was looking straight ahead with a blank expression.

"He's not smiling too much there, with Cristina," I commented.

"He manages his facial expressions very well," Marcó said.

I went back to the question about the pope's happiness. "Did we lose the question about whether he was happy as cardinal?"

"He's happy as pope," Marcó replied. "Let's see, when he was cardinal, he had a lot of problems with Rome. A lot. Because Rome made his life impossible."

"Impossible?" I asked.

"Yes, all the Roman Curia was dedicated to, as we say in Argentina, wearing him down," Marcó explained. "They didn't like the way he was. Bergoglio wouldn't use the official car. When we went for the first time to Rome, they called him and asked, 'Why don't you use the big car with a chauffeur?' And he replied, 'Because I like to walk.'"

Marcó sighed, raised his hands, and shrugged. To further illustrate how different Bergoglio was from other cardinals, he then told me what happened the day Pope John Paul II made Bergoglio a cardinal: "When he was made cardinal, in the morning, I went to the place where he was living, right? And he came down, with his red clothes on. And downstairs comes another cardinal who got in a Mercedes Benz and left. And I was with Bergoglio standing in the door and I asked him, 'In what are we going to go to the Vatican?' And he looked to me and said, 'Walking.'"

"Walking?" I asked, thinking of Skorka's point about Abraham and all the others who told me how much Bergoglio walked.

"Walking. But he was dressed all in red, and it was embarrassing for me," Marcó said, laughing at the memory.

"Why was it embarrassing?" I asked.

"Because it was like going to a costume party, you know, so I told him, 'Okay, look, it's like a film from Fellini. We can't walk in the streets of Rome with you dressed like this!' With the little cap, you know . . .

"'Oh, no,' Bergoglio replied. 'Don't worry, because one of the things I like so much about Rome is that you can go out with a banana on your head and nobody will say anything.'

"And so we began walking, with the red outfit, through the streets of Rome. He always went the same way, Via dei Coronari, and he looked at his watch and told me, 'It's early. I will invite you to take a coffee so that you overcome your embarrassment.'" Marcó laughed again.

"So, did you have a coffee?" I asked.

"We went into a little bar," Marcó said.

"With the hat on?" I asked.

"With the hat on, and with all his red vestments," Marcó replied. "And the owner—" He paused to laugh at the memory. "So the Italians like all these Vatican things, right? They did not want to charge us for the coffee. We were both standing at the counter of the little bar drinking coffee. It was very funny."

"Did he pay for it?" I asked.

"No, the owner of the bar didn't want us to pay. 'It's an honor for me to have a cardinal here,' he said."

Marcó was on a roll.

"And then we continued to walk. There is a little painting in the

Via dei Coronari called the *Madonna dell'Archetto*. He always prays to that little image, to the Virgin.

"And then we entered to St. Peter's Square. The cardinals have another door to enter the Vatican, so they were not expecting him at that place, and when we were in the square he looked at the clock and said, 'It's still early, so we are going to stay here a few minutes, and then we will enter.'

"And we were speaking, and some Japanese came and stood near him"—Marcó gestured, showing how the Japanese tourists jammed close to this unknown soon-to-be-cardinal for a picture—"to take photographs and they come one and two and three and I tell Bergoglio, 'Okay, put on your cap, and perhaps we make some money.'

"He thought that was funny. And when the Swiss Guard saw him, they were confused, because that place was not the place where the cardinals enter. They enter through another door, with their cars and all the people from the delegations."

We chatted for a few more minutes before I asked him if he had ever had disagreements with Bergoglio. "Many times," he said, smiling. "Because I was pestering him. I would always be telling him things, but he was very kind with me. But I resigned because I had a fight with President Kirchner."

Marcó went on to tell me the story of a local political battle that had national implications. In 2006, Governor Carlos Rovira of Misiones, who was an ally of President Néstor Kirchner, wanted to amend the constitution of the province to allow indefinite reelections. The retired bishop of a diocese in the province, Joaqín Piña, led an opposition group called the United Front for Dignity that included more than fifty nonprofit organizations and representatives of Jewish and Protestant groups. Kirchner thought that Bergoglio had encouraged Piña, who was a Jesuit, to oppose Governor Rovira's bid because of Rovira's relationship with Kirchner. Secco told me that "some people thought that Kirchner's ultimate goal was to change the national constitution to allow for the indefinite reelection of the president."

Tensions between Bergoglio and Kirchner peaked a few weeks before the October 29 election. In a homily on October 1, Bergoglio warned about those who sow discord: "If already at the moment of the cross there were people who sowed discord, throughout history there always were those people. The devil does not remain idle, he is the father of lies, he is the father of discord, the father of division, the father of violence. And we do not want that father because that father does not make us brothers, he divides us."

His statement was widely interpreted as a criticism of Kirchner, and Marcó received numerous calls from journalists asking whether Bergoglio's words were indeed directed at Kirchner. "I spoke all the day with journalists," Marcó told me. "In the afternoon—I was so tired that day—one journalist tells me, 'Okay, not Bergoglio, you. Do *you* think that the president is making the division in Argentina?' And I tell him, 'I think that this is not in his heart and in his mind, but if a president promotes hate and division, it is trouble for us.' The press transformed this and put 'Marcó says the president promotes hate and division.' In other words, an affirmation."

Marcó thought the incident would pass quickly, but Kirchner's allies kept the story alive. Speaking at a political event on October 5, Kirchner said, "There is a God and God belongs to all, but be careful, because the devil also reaches everybody, those of us who use trousers and those of us who use cassocks, because the devil slips in everywhere."

The next day, Marcó offered his resignation, but Bergoglio did not accept it. Rovira's measure lost by a wide margin, but the pressure on Marcó continued, and Bergoglio finally accepted his resignation in December. As I stood up to leave, Marcó said, "Yes, I left. I am a priest. I am not a politician or a journalist, so if I have to die for Jesus Christ, I will. But to die for a president fighting with an archbishop, no, it's not worth it. I don't like politicians much. . . . I provided a service for eight years, and he was my bishop, I was a priest. We had an excellent relationship."

Bergoglio did not behave like a normal cardinal in so many ways. He had upset the hierarchy in Buenos Aires political circles and the hierarchy in Rome.

But the ongoing economic crisis and the corruption in Buenos Aires presented more opportunities to go to the periphery, to go where he felt most comfortable, to deepen the theology of the people in new ways. I would learn even more about Bergoglio from two unlikely teachers.

22   The Fire

I THOUGHT THAT Miguel had gotten lost. We were stuck in traffic yet again, and it was hot. Miguel's air conditioner worked,
but his car was small and cramped and all I could see was more
traffic ahead.

"This is a mess," I said.

"This is Once, one of the busiest railway stations in Buenos
Aires," Miguel replied. "Almost a million people a day pass
through this area. Maybe you should get out and walk up two or
three blocks. You will see the Cromañón memorial there."

I popped out of the car, hoping that two or three blocks meant
close by. I just couldn't picture how a memorial to one hundred
ninety-four young people killed in a nightclub fire was going to
fit into this latest scene of chaos. Miguel was right, though. I
walked a couple of blocks and stumbled upon the memorial site.

Although the site is more than ten years old, it still has a very
makeshift feel. A crude, pergola-like structure houses the memorial, with a blue tarp and corrugated metal sheeting serving
as the roof. There are no walls. The entire structure appears
very unstable, as if a strong breeze could easily knock it over.

Pictures of the victims were everywhere inside the memorial.
Dozens of pairs of sneakers were placed throughout the space,
some with the laces tied together and thrown over a rope.

Small concrete benches offered a place to sit and gaze at the
seemingly countless pictures of all of those lives lost: young men

and women and even one little girl with soap in her hair who looked as if she had just gotten out of her bath.

Plastic flowers were scattered about, and plants grew out of cinderblocks. And of course, candles, crosses, and rosary beads were everywhere.

There, in front of this memorial, was Nilda Gómez, mother of Mariano Benitez, a twenty-year-old who had gone to the República Cromañón nightclub for a concert by a band called Callejeros on December 30, 2004, and lost his life.

Mariano perished with one hundred ninety-three other young people that night. Hundreds more were injured; an official number is not available, but estimates are between seven hundred and fourteen hundred. The club, which opened in April 2004, was a very short walk from the Once station—a perfect location for young people to travel to by train or bus to see a show and then get home easily.

A series of errors and oversights occurred that evening that led to the tragedy. Roughly three thousand people were jammed into the club, which had a maximum capacity of just over one thousand; emergency doors were chained closed so that nonpaying kids couldn't sneak in; decorations inside were highly flammable; and then someone lit a firework that sparked the blaze. Chaos ensued, and many died from poisonous gases and carbon monoxide.

Nilda has silver hair streaked with black. She spoke in Spanish with almost no emotion. "Come this way and I will show you where the fire took place."

She turned around, and within a few yards, we were on a street that was no longer in use. Maybe fifty yards down that street, she stopped.

"This is the club."

The area looked as if a bomb had just gone off—debris was everywhere. It looked as if no one had touched the place since the tragedy some ten years earlier. The street and the sidewalk were covered in fragments of broken concrete. The ground floor of the building was boarded up; there were holes in the walls. The second floor was boarded up as well. The top three floors of the building, though, looked fine.

There was a row of trees across the street and a second street beyond the trees. The second street was filled with buses and cars.

The area was at once alive with people and movement and noise, and abandoned and lonely and sad. The scene evoked contrasting emotions—like Buenos Aires in miniature.

I took a couple of pictures of the building and of Nilda. And then I just stared.

I had seen pictures of the bodies on the street and imagined that gruesome scene as I stood in the warm sun and looked at this sad woman standing amid the wreckage and memories.

After a few minutes, Nilda had had enough. "Come to my office and we can talk, but we have to hurry," she said. "I have another meeting."

Nilda turned around and walked back up the abandoned street toward the makeshift memorial and Once station. She walked by the memorial without stopping and across a busy intersection. I trotted to keep up.

We hustled by the buses, food vendors, and newspaper stands that sold everything from snacks to trinkets to prominently displayed dirty magazines. I felt as if I was in Times Square in early summer.

Nilda had a small office in one of the buildings near the train station. She went over to a desk, grabbed a newspaper in a plastic sleeve, and headed toward the table where I was sitting. She tossed the paper in front of me. It was an article from *La Nación* newspaper describing the mass held on the first anniversary, with a photo of family members wearing T-shirts picturing their deceased loved ones, lighting candles in the cathedral. The article also contained multiple photos of a gaunt and somber-looking Cardinal Bergoglio hugging relatives of the deceased.

Nilda was in no mood to exchange pleasantries. She was serious and in a rush, and like so many others who had interacted with Bergoglio, she wanted to tell her story.

I knew that Bergoglio had appeared on the scene—on the street that I had just walked—in the early dawn, shortly after the fire. He comforted the injured and the families of the victims until dusk. During my trip to Argentina, almost everyone with whom I spoke told me how much Bergoglio's presence meant not only to the grieving, but to the entire city as well. And it meant so much partly because the political leadership did so little.

"It's not that we ended up being friends of Bergoglio," Nilda told me, "but rather that when all this happened, he saw the pain, the tears, and as a church, he approached us to provide all his support, all of it."

Nilda then told me about the annual pilgrimage to the basilica in Luján to celebrate the feast day of our Lady of Luján, the patron saint of Argentina. The story goes that a statue of the Virgin Mary, made in Brazil, was being transported to Argentina in a cart and the cart got stuck in the road in Luján.

"When they took the Virgin off the cart," Nilda explained, "the cart would move, but when they put it back on, the cart would no longer move, so they decided that the Virgin wanted to stay there. So a church was built there. All those who travel ask for the protection of the Virgin of Luján. If one needs to have an operation, one promises to go to Luján if everything turns out well. So people walk to Luján. Luján is considered the capital of faith, all the pilgrims go there. So people perhaps that did not go before, if something happened in their family, they would gather relatives, friends, and neighbors, and organize a walk to Luján. And that is the history of faith in Argentina."

I couldn't quite understand what this story had to do with the fire, but Nilda explained. "Every year, we would go on the pilgrimage to a bridge on the way to Luján, and we would set up a table under that bridge and hand out cards, with the image of the Virgin and the names of the kids who died, to the pilgrims. And we would take the wishes of the people to God, the intentions, we would take down their names, their wishes, and put them in an urn. And then we would take the urn with all the wishes to the mass that Bergoglio would celebrate there. When we arrived at the plaza, Bergoglio's attendants accepted the urn, and they placed it at the foot of the stage with the altar where Bergoglio celebrated mass."

She told me that at the pilgrimage in 2005, "Bergoglio included us in the mass. He included the mothers of Cromañón in that service because he understood that from a position of faith, he could help. That was his way of helping us."

As I sat and listened to Nilda tell the story, I could not help but think of Bergoglio's grandmother Rosa and her faith. Rosa's Catholicism was filled with similar rituals and gestures and images—this was Catholic theology from below, not theology handed down from on high. And I harkened back to my own conversation with my grandma Rose about the Shroud of Turin and her words of wisdom: "Whatever brings people closer to God is a good thing."

Nilda told me how Bergoglio had arranged a monthly memorial service for the families and victims. "Throughout the year, there were, in different parishes, gatherings of family members, meetings where people would talk, reflect. Bergoglio would come as well as other priests. We would then conclude the gathering with a moment to share sandwiches and soft drinks, then the mass and then everyone would go home. This was a way always, not for us to feel resignation, but rather for many of us to find consolation in the word of God."

And there is the anniversary mass held in the Buenos Aires Metropolitan Cathedral.

"Every December thirtieth we march from the Plaza de Mayo to the sanctuary and we stay there until eleven fifty P.M. [the date and time of the fire]. First we celebrate mass from six o'clock to seven o'clock P.M. Bergoglio celebrates the mass. He hugs the parents. . . ."

"He had called us to help us organize the mass. One of us would read, another would read out the intentions, another would take the candles. In other words, he would always have all of us participate, not only one person, everyone."

At that first anniversary mass, Bergoglio delivered some of his most powerful words:

Today we are here to enter into the heart of that mother who went to the temple full of hope and who returned with the certainty that those hopes would be shattered, cut short. Entering into this heart let us remember the children of the city, of this city that is also a mother, that they be recognized by her, that she realize that these, like the children of Abraham in the First Reading, are the children of her inheritance; and the inheritance that those children who are no longer with us give us, is a very clear one: *Harden not your hearts!* Their photos here, their names, their lives symbolized in these candles, are shouting at us not to let our hearts harden. This is the inheritance they have left us. They are the children of an inheritance that tells us: "Cry!"

Distracted city, spread-out city, selfish city: Cry! You need to be purified by tears. Those of us here praying, we give this message to these our brothers and sisters of Buenos Aires: Let us together cry—we so need to cry in Buenos Aires. . . . Let us cry here. Let us cry outside, too. And let us ask the Lord to touch each of our hearts, and the hearts of our brothers and sisters of this city, that they, too, may cry; and that with our tears we might purify this, our superficial, flighty city.

Those words—"Let us cry here. Let us cry outside, too . . . that with our tears we might purify this, our superficial, flighty city"— shock me every time I read them because I was raised in a family that encouraged me *not* to cry. There's a famous story within our family that involves football and tears. The story goes that my brother Bobby was playing touch football with our cousins and was knocked down. He started to cry and Uncle Bobby said to him, "Stop crying. Kennedys don't cry."

My dad picked my brother up and said, "That's okay. You can cry. You are a Shriver."

In a family that values toughness, I am not sure whether my dad's words resonated at all. Having been raised in that culture, and in an American culture that highly values toughness as well, I am surprised by Bergoglio's plea to cry, to cry so as to soften one's heart. He is calling us all to change our perspective and to soften our hearts.

Nilda went on to say, "The fact was that in Bergoglio's speeches, he never asked us to give up or to stop crying. He would say to the people that they had not cried enough, and that the city of Buenos Aires, which was a flippant and corrupt city, was to blame for the deaths of our loved ones. That was what Bergoglio would say. He was never one to hold back, no."

But Bergoglio didn't hold back his spiritual consolation from anyone, either. He reached out to members of the band who were criminally prosecuted, and that upset Nilda. "I was very angry because he had spoken to them. I had gone out to the media and I had criticized him publicly very strongly. So he sent me an invitation to meet at the Curia."

Nilda looked like a tough woman, but still I was surprised that she had publicly criticized the cardinal of Buenos Aires and then even more surprised when she told me that she had refused to meet with him. Like many family members, she thought that the band was also responsible for the tragedy.

"At that time, we did not understand the power of the word, and his point of view. We were so angry that we considered all those who were supporting those whom we considered to be responsible—we saw them as our enemies.

"But Bergoglio just told the band members to be strong, to keep on moving forward. He never said they were innocent or anything of that nature. He is a pastor, and I understand that now, that God is there for everyone, for the just and for the sinners. For those who are good and those who are bad. He was doing the right thing. But we, at that moment, reacted, thinking, *What's up with this guy? How can he be supporting the bad guys?* But we came to understand that he has a broader view."

Nilda told me that Bergoglio even sent rosaries to the band members. "He is coming from the view that, as I say, God forgives everything. And that speaks to his humility and his love.

"Why is he pope now?" Nilda asked, shrugging. It was not so much a question as a statement. She pointed at the newspaper and said, "So that's where one understands he is something special."

The man has an uncanny sense of universal suffering. I think that it is rooted in the capacity for compassion that his grandmother Rosa instilled in him; in the family quarrels that made him cry in secret as a young child; in his own near-death experience as a young man.

But, more theologically, it is rooted in his identity as a Jesuit. Because he had taken Ignatian spirituality so seriously, he had made the suffering of Christ a part of who he is. He processes the pain of a mother who has lost her son in a catastrophic fire through the lens of Jesus on the cross, looking at his mother, Mary, as she watched him suffer an agonizing death. And Bergoglio reaches out with loving mercy and forgiveness to the band members, just as Christ on the cross did to the soldiers who had crucified him, saying, "Father, forgive them, for they know not what they do." Because he sees Christ in each human, he sees their suffering, too. The more people told me about his seeming ability to feel and share in their pain, the more I believed the Ignatian influence was at work—he feels with his brain and his heart, with his spirit and his gut.

FIVE DAYS AFTER the fire, the embattled mayor of Buenos Aires, Aníbal Ibarra, called Diego Gorgal and asked him to join his administration as secretary of security. Diego has a background in security issues and criminal policies and previously served as undersecretary for security planning for the province of Buenos Aires. He started work ten days after the fire, hired, essentially, as an outsider tasked with cleaning up the mess and working to ensure that such a tragedy never occurred again.

"A big change was needed," Diego told me over the phone. "Everyone felt that there was corruption before the event and that it needed to be cleaned up. And people were afraid that another mass incident could happen any day.

"In the Israeli embassy bombing in 1992, twenty-nine people were killed; in the Jewish community center bombing in 1994, eighty-five people died. Those were big tragedies," Diego said. "The Cromañón fire killed almost two hundred people and injured many more. This was a big, big deal in Argentina."

I asked him about Bergoglio's role in the aftermath of the tragedy. "Was he helpful to you?"

"Yes, very," Diego said. "He helped me build bridges to the families. Look, I was not a public official when the fire happened. But I was appointed by the mayor who was responsible for it. There were a lot of raw emotions at the time and a lot of mixed emotions directed at me. I was the guy trying to carry out change, but I worked for the guy they wanted to kill. I could not have done my work without Bergoglio's help. He helped me to be accountable to the families, but he helped me to talk to them, too. Bergoglio and I wanted to ensure justice, but we wanted to create a positive environment at the same time."

I told Diego that I had met with Nilda. I asked him what it was like working with the families of the deceased and injured.

"The families of the victims became a political movement. They wanted justice and accountability. There was corruption in the police force and corruption in the city government. The people who were supposed to ensure safety and security at events were not doing their jobs. They were getting paid off.

"Some of the parents wanted to use Bergoglio to advance their cause. They wanted Bergoglio to take a political stance against the government and against the band. But Bergoglio never got engaged in partisan politics; he never took one side over the other. In fact, a lot of the families got upset with him because he had contacted the musicians, who the families felt were also responsible for the tragedy. But Bergoglio never allowed himself to be used politically. He offered spiritual assistance for both sides, even the guilty ones."

Diego went on to tell me that Mayor Ibarra was impeached and left office in early 2006. He was succeeded by the vice mayor, Jorge Telerman, who fired the entire cabinet except for Diego. Telerman had a very good relationship with Bergoglio before he took office and they worked well together going forward.

A trial was eventually held in August 2008 and concluded one year later. The owner of the nightclub received a nearly eleven-year prison sentence; employees of the city government and the club also received prison sentences. The band was acquitted but retried in 2011, and its members received sentences ranging from five to seven years, which have been appealed.

"It was a very, very difficult time," Diego said. "So much pain and anger . . ."

His voice drifted off. There was silence on the line.

I thanked him for his time, and as I started to hang up, Diego said, "Remember, it was such a tragedy and had such a heavy impact on people that today, many try to just avoid it altogether."

I mentioned that a few months into his papacy, Pope Francis wrote to one of the band members in jail. The letter reads, in part, "Though I am physically far away I am close to you and your group in spirit, it is as if I can hear everything you hear and say, from a distance." He ended the letter with, "When you are able, please pray for me. A hug. Fraternally, Jorge."

Diego laughed and said, "Bergoglio."

"Bergoglio," he said again. The way he said it made me imagine that he was shaking his head in wonder on the other end of the phone line.

We then discussed the message that Pope Francis sent later that same year to the families of the victims. The message, sent for the annual December 30 liturgy, included these words: "In these days in which hope is renewed, I cannot forget the young people of Cromañón, their parents and relatives. . . . The wounds hurt and they hurt even more when they are not treated with tenderness. . . . Only a tender caress, from our heart, in silence, with respect, can give comfort."

"That's Bergoglio," Diego said again. "You have to remember that he doesn't avoid the issues, but he doesn't take sides. He always tries to go beyond the historical fight, the particular problem at hand, to try to move us all ahead."

I thanked him again for his time and hung up the phone.

He always tries to go beyond the historical fight, the particular problem at hand, to try to move us all ahead. I realized that Diego had just summed up the man as clearly as any theologian, writer, politician, or journalist I had encountered.

It sounded like the same advice Bergoglio gave his young scholastics when they went out in San Miguel on Saturdays and Sundays: Do your work and avoid fights. It sounded like his approach during the Dirty War. It sounded like his approach during the internal Jesuit battles over curriculum and economic justice.

Had he always done it perfectly? No, he had not, but he had learned from his mistakes and had evolved. When he was cardinal, however, the chief pastor of his city with no real other authority over him other than Rome, he could more fully exercise his philosophy. Go beyond history to faith. That was it. Go beyond history to faith and hope and love.

A few hours after my call with Diego, my wife, Jeanne, telephoned me to tell me about a conversation she had had with a friend whose parents were from Cuba. Pope Francis had left Washington, D.C., the day before.

"I can't stand Pope Francis," the friend said to Jeanne. "I can't wait for him to leave America. You don't understand what happened in Cuba. And neither does he. What he has done in Cuba with those bastards is an outrage."

I couldn't help but think of Nilda and her anger, her confusion, her sadness—emotions so strong that she blasted Cardinal Bergoglio in the press and refused to meet with him. I hope that Jeanne's friend will come to understand what Nilda learned from Cardinal Bergoglio: "God is there for everyone, for the just and for the sinners. For those who are good and those who are bad. He was doing the right thing. So it does not matter. Because God is there for everyone. We came to understand that he has a broader view."

Amen.

23 Cartoneros

I HAVE SEEN plenty of homeless people on the streets of Washington, D.C., New York City, and during my visits to Santa Monica, California, where my brother Bobby and sister Maria live with their families. Often, the homeless beg for money with their lifelong belongings jammed into a knapsack or a shopping cart. Sometimes they have a companion, but most of the time they are alone. And many seem to be suffering from mental illness.

So on my first night walking the streets of Buenos Aires in search of a place to eat, it was not a total shock to see what I thought were two homeless men pushing a cart full of what I thought was trash. This was a world capital, of course, and homelessness has become an unfortunate part of urban life worldwide. Bergoglio had devoted massive energy and resources to helping the poor, and men like Toto and Pepe were continuing the battle. But the economic crisis in Argentina had left the country wobbly, and now, in 2014, things were looking bleak again. All over the city, locals had told me, people were falling through the cracks.

What did surprise me, though, was the speed at which these people were moving. They were hustling down the street, yelling at each other, but the yelling wasn't angry as far as I could tell.

After dinner, on the walk back to the hotel, I saw another

group of people hustling down the street, pushing not one but two carts full of trash. Again, they were shouting back and forth. They stopped to sift through trash in front of apartments and businesses. And this time it wasn't two men, but a man, a woman, and a young girl.

When I got back to the hotel, I asked the concierge, "Is there a big homeless population here in Buenos Aires? I saw people rifling through trash just a few blocks down the road. Do they tend to be mentally ill?"

"No, not at all," he replied. "They are *cartoneros*. That's their job—they pick up cardboard and plastic bottles all night long and they sell it to the recyclers. They are all over Buenos Aires. They are hard workers."

"That's their job?" I asked. "Doesn't Buenos Aires have a recycling program? What about that kid with those two older people?"

The concierge replied, "It's probably a mom and a dad with one of their children. Families work together. Buenos Aires's recycling program is the *cartoneros*."

The next day, I had the good fortune to have breakfast with Marcos Peña, the chief of staff to Mauricio Macri, who was then mayor of Buenos Aires. Today, Macri is president of Argentina.

I asked, "What's the story with the *cartoneros*? Is the mayor working on that? I have never seen families rifling through trash to recycle it."

"Ah, yes," Marcos replied in English. "Bergoglio worked with the *cartoneros* when he was the cardinal. I will introduce you to Sergio Sanchez. He is in charge of the Movimiento de Trabajadores Excluidos—the Movement of Excluded Workers, or MTE for short—and is a friend of Pope Francis."

As THE 2001 economic crisis continued, thousands of Argentines were forced into low-paying work—from sweatshops to prostitution to child labor to picking up trash to be recycled. The situation was terrible.

"People who lived on the outskirts of Buenos Aires would use public trains and buses to come into the city to pick up the recyclables," Javier Ureta Saenz Peña, environmental management coordinator for the government of the city of Buenos Aires, told me. "They were all independent workers."

Initially, residents and businesses complained when those workers ripped through their garbage, often leaving a mess behind. "Over time, the city started to work with the *cartoneros* to get them to become a cooperative. We went block by block to recruit leaders. For the most part, these workers had no background in industry. They had no structure for their work. We wanted to help them get organized so that the recyclables were collected in a timely fashion. We wanted it run like a business. We wanted to turn it into an actual service with health and safety requirements," Javier said. "There are about ten thousand *cartoneros* working today, about five thousand of whom work in organized cooperatives. And more than half of the five thousand work for MTE. The rest are on their own.

"There are seven companies that pick up trash in Buenos Aires. That is a much more structured business," Javier continued. "MTE is a cooperative, not a union. MTE is registered with the national government but unions have clear rules. We are writing and negotiating new terms and conditions with the cooperatives."

"Did the government appoint Sergio Sanchez to his role?" I asked.

"Sergio was elected by his peers," Javier replied. "He negotiates the pay and working conditions and benefits for the MTE members. Many *cartoneros* are trying to organize themselves into cooperatives all across Argentina. We are a little further along here in Buenos Aires but we have much more work to do."

I HAD NEVER been to a recycling plant, so I was surprised to see a security gate around the Centro Verde Barracas plant on Herrera Street. *Why would anyone want to break in to a place that only has trash?* The guard directed us to park off to the right, away from the trucks and trash containers. "Go over there and wait," he said. "Sergio will come get you."

I was right on time, for a change.

But Sergio was not.

As ten minutes dragged into fifteen, I got out of the car and walked around the one-square-block facility. Cardboard and plastic bottles were strewn all over the place. Most of the cardboard was bundled up and most of the bottles were set off to one side, but there was still trash everywhere. A discarded swingset stood to the side next to dumpsters overflowing with garbage. But even though the place was messy, there appeared to be a clear system for processing the material.

Two backhoes, with two men on each of them, were moving cardboard from one section of the facility to another, and in one of the two large warehouses, seven people were sorting through the cardboard, picking out what was valuable and discarding what was not.

I wandered about and was greeted only by nods and smiles. People were working hard. I could hear cars zooming by on the highway that bordered one side of the plant; pigeons flew about, and in the midst of all of this organized chaos stood a beat-up-looking tree. There was, however, no nasty odor. I had expected the place to stink, but it did not.

Sergio caught me by surprise. I was standing just outside one of the warehouses looking in, watching the backhoes coming and going, the drivers shouting at the workers sifting through the recyclables. The whole scene was mesmerizing, but I had to focus to stay out of the way.

I jumped and turned when I was tapped on the shoulder.

The guy staring at me laughed, revealing no front teeth.

"Are you Mark? I am Sergio," he said in Spanish.

Sergio is about five feet four and two hundred pounds; he has a fleshy face with big cheeks and a generous double chin. His meaty forearms are covered in tattoos, one of which appeared to be of Mary, the mother of Jesus. He had a stud in his left earlobe, and a baseball cap covered his salt-and-pepper crewcut.

He wore a dark blue T-shirt with a neon green stripe across the chest. In the middle of the neon green stripe was a white strip. I had seen that same shirt on a couple of the workers.

On the sleeve was written MTE 10 AÑOS / MOVIMIENTO DE TRABA-JADORES EXCLUIDOS (MTE 10 Years/Movement of the Excluded Workers). Khaki cargo shorts and neon green sneakers completed his outfit.

His left calf was bleeding but he didn't seem to notice.

"Come on, I will walk you around," he said with a deep, raspy voice. He held a pack of cigarettes in one hand and twirled a keychain with the other. "Let's go this way."

We walked into the big warehouse where men and women were on their hands and knees sorting through the recyclables.

"Here, we sort what is sellable and throw out the trash. We are cleaning out the space now so that later tonight, there will be room for all the cardboard and plastic that our members bring in off the streets."

"So this is the day shift?" I asked.

"We are working here all the time," Sergio answered. "We are moving cardboard and plastic at all hours. And we feed our members, too. I will show you the eating area next."

I looked around and pointed at what appeared to be a statue of a woman. Placed on a small, beat-up refrigerator about the size of one you would see in a college dorm room, the statue was clad in an outfit similar to the workers' uniform, including that neon green stripe on the shirt. Fake flowers tied with ribbon sat at her feet, along with a small trophy and a sign that informed the workers when meals were served.

"Is that in honor of a woman who worked here?" I asked.

Sergio chuckled. The cigarette in his mouth didn't move.

"No, that's Our Lady of the Cartoneros. She looks out for us and blesses us in our daily work."

Our Lady was made out of cardboard.

"She's beautiful, no?" he said as he waved his hand at her. "Everyone loves her. Come on—let's go inside so we can talk. I have a lot to tell you."

. . .

SERGIO LED ME into a small building made of cinder blocks. It was uncomfortably warm inside. The overhead fan was working hard, but it wasn't cooling the room very much. A TV hung on the wall playing just static.

Four or five long tables were scattered around the room with an array of plastic chairs around them. Some were broken, some were in decent shape; it was a random collection. Sergio told me that the room serves as a dining hall, feeding three to four hundred people each night.

I asked Sergio if he had been living on the street when he started to collect cardboard.

"No, no," he said. "I was a regular person. I had a good job, doing landscaping in the country clubs. The owner went bankrupt. I was left without a job. I couldn't find work. And so I started with the cardboard with my family."

He told me that he had grown up outside Buenos Aires in a town called Mar del Plata with two brothers, one of whom died in an accident, the other of AIDS.

Sergio now lives in Villa Fiorito, which is on the outskirts of Buenos Aires and is considered one of the poorest places in Buenos Aires. It is considered a "red zone," according to Alfredo Abriani, the director general of religious affairs of the government of the city of Buenos Aires: "A stretch of the River Riachuelo has untreated industrial waste and sewage accumulated there, generating health, nutritional, and toxicological problems in children, youths, and adults."

"How did you meet Bergoglio?" I asked Sergio.

"We met as a result of the movement," he replied. "When we started to fight to have our rights recognized as workers, nobody knew us because we worked in the informal sector, so Bergoglio started to get to know us through the church, because when one is discriminated against and when one wants to baptize one's child, it became complicated because there were many bureaucratic steps, much paperwork, and we didn't have documents. Bergoglio would baptize them anyway.

"He approached the movement and started to support the work

that we were doing. We, as an organization, would organize demonstrations. For example, if we found out that in one house, there were slave workers, we would go there and demonstrate, and these were things that he was observing about the movement."

In March 2006, a fire in a sweatshop in the Caballito district of Buenos Aires killed six people, all of whom were trafficked Bolivians. Four of the six were children who were locked in a room so as not to interfere with their parents' work. "Bergoglio came to provide support when the situation occurred and then celebrated mass in the street," Sergio explained.

The movement continued to grow and Bergoglio continued to help. In 2008, he celebrated mass at Our Lady of Emigrants in front of a crowd brought there by MTE and a partner organization called La Alameda that worked with exploited textile workers.

That mass turned into an annual event celebrated every July in the Plaza de la Constitución—the plaza where Father Toto set up his missionary tent. Sergio and his colleagues always attended.

"We would go with him when he celebrated mass in the *villa*, too. He always remembered us, and always blessed someone. You would see the man so humble. When he would visit us, he would sit at the table, or chat with us in a corner. He was a humble guy, who would approach us, and when we saw him in the street, it was like a priest, not like any cardinal."

Sergio stopped talking only to take a big drag on his cigarette. The TV was still on but the screen was still just static. The heat and humidity were almost unbearable. I had sweat stains on my shirt.

"When we found out that he was pope, it made us a little sad, because we would be losing the link we had with him, we would be seeing him at a distance. But when he took office as pope, he said that he wanted a *cartonero* to be there."

"Really?" I asked. "At the papal installation mass?"

"It was not a normal thing for a *cartonero* to have a passport," Sergio explained. "Well, I had the good fortune of having a passport. So I went to Rome."

"Was this for his first mass as pope?" I asked.

"Yes, when he was sworn in," Sergio replied. "In truth, it was one of the places of privilege. I was there with José, who is a teacher, and a sister who is a missionary. And I saw the presidents go by, the kings, and they would pass by back there." Sergio gestured to show that the presidents and kings were seated behind him.

"I had my *cartonero* uniform on, to show him that the *cartoneros* were by his side. Well, after that, once all the ceremony is over, he comes in, and we enter behind him. We were the first ones that he greets, in a room, not the main room where all the presidents go—the presidents go to a room where there was a railing on the side, and from behind that little railing they would greet the pope. I felt very proud. And I thought to myself, *How many would pay to be inside in that place?* He greeted each one of us. He gave me a hug, then he told me, 'Keep up the good work, keep on strong, working hard.'"

Sergio was on a roll. I couldn't have stopped him if I wanted to.

"Let me tell you more. When he was in Brazil, in the event for the youth, he recognized that the *cartonero* youth had to be by his side."

Sergio explained that Bergoglio gave thirty-six *cartonero* youth a scholarship to attend the World Youth Summit in Brazil in July 2013. "Among them there were kids with all types of problems. Problems of addiction, problems of work, problems of alcoholism. We were out in a camping ground in tents. On the first day that he celebrated mass, we managed to make it into the church. We were about a hundred meters from him, but that was not where things ended."

The cigarette was still dangling on his lower lip, almost magically.

"On the second day, the general mass was celebrated, and to get in to see him, you had to have a series of identification cards, with photos and everything. Well, we were sort of lost, going from here to there, and the mass was about to begin, and a cardinal came down, or a person from the archbishop's office, who was looking for the pope's friends among the people, and found us, in the middle of the crowd, five hundred thousand people, and we went in and were next to him, a meter away from him. The archbishops were on one side, and all of us neatly sitting on the other side.

"When the pope entered he greeted each one of the thirty-six kids that I had brought, one by one. Then he had his photo taken with each one."

"One at a time?" I asked.

"One at a time," Sergio said.

He paused to take another drag on his cigarette. "And the other day," he continued, "he reached out to us, together with other organizations, to address three important problems in our country, and in all the world, that is, work, dignified land for all, and dignified homes for all."

"You just saw the pope in Rome?" I asked.

"Yes," Sergio replied, explaining that it was a three-day meeting.

"Cardinal Turkson came here before the meeting in Rome and we took him around the neighborhoods, inside the barrios, to see our work, and the craziest thing that I remember is that when we went to fetch him, he was looking out to see what type of car I'd be driving to pick him up, and I arrived in an ambulance, and you ought to have seen the cardinal, being taken around all the city in the ambulance!"

I had heard of Turkson but I didn't know much about him, other than that he was from Africa and had an important job in Rome.

Sergio drives an old ambulance "for all sorts of uses. To take people to the hospital or if something happens. I bought the ambulance to do solidarity work. When one lives in the *villas*, the regular ambulance does not come in to pick you up."

But Sergio goes into the *villas* despite the danger. "Thank God, nothing has happened to me yet," he told me. "For Turkson, it was a crazy thing. When I saw him in Rome, he was laughing about how he had been taken around the city."

Sergio smiled at me. He now had an unlit cigarette sitting in his mouth, dangling there, waggling up and down as he spoke. But it never fell.

I was in no hurry to leave despite the heat. The stories were unbelievable, really, especially the last one—a three-day meeting in Rome with cardinals and Pope Francis to discuss work, land, and housing? I had not read anything about this get-together in the popular press. I figured it was worth hearing Sergio's take on it—I could verify it all afterward.

"The meeting was held, and social organizations from seventy or eighty countries attended, workers like *cartoneros* and those working on housing and with farmworkers. The meeting lasted three days. One day was all the social organizations, one full day in the Vatican with the pope, and another full day in the hotel. And I will tell you a story that will make you laugh."

"Did you see the pope? Did you talk to the pope?" I asked.

"Yes, yes, I'll tell you. You will laugh at the story. Well, shall I tell you?"

He smiled. The guy was stringing me along.

"Yes, please." I smiled back.

He knew that he was a master storyteller. He didn't say anything for a couple of seconds. Just to draw it out.

"Okay," he finally said. "The first day we had the meetings in the hotel. Fine. On the second day, we had to go to the Vatican, where the pope was going to be, where he would speak. Well, on the second day, we took the *cartonero* cart that we had taken with us from here and the big bag with the cardboard and many did the same. The farmworkers took their baskets filled with crops they had harvested and things like that. We went all the way through the Vatican, from place to place."

Maybe I was tired, but Sergio's story was confusing me—*more than a hundred people in a three-day meeting that I had never heard of? Crops and recyclables being carried around the Vatican?*

Questions were spinning through my head: *Did Pope Francis invite the head of the AFL-CIO, or the head of the American Red Cross to this meeting? What child advocates from the United States or the United Kingdom were invited? What powerful leaders from the World Bank or big nongovernmental organizations were invited? What American cabinet secretaries or governors were invited? If the pope wanted to make structural changes, he must have invited some of those important, powerful people to help the Sergio Sanchezes of the world, right? I can make a few phone calls when I get home and get the inside scoop on the meeting.*

Sergio kept talking. "Well, at a certain point, the pope was there, he was talking about these problems, inclusion, dignified housing for all, and then about the land. After he spoke, the pope greeted each of us and had his photo taken with every one of us, all one hundred!

"We left with the commitment to work with all the organizations in the world. The pope said that there has to be a house for everyone, and regarding social inclusion, that this struggle is not the struggle only of us, the *cartoneros* that are working here, but there are people wearing a suit and a tie that are also excluded because they work in the informal economy. That is the struggle that we are engaged in, and he knows that we will make a noise."

He paused, the unlit cigarette still perched between his lips, and said, "The other day, I managed to get my son in to see Pope Francis, and the pope said, 'Yes, your father was rattling things up in Rome, right?'"

Sergio smiled. "Because I always go to rattle things up. Those people who don't shake things up a little never have anything!"

WHEN I RETURNED home to America, I started to research this three-day meeting, hoping, frankly, that it had really happened and that Sergio had not made it up. If he had, it would cast doubt on all of his stories.

I struggled to find anything at all on the meeting until I stumbled upon an article written by a man named Joe Gunn in a Catholic journal called *The Prairie Messenger*. Gunn was identified as the Ottawa-based executive director of Citizens for Public Justice, an ecumenical organization that promotes justice, peace, and the integrity of creation.

Gunn's first sentence grabbed me: "Chances are that you will never have heard of this encounter."

He was right about that!

Gunn went on, "There is no document about it in English. Only one person attended from Canada." He told the story of a Canadian woman named Judith Marshall, who was invited to the three-day meeting, the World Meeting of Popular Movements, held at the Vatican in October 2014. Marshall was identified as a Toronto-based trade union activist.

Gunn wrote, "One of the main organizers, Sergio Sanchez, is a robust man from a shantytown of Buenos Aires who transformed the lowly occupation of collecting cardboard waste into a new social movement. . . . Apparently, Bishop Bergoglio had been involved with these mainly undocumented migrants since 2006, saying mass and baptizing their children, while affirming their dignity."

I tracked down Marshall and asked if she would consent to a phone interview. She emailed back saying no, but she included an article that she had written on the experience entitled "Challenging the Globalisation of Indifference: Pope Francis Meets with Popular Movements." It was published in a journal called *Links, the International Journal of Socialist Renewal*. Marshall quoted a statement issued by the organizers of it to set the stage of who was invited and the focus of their get-together:

> In the main, these movements represent three increasingly excluded social sectors: (a) workers who are at risk or lack job security, in the informal sector or self-employed, migrants, day-labourers and all those unprotected by labour rights or trade unions; (b) landless farmers, family farmers, indigenous people and those at risk of being driven out of the countryside by agro-speculation and violence; (c) the marginalised and forgotten, including squatters and inhabitants of peripheral neighbourhoods or informal settlements, without adequate urban infrastructure.

One hundred fifty delegates attended the meeting, including thirty Catholic bishops from all over the world. The meeting had been organized by the Pontifical Council for Justice and Peace, headed by Turkson, and the Pontifical Academy of Social Sciences, headed by Dr. Margaret Archer. *Who were these delegates*, I thought, *and where did they come from?*

Marshall then described her fellow participants, including someone named Pancha Rodriguez from the National Association of Rural
and Indigenous Women in Chile who "had strong words about the
relentless pressures on rural producers from the transnationals—and
their own governments—to plant genetically modified seeds."

Marshall also wrote about Agostinho Bento from UNAC (National Union of Peasants). Agostinho was from Mozambique and
"talked about land grabs for mega-projects such as Pro-Savana for
agro-exports and major mining, oil and gas projects. He also called
for more supportive action from the Catholic Church."

There were Ghanaians who "talked about mining devouring Africa" and "the woman representing U.S. organic farmers [who]
warned about weasel words used to manipulate farmers, like the arguments about 'sound science' from big agricultural companies and
well-funded corporate think tanks denying global warming."

I read on and learned that the other delegates represented organizations such as the South African Waste Pickers Association, the National Slum Dwellers Federation of India, the Landless People's
Movement in Brazil, and the Malawi Union for Informal Sector.

I didn't know one person mentioned, nor had I heard of one of the
entities.

Not one.

Marshall vividly described day two of the World Meeting of Popular Movements.

[It] took the throng of grass-roots activists into the heart of the
Vatican, some in aboriginal dress, some in their work overalls for
collecting recyclables, some with T-shirts with political slogans,
many carrying organisational banners. The day began with a
mass in St. Peter's Basilica celebrated by Cardinal Turkson. Participants from our meeting had been chosen to read the scriptures in different languages. The symbolism was to be found not
only in the very visible presence [of] more than one hundred
grass-roots activists moving about in the Basilica but also in the
presence of the tools and the products of our struggles which we

had brought to Rome. The most prominent was the huge metal waste bin on wheels brought by the recyclers from Argentina. It was quickly filled, not with recyclables but with the contributions from other activists. Those working on land questions had brought seeds and tools and even produce. Travel memos prior to arrival had included reminders about border regulations on such things. A replica of a slum dwelling was included to symbolise housing struggles. . . .

Following the Mass, we proceeded to our meeting with the pope. Cardinal Turkson welcomed us and then Pope Francis quietly joined us.

I had to find a copy of the pope's comments. Surely they had been published in English somewhere.

I finally found them on the Vatican's website.

His first words were "Good morning again, I am happy to be with you. Besides, let me tell you a secret: This is the first time I have come down here to the Old Synod Hall, I have never been here before. As I was saying, I am very happy to see you here, and I welcome you warmly."

I have been told time and again that one of the best ways to win over an audience is to touch them at the outset with humility or humor or a story that pulls them close to you. A little secret from the most popular man in the world was a deft start!

I thank you—you who suffer exclusion and inequality in the first person—for accepting the invitation to discuss the many very serious social problems that afflict the world today. I also thank Cardinal Turkson for his welcome—thank you, Eminence, for your work and your words of greeting.

It is worth quoting the pope's unknown speech at greater length:

This meeting of grassroots movements is a sign, it is a great sign, for you have brought a reality that is often silenced into the presence of God, the Church, and all peoples. The poor not only suffer injustice, they also struggle against it!

You are not satisfied with empty promises, with alibis or excuses. Nor do you wait with arms crossed for NGOs to help, for welfare schemes or paternalistic solutions that never arrive; or if they do, then it is with a tendency to anesthetize or to domesticate . . . and this is rather perilous. One senses that the poor are no longer waiting. You want to be protagonists. You get organized, study, work, issue demands, and, above all, practice that very special solidarity that exists among those who suffer, among the poor, and that our civilization seems to have forgotten or would strongly prefer to forget.

"Solidarity" is a word that is not always well received. In certain circumstances it has become a dirty word, something one dares not say. However, it is a word that means much more than an occasional gesture of generosity. It means thinking and acting in terms of community. It means that the lives of all take priority over the appropriation of goods by a few. It also means fighting against the structural causes of poverty and inequality; . . . the lack of work, land and housing; and . . . the denial of social and labor rights. It means confronting the destructive effects of the empire of money: forced dislocation, painful emigration, human trafficking, drugs, war, violence, and all those realities that many of you suffer and that we are all called upon to transform. Solidarity, understood in its deepest sense, is a way of making history, and this is what the popular movements are doing.

This meeting of ours is not shaped by an ideology. You do not work with abstract ideas; you work with realities such as those I just mentioned and many others that you have told me about. You have your feet in the mud, you are up to your elbows in flesh-and-blood reality. You carry the smell of your neighborhood, your people, your struggle! We want your voices to be heard—voices that are rarely heard. No doubt this is because your voices cause embarrassment, no doubt it is because your cries are bothersome, no doubt because people are afraid of the change that you seek. However, without your presence, without truly going to the fringes, the good proposals and projects we often hear about at international conferences remain stuck in the realm of ideas and wishful thinking.

The scandal of poverty cannot be addressed by promoting strategies of containment that only tranquilize the poor and render them tame and inoffensive. How sad it is when we find, behind allegedly altruistic works, the other being reduced to passivity or being negated; or worse still, we find hidden personal agendas or commercial interests. "Hypocrites" is what Jesus would say to those responsible. How marvelous it is, by contrast, when we see peoples moving forward, especially their young and their poorest members. Then one feels a promising breeze that revives hope for a better world. May this breeze become a cyclone of hope. This is my wish.

This meeting of ours responds to a very concrete desire, something that any father and mother would want for their children—a desire for what should be within everyone's reach, namely land, housing, and work. However, nowadays, it is sad to see that land, housing, and work are ever more distant for the majority. It is strange but, if I talk about this, some say that the pope is communist. They do not understand that love for the poor is at the center of the gospel. Land, housing, and work, what you struggle for, are sacred rights. To make this claim is nothing unusual; it is the social teaching of the Church.

I got goosebumps reading these inspiring words. Pope Francis masterfully wove together his faith—"love for the poor is at the center of the gospel"—with an apolitical approach—"this meeting of ours is not shaped by an ideology"—that relied upon the theology of the people: "You have your feet in the mud, you are up to your elbows in flesh-and-blood reality. You carry the smell of your neighborhood, your people, your struggle!" And he used concrete images: the desires of a mother and father to address their children's basic needs, and "a promising breeze that revives hope for a better world. May this breeze become a cyclone of hope."

It is an inspiring political (with a small *p*) call to action, a call to continue to be "protagonists" who organize, work, issue demands, and practice solidarity, a call grounded in faith.

But the call is challenging, too. Am I a member of one of those NGOs that is "anesthetizing" and "tranquilizing" the poor? And "rendering them tame and inoffensive"? And that word "solidarity"— Pepe had used it, and Sergio used it to describe the work he did with his secondhand ambulance. "Solidarity" for Pope Francis means "much more than an occasional gesture of generosity. It means thinking and acting in terms of community. . . . It also means fighting against structural causes of poverty and inequality."

Am I in solidarity with people like Sergio Sanchez and Judith Marshall—or am I helping to create a system that is hurting the poor more than it is actually helping them? Surely the pope isn't criticizing me, a man who has dedicated his life to working with the poor—is he? Am I one of those whom Jesus would have called a hypocrite?

Pope Francis went on to discuss the three themes of the meeting— land, housing, and work. These next words softened the challenge issued at the outset because, honestly, my mind could not comprehend the immense task of providing land and housing and work for every human being in the world. I am very task-focused and I just couldn't figure out what the next step would be. It was just too overwhelming. I started to think that the pope was naive, too idealistic for the real world. Did he really think that Sergio Sanchez and the others in front of him were going to accomplish this towering task?

Having spent time with Sergio and picturing all of "those people" in their native clothing with their produce and that cart sitting in Synod Hall, I thought that nothing more would come from the three-day experiment. Their very presence—these folks from the fringe— their very presence would guarantee that "the good proposals and projects" discussed would "remain stuck in the realm of ideas and wishful thinking." The pope was right that that was the result of many international conferences—and that would be the result of this three-day meeting, too, I thought. It would be nothing more than a nice get-together that failed to generate concrete action and much press in the powerful, developed world.

Pope Francis must have known many would have those feelings, because his final words were:

> With all this I attach great importance to the proposal which some of you have shared with me, that these movements—these experiences of solidarity which grow up from below, from the subsoil of the planet—should come together, be more coordinated, keep on meeting one another as you have done these days. But be careful, it is never good to confine a movement in rigid structures, so I say you should keep on meeting. Even worse is the attempt to absorb movements, direct or dominate them—unfettered movements have their own dynamic; nevertheless, yes, we must try to walk together. Here we are in this Old Synod Hall (now there is a new one), and synod means precisely "to walk together." May this be a symbol of the process that you have begun and are carrying forward.
>
> Grassroots movements express the urgent need to revitalize our democracies, so often hijacked by innumerable factors. It is impossible to imagine a future for society without the active participation of great majorities as protagonists, and such proactive participation overflows the logical procedures of formal democracy. Moving toward a world of lasting peace and justice calls us to go beyond paternalistic forms of assistance; it calls us to create new forms of participation that include popular movements and invigorate local, national, and international governing structures with that torrent of moral energy that springs from including the excluded in the building of a common destiny. And all this with a constructive spirit, without resentment, with love.
>
> I accompany you wholeheartedly on this journey. From our hearts let us say together: No family without housing, no farm-

worker without land, no worker without rights, no one without the dignity that work provides.

The image of walking harked back to the many stories I had heard of Bergoglio walking at Colegio Máximo and in the *villas*, and especially to Rabbi Skorka's comment that Pope Francis loved the story of a walking Abraham. As Skorka told me, Pope Francis believes that "faith requires constantly moving, developing."

Indeed, movement is a constant theme in his words—"it is never good to confine a movement in rigid structures"; "unfettered movements have their own dynamic"; "moving toward a world of lasting peace and justice calls us to go beyond paternalistic forms of assistance"—and in his life.

Pope Francis himself was becoming "a torrent of moral energy," challenging my own rigidity. Am I just a cog in the wheel that makes my life comfortable, while my work does little more than anesthetize the poor?

Do I really believe that the Sergio Sanchezes and the Judith Marshalls of the world should be active participants in the decision-making process? Do I really believe that they have the ability and know-how to be protagonists for their own change?

I reread his speech. I agree that Sergio's efforts are manifestations of solidarity that grow from below, from the subsoil of the planet. But do I really believe that change is going to come from people who toil in the subsoil?

I am a firm believer that to make a difference, nonprofits have to be big enough not only to help a lot of people, but also to be influential with policymakers.

Yet Pope Francis was saying the opposite.

Deep down, I really didn't believe that even if the groups kept meeting or walking together, as Pope Francis asked them to do, that any change would come of it.

And since this first meeting generated almost no publicity, what were the chances that these ragtag people would ever come together again, anyway? Surely Pope Francis has more important work to do.

I put the speech aside. I was relieved to learn that Sergio's stories were true, but I was busy with many other projects. I had a job running a fledgling organization. We were developing our strategy for the next year, and one of our goals was to secure a few more powerful board members. Isn't that the best way to make systemic change in the United States?

I had had a successful trip to Argentina and even had what I thought was one of the best stories of the new pope's reign—he had invited a trash collector, a teacher, and a nun to sit in seats of honor at his installation mass. All three of them were with the new pope in the "back room" right after the mass while presidents and prime ministers and other bigshots waited in another room.

All I needed now was to secure an interview with Pope Francis and my portrait of him would be complete.

Yes, what I had learned about him had challenged me—from my idea of what constitutes a good Catholic to the value of interfaith relationships; from the very essence of the work I do day in and day out to the way I live my life.

But I had hundreds of emails to answer, critical work to do.

And I needed to get that interview.

I had learned enough from the Totos and Pepes, the Gomezes and Sanchezes of the world.

Or so I thought.

24 The Interview

AFTER MY TRIP to Argentina, after verifying that Sergio Sanchez's story about his meeting in the Vatican was true, and after
reading more of Bergoglio's homilies and writings, I finally felt
that I was prepared for an interview with Pope Francis. I knew
that it would take months to arrange, so I had gone to work in
early 2015.

I reached out to Cardinal Sean O'Malley of Boston. "Cardinal Sean," as he is called, is one of the nine cardinals on Pope
Francis's Council of Cardinals, essentially his kitchen cabinet. I
understood that Cardinal Sean had perhaps the closest relationship of any American cardinal to Pope Francis. Cardinal Sean
had attended my mother's wake and was on the altar for my
uncle Ted's funeral. I thought that that was a good connection.

Before calling him, though, I reached out to a couple of
prominent Bostonians who supported the Catholic Church and
asked them to call Cardinal Sean on my behalf. They agreed to
do so. I then called and spoke to Cardinal Sean's secretary, who
arranged for me to meet with the cardinal during his next trip to
Washington, D.C. Cardinal Sean said that he would raise the
issue, but he told me that he had received many interview requests and it was going to be difficult to arrange.

At the same time, I reached out to Cardinal Donald Wuerl of
Washington, D.C., who had presided at my father's funeral
mass and encouraged me over dinner one evening a few weeks

later to write a book about Dad. The result was *A Good Man*. My high school friend and college roommate, Fr. Bill Byrne, worked directly for him. With Father Bill's advice, I called him and made the request for a papal interview, adding, "You know that I would never have been asked to write this book if I had not written the one on Dad. And you know, Cardinal, that book was your idea, so this request is really all your fault!"

We both laughed. I don't know if Catholic guilt works on a cardinal, but Wuerl said he, too, would put forth the request, though he, too, warned that it was going to be tough to arrange.

But that was still not enough. I reached out to the apostolic nuncio (the ambassador from the Vatican) to the United States, Archbishop Carlo Vigano, and asked for a meeting. I had met him in February 2014 when I gave a speech to the Association of Catholic Colleges and Universities. He agreed to see me and at the end of our meeting said that he, too, would make the request to Pope Francis on my behalf.

I made several other phone calls to see who else could help. I contacted a friend of my family who lives in Rome and does some work for the Vatican. She had arranged a few audiences with Pope Francis and told me in English with a heavy Italian accent, "The pope will speak to you. You come from a famous Catholic family. Yes, this will happen. Your mom and dad will also help us make this happen!"

Help from above and help here on earth—I was thrilled!

And then another stroke of good luck: Pope Francis agreed to have an audience with Special Olympics athletes from Italy prior to their departure for Los Angeles to compete in the Special Olympics World Summer Games. Two hundred athletes would be there, and I was invited to join them. It wasn't an interview, but I would see him, and the audience would give me an excellent excuse to meet and pay my respects to the right people in the Vatican Curia.

When I traveled to Rome in June 2015, I landed with just enough time to rush to my hotel, shower, and head to the Vatican for the papal audience. It was a thrill to walk through the back corridors of the Vatican and to sit in the ornate Clementine Hall waiting for Pope Francis's arrival.

When Pope Francis walked into the room, he received a standing ovation from the athletes and the hangers-on like me. I felt that he looked directly at me for what seemed like ten seconds—*maybe he picked me out of the crowd, just as he picked out Rabbi Avruj!* He turned and headed to his chair and I shook my head, realizing that my ego had gotten the better of me.

Special Olympics athletes Filippo Pieretto and Irene Luigini stood up together and approached the microphone. Filippo spoke first, thanking Pope Francis for the audience. He then asked the president of Special Olympics Italy, Maurizio Romiti, to present a "Play Unified" soccer ball to the pope, a symbol that "aims to create a generation united to fight, through sports, exclusion and discrimination."

Filippo then asked my brother Timothy, the chairman of the board of Special Olympics International, to present the pope with an Olympic torch, which is a "symbol of peace and brotherhood." Filippo went on to say that "we hope that this flame will be a light of hope for a better world and for a future of respect and inclusion for all, no one shut out!"

The pope clapped heartily for Filippo and accepted both gifts with a big smile. Then Irene recited the Special Olympics oath: "Let me win, but if I cannot win, let me be brave in the attempt." Again, the pope applauded; he then walked over and gave both athletes big hugs.

Pope Francis spoke to the athletes:

I encourage you to remain committed to helping one another discover your potential and to love life, to appreciate it with all its limitations and especially in all its beauty. Never forget beauty: the beauty of life, the beauty of sport, that beauty which God has given us. Sport is a very suitable path for this discovery, to open ourselves, to go outside of our own walls and get in the game. This is how we learn to participate, to overcome, to struggle together. And all this helps us to become active members of society and also of the Church; and it helps society itself and the Church to overcome all forms of discrimination and exclusion.

Toward the end of his short talk, he said, "Sport must instead be safeguarded and protected as an experience of human values, of competition yes, but in loyalty, in solidarity. Dignity for every person: always! Let no one feel excluded from playing sport."

He blessed us all and asked everyone to pray for him. The room erupted in applause. He then shook hands with every Special Olympics athlete—just as he shook hands with every one of those *cartonero* kids in Brazil and every one of those participants at the World Meeting of Popular Movements in Rome in October 2014.

After the audience, I met with a few high-ranking members of the Curia. A few days later, I had a late dinner with my Jesuit friend Fr. Michael Czerny at the same residence where Fr. Federico Lombardi, the director of the Holy See Press Office, lives. Czerny and I were the only ones in the dining room when Lombardi walked in. He sat down and joined us. When Czerny introduced us, Lombardi smiled and said in halting English, "I know you. I've heard a lot about you."

We laughed.

"I will bring your request to the Holy Father, but I cannot guarantee anything," Lombardi said. "I receive so many requests for interviews. I turn down *The New York Times*, *The Washington Post*, ABC, NBC—everyone. And then I hear that Pope Francis has done an interview with a small radio station in one of the *villas* in Buenos Aires. I did not even know that he was going to do it!"

He shrugged and smiled. "That is Pope Francis. It is all good. I will ask about your request, but one never knows."

I sent a thank-you email to Lombardi and continued to push with both cardinals, the apostolic nuncio, and the connections I had made in the Curia. Although no one would commit to arranging a papal interview, I was told that my best chance would be in early September, after the summer holidays.

. . .

DURING THE SUMMER, I wrote page after page about all my experiences in Argentina, but I could not stop thinking in particular about Sergio Sanchez and what the pope had said to Sergio and his colleagues at the Vatican, nor could I forget the faces of Father Toto and Father Pepe and Nilda Gómez. I loved all the other stories I had heard and the other characters I had met, but what these people had said and done, and what the pope had said to all of them, just stayed with me. I tried to discern what was happening in my head and in my heart, but with summer vacation, work, and the pressure to write, it was all muddled.

I didn't hear much from my contacts. I was told not to worry. "Things are quiet in July and August, but be ready to come to Rome in early September." I was excited but apprehensive. *This is the most important man in the world, after all.*

AS LATE AUGUST approached, I was asked to appear on national and local television to comment on Pope Francis's trip to the United States in September. It was a great opportunity to get my name "out there" and to generate publicity about the book, but it was a huge time commitment. I was asked to be in the studio for almost three whole days. Nevertheless, I said yes.

A few days later, I received an email from Lombardi. Pope Francis had declined my request for an interview.

I was disappointed. I had worked so long and hard—and politely—to get the interview. *There goes my chance of getting the ultimate nuggets of insight.*

I was also confused. *What do I do now? How am I going to end this book?*

I went back to writing. As I finished the Sergio Sanchez story, my chief of staff, Betsy Zorio, handed me a seven-page document. "He met with Sergio Sanchez and his colleagues again when he was in Bolivia this summer," Betsy said. "You should read his speech."

He met with Sergio Sanchez again? And he couldn't work in just a little bit of time for me? I thanked Betsy and put the speech aside.

WASHINGTON, D.C., WAS abuzz about Pope Francis's visit in September 2015. I, too, was excited to see him in my hometown, but my deadline was looming: The book was due on September 30, 2015, three days after the pope was to leave America.

I backed out of the television interviews just five days before Pope Francis landed in Washington, on September 22. I was still trying to piece together chunks of stories and needed the time to write.

I was thrilled when our oldest child, Molly, a high school senior, was asked to join other students to welcome Pope Francis when he landed at Andrews Air Force Base outside Washington. She was within ten yards of him, took some amazing pictures, and was over the moon about seeing him. I watched his arrival on television, but only for a few minutes. I went back to writing.

And I wrote the next morning as Pope Francis visited the White House and toured downtown Washington in the popemobile. I got choked up when I saw him on television stopping the car and waving a young girl over to see him. The girl had run out into the street but was whisked back to her parents by security agents. Those same security agents brought the child back to the pope, who hugged her. That gesture touched many a heart in Washington, mine included. We all later learned that the girl was five-year-old Sofia Cruz, the daughter of undocumented immigrants.

There were more simple yet profound gestures—he hugged one of our son Tommy's high school friends who was waiting outside the Vatican embassy to wish him a good morning. The kid, a tough football player, was quoted on local radio as saying that he "loved" the pope. Our children were just as mesmerized.

When Jeanne, the kids, and I had to wait in line for an hour and a half and then sit in the hot sun for another hour and a half along with thirty thousand others for an outdoor mass at Catholic University, I was surprised that not one of our children complained. Tommy even climbed a small tree to get a better view as the pope went by in that ever-present popemobile. He was all alone in that small tree, a sight I will never forget. And Emma, our ten-year-old, who couldn't see the pope as he drove by and couldn't understand the sermon in Spanish or read the subtitles on the big screen, never complained.

The next day, when the pope spoke to Congress and visited the homeless at a soup kitchen run by Catholic Charities, he created even more of a glow around Washington. I was born and raised and have worked most of my adult life in the nation's capital, and no event, no person, has made the city feel friendlier or happier than the pope's forty-eight hours in our presence.

But I watched that second day from my desk, where I continued to write.

The good feeling soon abated, particularly when I read an article about a boy who had been sexually abused by a priest. He became a drug addict as a young man and died of an overdose the day before he was scheduled to face his alleged abuser in court. I wondered if the Church really was doing enough to address this type of tragedy. I smiled when the pope told a nun on national television that he loved her, but what concrete steps had he taken to include women more in the life of the Church?

A few days later, I picked up the phone and called Father Paredes, Bergoglio's former student. I asked him a few clarifying questions and then, just before hanging up, I asked him how long he had known his friends Father Nardin and Father Gauffin.

"I have known them for more than thirty years," he replied.

"Got it," I said. "Thank you again for all of your time and help."

Before I could hang up, Paredes asked, "Did Leonardo [Nardin] tell you about our classmate from Ecuador, Tarcisio Vallejo?"

"Yes, Nardin told me how Bergoglio made him wear Vallejo's sweater after Nardin made fun of him," I said.

"Did he tell you about Tarcisio's sister?"

"No," I replied.

"Well, I know he wouldn't mind me telling you, as people know the story," Paredes said. "Tarcisio comes from a big family with thirteen children. He grew up in the jungles of Ecuador. One day, while we were scholastics at Colegio Máximo and Bergoglio was the rector, Tarcisio got word that one of his sisters, Susana, was pregnant. And she was not yet married.

"Tarcisio was full of shame. He's a Jesuit, after all, and his sister is pregnant out of marriage. So he goes to Bergoglio and tells him the story.

" 'What am I to do?' he asks Bergoglio.

"And Bergoglio says to him, 'Embrace your sister. The Catholic Church wants everyone to get married and then have a baby, but she is going to have the baby. You can't condemn your sister or treat her as an outcast. Love her anyway.' "

On one level, I admired the loving mercy that Bergoglio showed Susana and her baby, and Tarcisio. It was the same loving mercy that he showed Sergio Sanchez and his colleagues and their babies.

But I had mixed emotions: Rules needed to be followed, right? You are supposed to go to mass at least on Sundays, and you are supposed to get married and then have a baby, correct?

Weren't these people breaking the rules?

I was confused on other fronts, too. I loved that Pope Francis had invited and paid for those thirty-six *cartonero* youth, many of whom were struggling and were not Catholic, but why not pay for well-behaved, active young Argentine Catholics to go to Brazil, also? And I was taught to show respect to God, but Bergoglio was celebrating mass in a shed? And what about letting dogs lap water at the foot of the altar?

This was not the Catholic Church that I knew.

My confusion was fueled by a nagging feeling of inadequacy when I compared myself to Pepe and Toto, who are putting their lives on the line for God, and to Nilda and Sergio and their struggle for justice. Yes, I am trying to create systemic change for kids, but I am doing it from a comfortable office in Washington, D.C., with a comfortable salary. I try to get children and parents involved with our work, but I am not living with them, I am not driving around in a used ambulance, struggling with them every day. My life isn't threatened by drug dealers, nor am I living in a bare room, sleeping in a single bed. I am pretty darn comfortable and content in my job, pretty darn comfortable and content in my life.

Am I doing enough? Should I drop everything and try to be like Pepe, Toto, Nilda, and Sergio?

And do I really believe in the theology of the people? That poor people are protagonists for their own change and that I needed to do more for and *with* them? Do they really have the skills to create change? I always thought that working to provide services for others was enough; do I really have to *be* with them?

I struggled with these questions, with these thoughts. I couldn't discern what they meant, but they stayed in my head and my heart.

Something was happening.

What I did know was that what had started as a journey to see whether the new pope was the real deal, to find out whether he was all that he appeared to be, had evolved into a very real challenge to the way I viewed Catholicism, but even more, it was a challenge to the way I viewed the world, myself, and how I made a living.

A few days later, as I sat in my office, I came across the transcript of the speech that Pope Francis gave in Bolivia.

A newspaper article about the meeting was attached to the speech. I read that first. This time the meeting was bigger, with fifteen hundred participants from forty countries. It was another three-day get-together, but Pope Francis's speech was fifty-five minutes long, one of the longest speeches he had given. Clearly, he was engaged.

I picked up the transcript and started reading it.

He bonded immediately with his audience: "During our first meeting in Rome, I sensed something very beautiful: fraternity, determination, commitment, a thirst for justice. Today, in Santa Cruz de la Sierra, I sense it once again. I thank you for that."

Then he quickly said that "change is needed." Change not just in Latin America but change "to humanity as a whole." And the reason change is needed is that a global system "has imposed the mentality of

profit at any price, with no concern for social exclusion or the destruction of nature."

He continued:

> Let us not be afraid to say it: we want change, real change, struc-
> tural change. This system is by now intolerable: farmworkers
> find it intolerable, laborers find it intolerable, communities find
> it intolerable, peoples find it intolerable. . . . The earth itself—
> our sister, Mother Earth, as Saint Francis would say—also finds
> it intolerable.
>
> We want change in our lives, in our neighborhoods, in our
> everyday reality. We want a change which can affect the entire
> world, since global interdependence calls for global answers to
> local problems. The globalization of hope, a hope which springs
> up from peoples and takes root among the poor, must replace
> the globalization of exclusion and indifference!

And then I felt he was speaking directly to me:

> Even within that ever smaller minority which believes that the
> present system is beneficial, there is a widespread sense of dis-
> satisfaction and even despondency. Many people are hoping for
> a change capable of releasing them from the bondage of indi-
> vidualism and the despondency it spawns.

He poked at those of us who want to study the problem but not
act:

> I do not need to go on describing the evil effects of this subtle
> dictatorship: you are well aware of them. Nor is it enough to
> point to the structural causes of today's social and environmental
> crisis. We are suffering from an excess of diagnosis, which at
> times leads us to multiply words and to revel in pessimism and
> negativity. Looking at the daily news we think that there is noth-

ing to be done, except to take care of ourselves and the little circle of our family and friends.

Five hundred years ago, Saint Ignatius of Loyola called upon each of us to be contemplatives in action. Pope Francis was making the same call now.

Pope Francis then addressed one of my concerns head-on: What can one person do? He addressed his remarks not to those with resources but to those who are struggling:

> What can I do, as a collector of paper, old clothes, or used metal, a recycler, about all these problems if I barely make enough money to put food on the table? What can I do as a craftsman, a street vendor, a trucker, a downtrodden worker, if I don't even enjoy workers' rights? What can I do, a farm wife, a native woman, a fisher who can hardly fight the domination of the big corporations? What can I do from my little home, my shanty, my hamlet, my settlement, when I daily meet with discrimination and marginalization? What can be done by those students, those young people, those activists, those missionaries who come to a neighborhood with their hearts full of hopes and dreams, but without any real solution for their problems? They can do a lot. They really can. You, the lowly, the exploited, the poor and underprivileged, can do, and are doing, a lot. I would even say that the future of humanity is in great measure in your own hands, through your ability to organize and carry out creative alternatives, through your daily efforts to ensure the three "L"s—do you agree?—(labor, lodging, land) and through your proactive participation in the great processes of change on the national, regional and global levels. Don't lose heart!

I was energized by his words, but I still felt overwhelmed at the immensity of the task—I couldn't imagine how someone struggling to make ends meet could feel that he or she could make a difference. Pope Francis offered more encouragement:

> You are sowers of change. Here in Bolivia I have heard a phrase which I like: "process of change." Change seen not as something which will one day result from any one political decision or change in social structure. We know from painful experience that changes of structure which are not accompanied by a sincere conversion of mind and heart sooner or later end up in bureaucratization, corruption and failure. There must be a change of heart. That is why I like the image of a "process," processes, where the drive to sow, to water seeds which others will see sprout, replaces the ambition to occupy every available position of power and to see immediate results. The option is to bring about processes and not to occupy positions. Each of us is just one part of a complex and differentiated whole, interacting in time: peoples who struggle to find meaning, a destiny, and to live with dignity, to "live well," and in that sense, worthily.

We are to sow and water seeds that others will see sprout? I am to do *that* rather than try to solve the problem now? I am to plant and water for future generations rather than do whatever I can do *now* to get power so that I can change the situation immediately?

He went on to call them "little acts of heroism"—acts that enable you to

> Practice the commandment of love, not on the basis of ideas or concepts, but rather on the basis of genuine interpersonal encounter. We need to build up this culture of encounter. We do not love concepts or ideas; no one loves a concept or an idea. We love people. . . . Commitment, true commitment, is born of the love of men and women, of children and the elderly, of peoples and communities . . . of names and faces which fill our hearts. From those seeds of hope patiently sown in the forgotten fringes of our planet, from those seedlings of a tenderness which strug-

gles to grow amid the shadows of exclusion, great trees will spring up, great groves of hope to give oxygen to our world.

What he is talking about is pretty much impossible, I thought. I was inspired, but once again overwhelmed. Couldn't he just tell me how to do this?

It is not so easy to define the content of change—in other words, a social program which can embody this project of fraternity and justice which we are seeking. It is not easy to define it. So don't expect a recipe from this pope. Neither the pope nor the Church has a monopoly on the interpretation of social reality or the proposal of solutions to contemporary issues. I dare say that no recipe exists. History is made by each generation as it follows in the footsteps of those preceding it, as it seeks its own path and respects the values which God has placed in the human heart.

The pope admits that he doesn't have all the answers, nor does the Church! This is not a typical model of leadership. I read on:

Popular movements play an essential role, not only by making demands and lodging protests, but even more basically by being creative. You are social poets: creators of work, builders of housing, producers of food, above all for people left behind by the world market.

Globalization of hope? Great groves of hope? Social poets?
The language was soaring, the images beautiful, but how do I become a social poet? How do I sow and water so as to really make a difference? I couldn't figure it out—it all seemed so abstract.

The next morning, I went to a breakfast organized by the Catholic Business Network of Montgomery County, Maryland. I had been asked months earlier to speak about my book on my dad, *A Good Man.*

I arrived and chatted with a couple of people. Grace was said and everyone headed to the buffet line. I got my scrambled eggs and bacon and headed to a table. On my way, I bumped into the woman who had offered the prayer and introduced myself. "That was a great prayer you wrote. I would love a copy of it."

She smiled and handed me a piece of paper. "This is it, but I didn't write it. It is part of a speech Pope Francis gave while he was in Philadelphia. I hope it brings you joy." She smiled again and walked away.

I unfolded the paper and read:

> Faith opens a "window" to the presence and working of the Spirit. It shows us that, like happiness, holiness is always tied to little gestures. "Whoever gives you a cup of water in my name will not go unrewarded," says Jesus (Mark 9:41). These little gestures are those we learn at home, in the family; they get lost amid all the other things we do, yet they do make each day different. They are the quiet things done by mothers and grandmothers, by fathers and grandfathers, by children. They are little signs of tenderness, affection, and compassion. Like the warm supper we look forward to at night, the early lunch awaiting someone who gets up early to go to work. Homely gestures. Like a blessing before we go to bed, or a hug after we return from a hard day's work. Love is shown by little things, by attention to small daily signs which make us feel at home. Faith grows when it is lived and shaped by love. That is why our families, our homes, are true domestic churches. They are the right place for faith to become life, and life to become faith.

I didn't need that interview after all. Bergoglio—great teacher that he is—knew that. He had already given me the answer to all my questions: Have faith in God.

His answer starts and ends with faith in God, a faith that opens the windows of your soul so that God can enter into you and do great things. And those great things are often little gestures—a cup of water, a hug, a blessing.

They are great because they are love. And love actualized creates great groves of hope.

Little gestures.

Quiet things.

Little signs.

Little things.

It's not power or money or prestige—no, it's not as complicated as I had thought it was, or perhaps not as complicated as I had made it out to be. Pope Francis is calling us all to love, to make our families and our homes true domestic churches built on faith, hope, and love.

Pope Francis is calling us all, rich or poor, Christian or non-Christian. Anyone can build churches—temples, synagogues, mosques, whatever you want to call them—because anyone can love.

And from that place—where do we go?

There is no known roadmap for the next step—just faith, hope, and love.

Without ever having spoken one word directly to me, this man had taught me by his consistent example—he lives daily what he preaches; he taught me by admitting his sins and shortcomings and asking for forgiveness—and by showing mercy; he taught me by living a joy-filled life. And like a great teacher, he provoked me to question my own beliefs and attitudes and the way I live and act. He did so not through guilt or shame but by showing that real faith frees one to live joyfully.

He had interviewed me.

AFTERWORD

A FEW WEEKS after my request for an interview with Pope Francis was turned down, both Father Federico Lombardi and Father Michael Czerny offered to try to arrange a later time when I could present the pope with a copy of my book and have a picture taken.

I thanked them both for the generous offer. During a later conversation with Father Michael, I said that the ultimate experience would be to attend Pope Francis's daily mass at Santa Marta chapel with Jeanne and our three kids.

"We shall see," Father Michael said. "No promises. That is very, very hard to arrange."

We finished our conversation, and that was the last time I thought about the request.

JEANNE'S MOM, ELIZABETH "Libby" Scruggs, died on March 23, 2016, at 1:30 in the morning. Jeanne and her six siblings were at their mother's bedside in Knoxville, Tennessee; our three kids and I were at home in Bethesda, Maryland.

I woke up to the news via a text Jeanne had sent in the middle of the night.

I told the kids the sad news that morning. Then I took Emma to school and headed to the office.

At 5:30 that afternoon, an email from Father Michael arrived in my inbox:

San Calisto, 23.3.2016
Dear Mark, the peace of Christ during Holy Week!
The Shriver family of five, accompanied by their friend Fr Michael, is warmly invited to Holy Mass at 7:00 A.M. on 16 June in the chapel at Santa Marta.
   Let the planning roll . . . very much looking forward. . . . God bless all the family, and happy, healthy, and peaceful Easter to everyone.

In our Lord, your dear Fr. Michael

The invitation arrived the day Mrs. Scruggs died. Mrs. Scruggs, a wonderful, generous woman who never said a bad word about anyone, was perhaps the kindest person I have ever known—I knew she had a hand in this unexpected blessing.

JEANNE, MOLLY, TOMMY, Emma, and I arrived in Rome on Wednesday morning, June 15. We spent the day traveling through Trastevere before going to bed early. The wake-up call on Thursday came at 5:30 A.M. Father Michael had told us to meet him at the Perugino Gate at 6:27. Our cab was waiting for us at 6:00; the ride was supposed to take about fifteen minutes—but we didn't stumble into the car until 6:15. We arrived at the gate at 6:28 to find Father Michael, dressed in a black cassock, smiling.

I gave him a hug and he warmly greeted Jeanne and the kids. We headed toward the gate, where Father Michael gave the guard our names in Italian. The guard flipped the pages on his clipboard, found our names, and then waved us in. There were no metal detectors, no security X-ray machines—nothing. We walked on a cobblestone road for about twenty yards before bearing right toward Casa Santa Marta.

Casa Santa Marta was built by Saint Pope John Paul II and opened in 1996. It serves as a guesthouse for clergy visiting the Vatican and as the residence for the College of Cardinals during papal enclaves. It also is Pope Francis's residence, where he celebrates daily mass at 7:00 A.M.

Two Swiss Guards were stationed at the entrance. We walked through the doors, and a gentleman showed us to a large waiting area. We were the first to arrive. Over the course of the next twenty minutes, a few priests walked in and sat down; a couple of laypeople also joined us.

At about 6:55, a priest entered the room and gave some instructions in Italian. Father Michael said, "Okay, let's head to the chapel."

We walked for a few seconds before he added, "Follow the priest. I will see you in the chapel."

We entered the chapel, a beautiful, light-filled space with a vaulted ceiling, a wall of windows on one side, and a simple altar at the front. We were directed to the third row of chairs on the left. We knelt, said a few prayers, and then sat. About ten people filed in behind us and another ten to fifteen sat on the other side of the aisle. Everyone was dressed in black except for two people in the last row: a man in an open-collared shirt and a woman in a bright multicolored dress.

After a few minutes, the priest in charge asked us to stand, and in processed sixteen priests, including Father Michael. Then, out of a door on the left, appeared Pope Francis, in green vestments and a white skullcap. He walked to the altar, kissed it, and began the mass.

It was a surreal moment. There he was, the man I had studied for almost three years, about twenty-five feet away from me. I knew many of his friends and colleagues; I had visited Buenos Aires and Córdoba, had seen his bedrooms, had seen where he ate meals and taught courses. I had read his letters, speeches, and homilies. I had seen where he preached in front of large crowds of the rich and powerful and small crowds of the poor and marginalized. I had walked the halls of his beloved Colegio Máximo and the roads of the villas he had frequented. He was physically so close now—yet still so far away.

He spoke in Italian. We did not understand a word he said, but on the ride to Santa Marta, the kids had taken turns reading aloud the day's scriptures, so we knew that the gospel recounted the story of Jesus teaching his disciples to pray the Our Father.

Pope Francis read the gospel and then preached. He started slowly but became more and more animated. I understood only a word or two, but it made little difference. For now, just being in the chapel with Jeanne and our three children, praying in the same room as Pope Francis, was more than enough.

The mass proceeded. Pope Francis did not distribute communion; he sat in his chair, bowed his head, and prayed during that portion of the mass. Then the mass was over.

Pope Francis exited through the same side door from which he had entered, and the priests all processed down the small main aisle.

The same priest who had welcomed us asked us all to sit down. You could have heard a pin drop. Two or three minutes later, Pope Francis emerged from the side room. He walked by Tommy, who could have reached out and touched him.

The room was completely quiet. After a minute, I felt as if someone was looking over my left shoulder; I slowly turned my head and there was Pope Francis, sitting in a chair about ten feet behind us, his head bowed, praying.

I turned back around and stared at the altar. We all sat in silence for a good five minutes.

And then he got up and slipped out of the little chapel.

The priest in charge came out again and motioned for us to follow him to the back of the chapel, where a small line formed, to shake Pope Francis's hand and have our picture taken with him.

I had purchased ten rosaries from Colegio Máximo when I had visited in 2014. I loved the simple plastic rosary beads, each one the shape of a heart. They cost less than fifty cents, and reminded me daily of the simplicity and faith of Pope Francis.

I had given them to my godchildren and a few close friends, but I had two left and wanted to give one to Pope Francis. I had the beads in my hand, ready to offer this small gift.

I was hoping not only that he would appreciate the rosary beads from the place he cherished and called home for thirty years but that maybe—just maybe—the gift would spark some sort of reaction, and he would say something that would prolong the encounter. Maybe—just maybe—he would ask me a question and we would have a conversation. Maybe he would then take a liking to us all and invite us for breakfast—something like that.

Maybe?

And then there he was, right in front of us.

Father Michael shook his hand first and they embraced and exchanged a few words. Then Father Michael turned around and introduced Emma to Francis. They shook hands. I was introduced next, and bent and kissed his ring. Jeanne and Tommy did the same; Molly shook his hand. I showed him the rosary and mumbled something about Colegio Máximo and Brother Mario Rausch.

The pope nodded his head and said, "Yes, yes, Mario Rausch." He blessed the rosary, closing my fingers over it. He wanted me to keep it. I had prepared some thoughts, but they all vanished when I looked into his eyes. I mumbled something about the Jubilee Year of Mercy—I couldn't think of anything else to say!

He said in halting English, "Please pray for me." He paused and then said with a smile, looking at the kids, "Please don't forget!"

And then it was over.

AFTERWARD, WE WALKED out of Casa Santa Marta, profusely thanking Father Michael. St. Peter's Basilica was across the road, some fifty yards away. The basilica was massive, made even more so by the fact that no one was around except those two Swiss Guards. We seemed to have Vatican City to ourselves.

As we strolled, Father Michael pointed out a few sites, but my mind was still focused on the mass and that beautiful moment with Pope Francis. Despite my longing to make a new friend—or at least to have something more than a brief encounter with the man I had studied for so long—I was overwhelmed by the sweetness in his eyes, the joy on his face, and the power of his few words. . . .

We soon slipped into a nearby coffee shop and ordered chocolate croissants and cappuccinos. Father Michael spent about ten minutes with us before he left to attend a meeting. A few minutes later, Father Lombardi appeared. "I just saw Michael," he said in English with a heavy Italian accent. "He told me you were here. How was your visit with the Holy Father?"

I stood up and hugged Father Lombardi, then introduced him to Jeanne and the kids. He shook their hands and made us all feel so welcome.

We thanked him for all of his help and then he, too, was gone.

As we were finishing our croissants, the woman in the bright multicolored dress and the man in the open-collared shirt walked in. We recognized one another.

"Hi there! How are you?" Jeanne said.

"What a great morning," the man replied in English with a Spanish accent. They sat down at the table beside us. I introduced the kids, Jeanne, and myself.

"My name is Leandro Lurati, and this is my fiancée, Agustina Balduzzi. We are from Argentina."

"Where in Argentina?" I asked.

"Buenos Aires," Leandro replied.

"I was in Buenos Aires about two years ago," I said. "I am writing a book on Pope Francis. I traveled around to see his work and to meet some of his colleagues."

"Did you like Buenos Aires?" Agustina asked, and before I could answer her, Leandro said, "That is my hometown. I love it! I met Pope Francis on the subway there when I was just twenty-three years old. Afterward, we met several times at the curia to discuss the Church, Argentine politics, and spirituality. We always met at 7:00 A.M. He encouraged me to volunteer in Villa 21-24, which I did."

I told them that I had visited Villa 21-24. We talked about Pepe and Toto and their work with the poor and with drug-addicted youth. We talked about Cardinal Bergoglio and his work in the *villas*, too. Jeanne told Agustina and Leandro that we hoped that one day Molly and Tommy would visit the *villas* to work with, and learn from, Toto and Pepe and the people they serve.

"Please stay with us when you visit," Leandro said, "or if you stay with Pepe or Toto, please visit us. We will take you around Buenos Aires and have a wonderful time together."

We thanked them both for the generous offer.

"Did Pope Francis invite you to Rome to go to the mass?" I asked.

"No, no, not at all," Leandro replied. "Yesterday he had his general audience. We were in the crowd—there must have been ten thousand of us there. After the ceremony, he walked around and we were in the right spot, so we got to shake his hand. I asked him if he remembered me, because it had been almost six years since I had seen him. And he has a new job, right?" Leandro laughed and then continued. "Francisco immediately said, 'Leandro, I remember you perfectly. How are you doing?' He asked about a priest friend of ours, my community, and my family, too.

"It was amazing for me. I introduced him to Agustina. And then, surprisingly, he asked us, 'When do you leave Rome?'

"We said on Friday, so he tells one of his Swiss secretaries, 'They are my friends. Could they possibly come tomorrow to mass at Santa Marta?'"

Leandro took a sip of his cappuccino and shook his head. "The pope asked me for my mobile number. I gave it to one of his aides and then Francisco said, 'I'll see you tomorrow.'"

"Did he call you?" Molly asked.

"Funny you should ask," Agustina said. "At twelve o'clock, no call. One, two, three o'clock, no call at all. We thought that maybe he forgot about us. But then at five o'clock, the mobile phone rang. It was his aide. He told us to show up at 6:45 at the Perugino Gate."

"I didn't have a coat or tie," Leandro said, "and Agustina didn't have a black dress—this is all we had. It is kind of embarrassing, no?"

Before we could answer, Leandro said, "We were the last ones in line to greet him."

"What did he say to you?" I asked.

"He hugged us both," Leandro said, "and with a big smile on his face, he said, 'You crashed mass!'

"And then he hugged us again."

Acknowledgments

WHEN THE IDEA to write this book first surfaced, I had never been to Argentina. I knew a handful of Argentines, but little of the country's rich history. I didn't, and still don't, speak Spanish. I had a full-time job, and Jeanne and I had three kids under the age of sixteen.

This book only happened because I had so much help from so many people.

Greg Jordan, a writer from Baltimore who worked with me on *A Good Man*, collaborated with me in envisioning, shaping, and writing this book. Early on, he and I identified key themes in Bergoglio's life. Greg traveled with me to Argentina, working side by side with me on many of the interviews (even serving as my interpreter). Greg's research, ideas, and writing were indispensable, and I am indebted to him for his help.

Gina Centrello and Jon Meacham first broached the idea with me. Jon was the lead editor and supported me from start to finish. *Pilgrimage* would not have happened without the two of them. It's that simple. Thank you both.

I would not have met Gina if I had not been asked to speak at the 2014 commencement exercises of Loyola University Maryland. Thank you to Loyola president Fr. Brian Linnane for the invitation and to Fr. Tim Brown, who also works at Loyola. I have known Father Tim for almost thirty years and he is a constant source of books and articles and ideas; I appreciate all of that but most of all I value his friendship.

When I was struggling with the decision to write this book, I relied on the advice of my college roommate and great friend Paul Hardart. Paul encouraged me to write *A Good Man* and accompanied me throughout the process of writing this book as well. No one could ask for a better friend than Paul. He is the embodiment of goodness.

A few days after I decided to write the book, I bumped into a friend, Alan Fleischmann. It turned out that Alan loves Argentina and was hosting a dinner party a few weeks later for Buenos Aires's Bishop Óscar Vicente Ojea, who was visiting Washington, D.C. At the dinner, I was introduced to Bishop Ojea and his friend Eugenio Diaz Bonilla, a terrific translator and a fount of information who has become a friend. In Argentina, Ojea later introduced me to Magui Alonso and Paz Alonso, who took me to Villa 21-24. Paz was my translator when I met with Father Pepe and Sergio Sanchez, and her dad treated me to lunch between interviews. What a wonderful daughter, and what a gracious man.

I knew I needed to speak to many more of Pope Francis's colleagues and friends, so I started calling everyone I knew to ask for help.

Cardinal Donald Wuerl of Washington, D.C., was very helpful, as was his assistant, Stephen DeMauri. My high school friend and college roommate Fr. Bill Byrne was a tremendous resource throughout the process. I treasure our friendship.

Cardinal Sean O'Malley of Boston was generous enough to meet with me and provide advice; Fr. Robert Kickham, his secretary, was always kind to me. I appreciate the help of Fr. Mark Hession, Joe Feitelberg, and Tommy O'Neill, too.

Jack DeGioia connected me to Rabbi Abraham Skorka, and also found an email address for Fr. Miguel Petty. Fr. Otto Hentz and Fr. Tim Brown found other email addresses for Father Petty. I had no idea what a blessing that connection would be.

Father Petty was a tremendous help. He became my go-to Jesuit in Argentina, patiently answering my many questions, making phone calls on my behalf, and tracking down just about whatever information I needed. His constant laughter infused every conversation with joy and energy. I wish I had known Father Petty years ago—he is a wonderful man. And I will never forget the great lunch he organized with Fr. Alejandro Gauffin and Fr. Leonardo Nardin. That was so much fun and incredibly informative. I am grateful to all three men for their stories and thoughts.

The great Jesuit writer Fr. Jim Martin connected me to Fr. Hernan Paredes, an Argentine Jesuit living in New York who was another terrific resource. Father Paredes connected me to Jesuits in Buenos Aires, as well as to Maria del Carmen, who introduced me to Mario Maidana and Daniel Lemos. A big thank-you to all of them.

On the flight to Buenos Aires, I had a long layover in Miami. I spent the time with my brother Anthony and his family. That day, I met Jose Molla, an Argentine living in Miami. Jose offered to help me, and help me he did! Just a day later, he sent an email introducing me to Marcos Peña, who was then secretary general for the city of Buenos Aires; today, he is cabinet chief to the president of Argentina, Mauricio Macri.

It turns out that Marcos grew up in Bethesda, Maryland, just a few miles from where Jeanne and I now live. While I was running for the Maryland House of Delegates, I knocked on his family's front door and was, evidently, polite to his mother and father. When he told me that story and offered to introduce me to people who worked with then-Bishop and then-Cardinal Bergoglio, I knew someone was watching out for me!

Marcos went straight to work, introducing me to Luis Czyzewski, Fr. Guillermo Marcó, Nilda Gomez, Sergio Sanchez, Alfredo Abriani, Javier Ureta Saenz Peña, Fr. Gustavo Carrara, Fr. Alejandro Russo, Juan Tobias, Jorge Triaca, and Adriana Menendez de Triaca. So many of those introductions proved critical to the book and my journey. I am grateful to all of them for their time and insights, and I thank Marcos for his kindness.

In Argentina, I also had meaningful interviews with Sr. Martha Rabino, Fr. Juan Scannone, Fr. Juan Berli, Br. Mario Rausch, Br. Luis Rausch, Fr. Salva Veron, Miguel Mom Debussy, Fr. Rafael Velasco,

Leandro Manuel Calle, Rabbi Abraham Skorka, Fr. José Maria Di Paola (Pepe), Fr. Lorenzo de Vedia (Toto), Dario, Juan, Beto, Rabbi Alejandro Avruj, Sr. Liliana Badaloni, Dr. Gabriela Peña, Javier Cámara, Sr. Maria Jose, and German and Ana Laura Abdala.

I had a terrific time riding the subway in Buenos Aires with Fr. Roberto Cid, who also took me to San José Patriarch Church. Father Cid is from Buenos Aires but now lives in Miami and is the pastor of Anthony's church. Many thanks to Father Cid for that tour and for his connections and encouragement throughout the process.

I met the gracious Alurralde family in Córdoba through my friend Gabriella Smith. Ignacio "Nacho" Alurralde drove me around Córdoba and made me laugh a lot! He and his family could not have been more hospitable.

I could not have traveled around Buenos Aires without Miguel Calculli. I met Miguel through my friend Alex Hernandez Dessauer. Thanks to them both.

When I came back to the United States, I quickly realized that I needed more information about Argentine history and some of the events that shaped Jorge Mario Bergoglio's life. I called my good friend Hunter Biden, who I knew had been to Argentina. Hunter, in turn, introduced me to Gabriel Sanchez Zinny. What a discovery! Gabriel seemingly knows everyone in Argentina and I don't think there is a funnier, more self-deprecating, warmhearted Argentine alive.

Gabriel and his many connections led me to some of the interviews you read, as well as to others who offered insights into the pope's life, including Dr. Sergio Berensztein, Jose Maria Ghio, Diego Gorgal, Luis Secco, Christian Asinelli, Esteban Bullrich, Miguel Ángel Martínez, and Fr. Adolfo Granillo Ocampo. I am grateful to them all.

In Rome, I had terrific conversations with Cardinal Leonardo Sandri (who met with me a second time in Los Angeles), Cardinal Peter Turkson, Msgr. Robert Murphy, Fr. Flavio Pace, Msgr. Peter Wells (who is now archbishop and apostolic nuncio to South Africa and Botswana), Fr. Scott Brodeur (who showed me many sites in Rome, including the Church of the Gesu and Caravaggio's *The Calling of St.*

Matthew), Fr. Mike Rogers, Fr. Tom Powers, Fr. Andrew Small, Msgr. Lucio Ruiz, and Carol Glatz. Greg Burke, the director of the Vatican Press Office, was also very helpful, as was Fr. Federico Lombardi, who has since retired as the director of that office.

Many thanks to Msgr. Jim Checchio for the warm hospitality in Rome.

I met Fr. Michael Czerny on that trip, and within minutes, he seemed like a trusted old friend. His life work inspires me daily, and I will never forget his humility, generosity, and warm smile. How I wish that everyone could have a "Padre Michael" in their life!

Each chapter was enhanced by interviews, comments, or assistance from the following people: Martín Rey, Fr. Joseph Boenzi, N. J. Viehland, Prof. Rosa Carrasquillo, Michael May, Fr. Julio Merediz, Oscar Crespo, Dr. Fabian Garcia, Tim Royston, Fr. Kevin Burke, Fr. Andrés Aguerre, Fr. Enrique García, Jorge Milia, Dr. Massimo Faggioli, Angelo Moratti, Laura Gancia, Fr. James Kelly, Rabbi Abraham Cooper, Sergio Widder, Dr. Shimon Samuels, Dr. Judith Marshall, Sr. Teresa Maria Gallardo, Sr. Joan O'Shanahan, Sr. Veronica Rafferty, Sr. Rose Ann Schlitt, Archbishop Carlo Maria Viganò, Fr. Jim Greenfield, Fr. Tim Kesicki, Fr. Stephen Sundborg, Fr. Jim Hayes, Fr. Larry Snyder, Fr. Gerry Blaszczak, Fr. Ted Dziak, Fr. Matt Carnes, Fr. Joe Daoust, Fr. Steve Katsouros, Fr. Richard Fragomeni, Fr. Joseph Lingan, Cokie Roberts, Jeff Reppucci, Leandro Lurati, Agustina Balduzzi, Chris Maloney, Steve Neill, Rob Granader, Tony Williams, Neil "NAG" Grauer, and Lauretta and Bruce Stewart.

Fernando Massobrio, Dr. Jorge Di Paola, León Muicey, and Fr. Patrick Mulemi provided some of the beautiful photos found in the book. Alessandro Gisotti provided excellent advice and words of encouragement along the way.

A few chapters got cut out of the final text, but I am still grateful to Larry Lucchino and Billy Hogan for their help on all things soccer, and to José María del Corral, Martin Migoya, and Enrique Palmeyro at Scholas and David Evangelista at Special Olympics for their time and assistance.

It was an honor to speak with the late Fr. John Schlegel, who told me about the mass he attended at Santa Marta chapel with Pope Francis. He died a few months after we spoke.

Thank you to Greg Craig, John Kabealo, Cliff Sloan, and Catherine Whitney for their sage legal advice. What a team!

Writing this book while running a start-up wasn't easy. Thank you to Carolyn Miles and Carlos Carrazana for giving me the space and flexibility to research, travel, and write, and to the board of directors and staff at Save the Children Action Network (SCAN) for their hard work to make SCAN so successful.

All of the interviews were translated and transcribed by Susana Martin. She also translated emails, letters, and homilies—everything, actually, that was written in Spanish was translated into English by Susana—and she served as interpreter for a number of interviews that I conducted by phone. I quickly learned that the Argentine dialect of Spanish has some idiosyncrasies that require a trained ear. Susana is one of the best in the business, and her perspective on Argentine history was very helpful as well. She also enlisted her friend Maria Cairoli to help find answers to my questions. Susana was kind and incredibly responsive. She is an absolute treasure.

A special thank-you to Yayo Grassi for his assistance. Every time I have spoken with the man, I have smiled. Yayo just exudes joy. He always took my calls; he was not only helpful but he also encouraged me to persevere in writing. He has become a friend.

Francesca Ambrogetti and Sergio Rubin wrote the official biography of Pope Francis, *Pope Francis: His Life in His Own Words: Conversations with Jorge Bergoglio*. It is a must-read for anyone interested in the pope's life. Not only did they both graciously meet with me when I was in Buenos Aires, they made connections for me and answered countless questions via email. They were a huge resource—and so very friendly.

Father Czerny introduced me to the writer Austen Ivereigh. Austen wrote a biography of Pope Francis, *The Great Reformer: Francis and the Making of a Radical Pope*. I think it is the most comprehensive, best written, and best researched book on the topic. Not only did I rely on the book to better understand Pope Francis and the country's history, I also relied on Austen himself for help. He answered all of my emails and phone calls quickly and completely—I couldn't have asked for anything more. What an incredible help he was.

I am going to miss Fr. Kevin O'Brien. Throughout the writing of the book, he was based at Georgetown University in Washington, D.C.; he is now based at Santa Clara University in California. Kevin taught me so much about the Jesuits, particularly the Spiritual Exercises. If the words I write make any sense, credit Kevin; if anything is wrong or unclear, it is my fault! Kevin answered every email and phone call and silly question I asked him. I cannot thank him enough.

Fr. Gustavo Morello, an Argentine who teaches sociology at Boston College, was a huge resource on all things Argentina. He wrote the excellent book *The Catholic Church and Argentina's Dirty War*. He, too, answered every question I had, and taught me all about Argentine history, politics, and the Jesuits.

Mika Kasuga and Will Murphy at Random House were instrumental in making this book a reality. From smart edits to the text, including drawing out themes, to ensuring that drafts were in on time, they made the book much stronger—and got it to the printing press by its deadline. I hope Gina and Jon give them big pay raises!

A big thanks to my siblings, Bobby, Maria, Timothy, and Anthony, for their insights and support throughout the process.

No one worked harder on this book than Betsy Zorio. I have the pleasure of working with Betsy on a daily basis at Save the Children Action Network, where she is my chief of staff, and the best in the business in that role.

For this book, Betsy spent countless hours at night, early in the morning, and on weekends doing research. She suggested edits and added words; when I was tired, she was patient and kept me focused on each and every word. Betsy's careful eye and tenacity helped to make the book flow. She kept track of each and every footnote and lined up all the pictures as well. Those are very time-consuming, difficult endeavors. I could not have written this book if not for Betsy's help. She was my partner in this effort and I am eternally grateful.

Finally, I want to thank Molly, Tommy, and Emma for their love.

When I was about to pull my hair out or exhausted as a result of the writing, they always made me laugh and remember what was important in life. I am so proud of each of them.

And to my best friend, Jeanne, who read every draft of this book, offered edits and suggestions, and supported me throughout it all, I say thank you. You are the best and I love you.

Notes

1 Rosa

4 **"would give talks everywhere":** "Storia di una vocazione," *L'Osservatore Romano,* December 23, 2013, osservatoreromano.va/it/news/storia-di-una-vocazione.

5 **Bergoglio recalled that his father had befriended many Salesian priests:** "Storia di una vocazione."

6 **say the rosary before dinner:** Paul Vallely, *Pope Francis: Untying the Knots* (London: Bloomsbury, 2013), 25.

6 **"the spiritual father of the family":** "Storia di una vocazione."

6 **"a person who loaned them two thousand pesos":** Ibid.

6 **As Bergoglio said in a 2012 radio interview:** Vallely, *Pope Francis,* 25.

6 **"If someone close to the family divorced or separated":** Jorge Mario Bergoglio and Abraham Skorka, *On Heaven and Earth: Pope Francis on Faith, Family, and the Church in the Twenty-First Century* (New York: Image, 2013), 72–73.

6 **two women from the Salvation Army:** Ibid., 73.

7 **Rosa gave him a letter that she had written:** Austen Ivereigh, *The Great Reformer: Francis and the Making of a Radical Pope* (New York: Henry Holt, 2014), 99–100.

8 **"And the small . . . the small representation of women":** Pope Francis, meeting with young people during apostolic journey to Sri Lanka and the Philippines (January 18, 2015), w2.vatican.va/content/francesco/en/speeches/2015/january/documents/papa-francesco_20150118_srilanka-filippine-incontro-giovani.html.

8 **"When I told my grandmother":** Francesca Ambrogetti and Sergio Rubin, *Pope Francis: His Life in His Own Words: Conversations with Jorge Bergoglio* (New York: G. P. Putnam's Sons, 2013), 38.

9 **"I will build my church":** Matthew 16:18, usccb.org/bible/matthew/16.

9 **When Rosa died at the age of ninety:** Ivereigh, *Great Reformer,* 16.

2 Serenity

13 **one of Pope Francis's letters, written in 2013:** Robert Moynihan, "Letter #24, 2015: The Pope's Traumatic Childhood Experience," *Inside the Vatican,* June 25, 2015, insidethevatican.com/news/newsflash/letter-24-2015-the-popes-traumatic-childhood-experience.

3 Peronismo

16 **"Perón is the face of God in the darkness":** Eva Perón, *La Razón de mi vida* (1951).

4 El Porteño

22 **By 1908, Argentina's per capita income:** Jutta Bolt and Jan Luiten van Zanden, "The Maddison Project: The First Update of the Maddison Project: Re-Estimating Growth Before 1820" (January 2013), ggdc.net/maddison/maddison-project/publi cations/wp4.pdf.

5 The Scientific Method

25 **Bergoglio would later say that his mother "became paralyzed":** Ambrogetti and Rubin, *Pope Francis: His Life in His Own Words,* 11.

25 **enrolled as boarders at Colegio Wilfrid Barón de los Santos Ángeles:** "Ricordi salesiani," *L'Osservatore Romano,* January 29, 2014, osservatoreromano.va/it/news /ricordi-salesiani.

25 **Jorge would later write that the year he spent boarding:** Ibid.

26 **The talk would become Jorge's "point of reference":** Ibid.

28 **His father told him, "Now that you're starting secondary school":** Ambrogetti and Rubin, *Pope Francis: His Life in His Own Words,* 11.

28 **Reflecting on that time, Bergoglio mused:** Ibid., 12.

28 **"In the laboratory I got to see the good and the bad":** Ibid., 14–15.

29 **resulted in the "disappearance" or killing:** Gustavo Morello, SJ, *The Catholic Church and Argentina's Dirty War* (New York: Oxford University Press, 2015), 1.

30 **"When we read the account of Creation in Genesis":** Pope Francis, "Address to the Plenary Session of the Pontifical Academy of Sciences" (October 27, 2014), w2.vatican.va/content/francesco/en/speeches/2014/october/documents/papa-francesco _20141027_plenaria-accademia-scienze.html.

31 **"him the steward of creation, even that he will rule over creation":** Ibid.

31 **"Let us make human beings in our image":** Genesis 1:26, usccb.org/bible/gene sis/1.

31 **"We are not God":** Pope Francis, "Laudato Si: On Care for Our Common Home," May 24, 2015, w2.vatican.va/content/francesco/en/encyclicals/documents /papa-francesco_20150524_enciclica-laudato-si.html.

32 **"Everything that we did and learned also had a harmonious unity":** "Ricordi salesiani."

6 The Decision

34 **Inside the basilica is a painting of James Cardinal Gibbons:** Gibbons was the most influential Catholic of his day, and he was Dad's godfather, too. That portrait of Gibbons hung in our house until I was in my thirties, when Dad gave it to the Basilica.

36 **The story goes that he was knocked off the animal:** Acts 9:3–15, www.usccb.org /bible/acts/9.

36 **"I looked, it was dark":** Ivereigh, *Great Reformer,* 35–36.

37 **"Something strange happened to me":** Ambrogetti and Rubin, *Pope Francis: His Life in His Own Words,* 34.

7 Seminary

44 **"When I was a seminarian"**: Bergoglio and Skorka, *On Heaven and Earth*, 47–48.

8 Illness

48 **"she was daringly astute"**: Antonio Spadaro, SJ, "A Big Heart Open to God," *America*, September 30, 2013, americamagazine.org/pope-interview.
48 **He was drawn to *The Imitation of Christ***: John W. O'Malley, *The First Jesuits* (Cambridge, MA: Harvard University Press, 1993), 266.
50 **a diocesan priest goes to seminary for four years**: National Coalition for Church Vocations and National Religious Vocation Conference.
51 **"the Ignatian way to discover God's will"**: Mark E. Thibodeaux, *God's Voice Within: The Ignatian Way to Discover God's Will* (Chicago: Loyola Press, 2010).
51 **"Ignatius was a keen student of human nature"**: Ibid., xiv.

9 A Novice

54 **"I ultimately entered the Society of Jesus"**: Ambrogetti and Rubin, *Pope Francis: His Life in His Own Words*, 35–36.
55 **"I was always looking for a community"**: Spadaro, "A Big Heart Open to God," *America*.
59 **corroborated by Javier Cámara**: Javier Cámara and Sebastián Pfaffen, *Aquel Francisco* (Buenos Aires: Raíz de Dos, 2014), 72–83.
61 **"Gaviña was a very reserved, serious, good, and tactful man"**: Ibid., 54.
64 **He lived and worked in Japan prior to the Pearl Harbor attack**: Kevin Burke, *Pedro Arrupe: Essential Writings* (Maryknoll, NY: Orbis Books, 2004).
64 **"Nothing is more practical than finding God"**: Ibid.

10 The Spiritual Exercises

69 **"I think we, too, are the people"**: Pope Francis, Holy Mass in the Parish of St. Anna in the Vatican, March 17, 2013.
70 **The story goes that Jesus saw Matthew sitting at work**: Matthew 9:9, usccb.org /bible/mt/9:13.
70 **Bede wrote that Jesus's call to Matthew**: The coat of arms of Pope Francis, w2.vatican.va/content/francesco/en/elezione/stemma-papa-francesco.html.
70 **"contemplate the painting of *The Calling of St. Matthew*"**: Spadaro, "A Big Heart Open to God," *America*.
70 **"That finger of Jesus, pointing at Matthew"**: Ibid.
71 **Jubilee Years are typically called**: "Frequently Asked Questions About the Jubilee of Mercy," U.S. Conference of Catholic Bishops, usccb.org/beliefs-and-teachings /how-we-teach/new-evangelization/jubilee-of-mercy/frequently-asked-questions -about-the-jubilee-of-mercy.cfm.
71 **"Mercy is the very foundation of the Church's life"**: Pope Francis, "Misericordiae Vultus: Bull of Indiction of the Extraordinary Jubilee of Mercy," April 11, 2015, w2.vatican.va/content/francesco/en/apost_letters/documents/papa-francesco_bolla _20150411_misericordiae-vultus.html.
71 **In his opening address, he spoke about**: Richard McBrien, "Pope John XXIII's Opening Address to the Second Vatican Council," *National Catholic Reporter*, Novem-

ber 5, 2012, ncronline.org/blogs/essays-theology/pope-john-xxiiis-opening-address
-second-vatican-council.

72 **"I remember a mother with young children"**: Pope Francis, *The Name of God Is Mercy* (New York: Random House, 2016), 60.

73 **"The method for each hour's meditation is generally the same"**: Ron Hansen, "Spiritual Exercises," *Santa Clara Magazine*, Summer 2006, magazine.scu.edu/summer 2006/spiritual.cfm.

74 **"the state of being under the influence of the false spirit"**: Thibodeaux, *God's Voice Within*, 12–13.

74 **"We need to distinguish clearly what might be a fruit of the kingdom"**: Pope Francis, "Evangelii Gaudium," November 24, 2013, 44, w2.vatican.va/content/fran cesco/en/apost_exhortations/documents/papa-francesco_esortazione-ap_20131124_ evangelii-gaudium.html.

74 **"Manuel, you've got to live your own exile"**: Ivereigh, *Great Reformer*, 207.

11 Colegio Máximo

86 **"The real action at the Máximo in those years"**: Ivereigh, *Great Reformer*, 76.

12 Teaching Borges

90 ***"But forgetfulness does not exist, dreams do not exist"***: Federico García Lorca, "City That Does Not Sleep," *Lorca & Jimenez (Selected Poems)* (Robert Bly, translator, Boston: Beacon Press 1973), 159.

92 **Borges's secretary, María Esther Vázquez, had taught piano**: Ivereigh, *Great Reformer*, 77.

92 **"may have been the key to establishing direct contact with the writer"**: Jorge Milia, "Bergoglio and Borges: Truths and Tales of a 'Friendship,'" *La Stampa*, June 12, 2013.

92 **"Thousands of literature professors from prestigious universities"**: Ibid.

92 **"Bergoglio went to pick [Borges] up from the old station"**: Ibid.

93 **"probably the most generous preface ever"**: Ibid.

93 **"Borges had a genius's knack for talking about any subject without ever bragging"**: Ambrogetti and Rubin, *Pope Francis: His Life in His Own Words*, 151.

93 **"Before I ever wrote a single line"**: Fernando Sorrentino, *Seven Conversations with Jorge Luis Borges* (Troy, NY: Whitston, 1982), 25.

13 Vatican II

98 **Argentina had twenty-five novices in 1961**: Vallely, *Pope Francis, Untying the Knots*, 45.

98 **In 1965, the Jesuit order claimed some thirty-six thousand members**: Thomas Gaunt, SJ, Ph.D., "The Changing Jesuit Geography," Center for Applied Research in the Apostolate, Georgetown University, February 1, 2011, nineteensixty-four .blogspot.com/2011/02/changing-jesuit-geography.html.

99 **"The option for the poor goes back even to the first centuries of Christianity"**: Transcript of 2010 judicial inquiry, "Bergoglio Declara ante el TOF," abuelas.org.ar /material/documentos/BERGOGLIO2.pdf.

14 Father Bergoglio

103 **"May my grandchildren, to whom I gave the best of my heart"**: Ivereigh, *Great Reformer*, 100.

104 **"I want to believe in God the Father, who loves me like a son"**: "Credo de Jorge Mario Bergoglio, Papa Francisco," September 18, 2013, revistaecclesia.com/credo -de-jorge-mario-bergoglio-papa-francisco/.

15 Novice Master

108 **the five "simple" vows**: James Martin, S.J., "Final Vows? What's That?" *America*, October 30, 2009, americamagazine.org/content/all-things/final-vows-whats.

109 **From the early 1960s to 1973**: Ivereigh, *Great Reformer*, 106.

110 **"worker-based, social-justice Peronist platform of the 1940s"**: Ibid., 104.

110 **Yorio, a native of Buenos Aires**: Ibid., 153.

16 Provincial

116 **"Decree Four incorporated the pursuit of social justice"**: Ivereigh, *Great Reformer*, 120–21.

116 **"appeared to have few safeguards"**: Ibid., 121.

117 **Yorio, who had moved to the Ituzaingó barrio in 1970**: Ibid., 154–55.

117 **"There were Latin American points of reference"**: Transcript of 2010 judicial inquiry, "Bergoglio Delcara ante el TOF."

118 **"They had a balanced, orthodox view"**: Ibid.

118 **"In view of the rumors . . . I told them to be very careful"**: Ambrogetti and Rubin, *Pope Francis: His Life in His Own Words*, 204.

118 **"I am sure that he gave the list with our names to the Marines"**: Olga Wornat, *Nuestra Santa Madre: Historia Pública y Privada de la Iglesia Católica Argentina* (Barcelona: Ediciones B, 2002).

118 **"I myself was once inclined to believe that we were the victims of a denunciation"**: Jonathan Watts, "Pope Francis Did Not Denounce Me to Argentinian Junta, Says Priest," *The Guardian*, March 21, 2013, theguardian.com/world/2013/mar/21 /pope-francis-argentinian-junta-priest.

119 **An estimated fifteen thousand people**: Morello, *The Catholic Church and Argentina's Dirty War*, 1.

119 **Yorio maintained that he had "no reason to think [Bergoglio] ever did anything to free us"**: Wornat, *Nuestra Santa Madre*.

119 **Bergoglio later recounted that they were released**: Ambrogetti and Rubin, *Pope Francis: His Life in His Own Words*, 205.

119 **"I did what I could for my age and, with the few contacts I had"**: Ibid., 200–201.

120 **And it is a fact that not one Jesuit was killed**: Ivereigh, *Great Reformer*, 137.

120 **"We all are Political animals, with a capital P"**: Bergoglio and Skorka, *On Heaven and Earth*, 136.

120 **"What did the Church do during those years?"**: Ibid., 195–97.

121 **"In my experience as superior in the Society, to be honest"**: Spadaro, "A Big Heart Open to God," *America*.

18 Córdoba

142 **lost by less than twenty-five hundred votes:** "2002 Gubernatorial Election Official Results: Congressional District 08," State Board of Elections, Maryland, elections .state.md.us/elections/2002/results/p_cd08.html.

145 **He had stated, during his juniorate:** Ivereigh, *Great Reformer,* 72.

146 **In an essay entitled "The Exile of All Flesh":** Daniel Burke, "The Pope's Dark Night of the Soul," CNN, September 2015, cnn.com/interactive/2015/09/specials /pope-dark-night-of-the-soul/.

147 *"If you do not listen to this in your pride":* Jeremiah 13:17, usccb.org/bible/jere miah/13.

147 **"It's the prayer of a man who gave everything":** Burke, "The Pope's Dark Night of the Soul."

147 **"Spiritual consolation is an experience of being so on fire with God's love":** "Introduction to Discernment of Spirits," *Ignatian Spirituality,* ignatianspirituality .com/making-good-decisions/discernment-of-spirits/introduction-to-discernment -of-spirits.

19 Sons of Abraham

153 **"As far as I know, this has to be the first time in two thousand years":** Ambrogetti and Rubin, *Pope Francis: His Life in His Own Words,* xi.

153 **Nearly a quarter of a million Jews live in Argentina:** Congreso Judío Latinomari- cano, congresojudio.org.ar/comunidades_detalle.php?id=1; Simon Romero, "Out- post on Pampas Where Jews Once Found Refuge Wilts as They Leave," *New York Times,* June 9, 2013, nytimes.com/2013/06/10/world/americas/traditions-fade-in -argentine-haven-for-jews.html?_r=1.

159 **Three days later:** Associated Press, July 22, 1994, aparchive.com/metadata /ARGENTINA-REACTION-TO-SYNAGOGUE-BOMBING/918a6bedab40263 a764ba296b2894293?query=Argentina+bomb&current=6&orderBy=OldestFirst&hi ts=17&referrer=search&search=%2fsearch%3fquery%3dArgentina%2bbomb%26st artd%3d7%252F18%252F1994%26endd%3d7%252F18%252F1995%26orderBy %3dOldestfirst%26from%3d1%26allFilters%3d07%252F18%252F1994 -07%252F18%252F1995%253ADate%26g2ItemId%3d&allFilters=07%2f18%2f1 994-07%2f18%2f1995%3aDate&productType=IncludedProducts&page =1&b=894293.

20 Toto, Pepe, and the Rabbi

164 **Pepe explained that he went to work in a shoe factory for a year:** Stefania Falasca, "Padre Pepe: il Papa mi ha accompagnato nella mia crisi," *Avvenire,* August 28, 2013, avvenire.it/Chiesa/Pagine/padre-pepe-il-Papa-mi-ha-accompagnato-nella-mia-crisi .aspx.

21 Cardinal

200 **Menem had implemented a series of free-market reforms:** "Profile: Carlos Menem," BBC News, updated April 28, 2003, news.bbc.co.uk/2/hi/americas/1376100 .stm.

200 **He also doubled government spending and had to borrow heavily to pay for it:**

Timothy Borden, "Menem, Carlos Saul: 1930: Political Leader," in *Contemporary Hispanic Biography* (Gale Group, 2002).

200 **The unemployment rate was at 14 percent, and nearly 40 percent of the population lived in poverty:** "Unemployment," IndexMundi, indexmundi.com/g/g .aspx?c=ar&v=74; "Poverty," IndexMundi, indexmundi.com/g/g.aspx?c=ar&v=69.

200 **That day, Bergoglio challenged Menem and other political leaders:** Ivereigh, *Great Reformer,* 250.

201 **De la Rúa was elected president in October 1999:** Clifford Krauss, "Vote for Me, Declares Argentine, I'm Boring," *New York Times,* September 26, 1999, nytimes .com/1999/09/26/world/vote-for-me-declares-argentine-i-m-boring.html.

201 **"We need to recognize, with humility":** Ivereigh, *Great Reformer,* 25.

201 **in 1933, the height of the Great Depression:** Irving Bernstein, "Americans in Depression and War," U.S. Department of Labor, dol.gov/general/aboutdol/history /chapter5.

201 **in more modern times:** "A Brief History of U.S. Unemployment," *Washington Post,* washingtonpost.com/wp-srv/special/business/us-unemployment-rate-history/.

203 **"it becomes increasingly apparent that our social and political apathy":** Jorge Mario Bergoglio, Homily of the Archbishop, Te Deum, May 25, 2003, arzbaires.org .ar/inicio/homiliasbergoglio.html.

204 **"Today, as always, Argentines must choose":** Jorge Mario Bergoglio, Homily of the Archbishop, Te Deum, May 25, 2004, arzbaires.org.ar/inicio/homiliasbergoglio .html.

205 **In an interesting twist, a 2015 biography of Verbitsky:** Gerard O'Connell, "Main Accuser of Pope Francis Worked for Argentina's Military Dictatorship," *America,* May 18, 2015, americamagazine.org/content/dispatches/main-accuser-pope-francis -worked-argentinas-military-dictatorship.

205 **When his biographers asked him, "How did it feel to hear your name repeated":** Ambrogetti and Rubin, *Pope Francis: His Life in His Own Words,* 165–66.

206 **prompting Bergoglio to cancel the celebration at the cathedral:** "The Church Suspended the Te Deum in the Capital," *La Nacion,* May 24, 2005, lanacion.com .ar/706830-suspendio-la-iglesia-el-tedeum-en-la-capital.

209 **In 2006, Governor Carlos Rovira of Misiones:** Carlos M. Regúnaga, Center for Strategic and International Studies, Hemisphere Highlights, vol. 5, issue 10, November 2006, csis.org/files/media/csis/pubs/hh06_10.pdf.

210 **"If already at the moment of the cross there were people who sowed discord":** Jorge Mario Bergoglio, Homily of the Archbishop, October 1, 2006, arzbaires.org.ar /inicio/homiliasbergoglio.html.

210 **"There is a God and God belongs to all":** "Kirchner: 'El diablo también les llega a los que usan sotana,'" *Clarín,* October 6, 2006, edant.clarin.com/diario/2006/10/06 /elpais/p-00310.htm.

22 The Fire

216 **"Today we are here to enter into the heart of that mother":** Ivereigh, *Great Reformer,* 276–77.

221 **Pope Francis wrote to one of the band members in jail:** "Pope Writes to Rock Singer Jailed for Causing Fire," *CathNews New Zealand,* July 16, 2013, cathnews .co.nz/2013/07/16/pope-writes-to-rock-singer-jailed-for-causing-fire/.

221 **the message that Pope Francis sent later that same year to the families of the**

victims: "Pope Francis Sends Message of Consolation to Victims' Families of Buenos Aires Fire," *Vatican Radio*, December 31, 2013.

23 Cartoneros

233 **"Chances are that you will never have heard of this encounter":** Joe Gunn, "Pope Gives Blessing to Global Movements Striving for Change," *Western Catholic Reporter*, January 12, 2015, wcr.ab.ca/Columns/Columns/entryid/6260.

234 **"In the main, these movements represent three increasingly excluded social sectors":** Judith Marshall, "Challenging the Globalisation of Indifference: Pope Francis Meets with Popular Movements," *Links International Journal of Socialist Renewal*, November 21, 2014, links.org.au/node/4172.

236 **"Good morning again, I am happy to be with you":** Pope Francis, "Address to the Participants in the World Meeting of Popular Movements," October 28, 2014, w2.vatican.va/content/francesco/en/speeches/2014/october/documents/papa -francesco_20141028_incontro-mondiale-movimenti-popolari.pdf.

24 The Interview

245 **"I encourage you to remain committed to helping one another":** Pope Francis, "Address to a Delegation of Athletes of Special Olympics Italy," June 19, 2015, w2.vatican.va/content/francesco/en/speeches/2015/june/documents/papa-francesco _2015_0619_special-olympics-italia.html.

249 **I read an article about a boy who had been sexually abused by a priest:** Karen Heller, "A Papal Visit Can't Heal These Wounds," *Washington Post*, September 17, 2015, washingtonpost.com/sf/local/2015/09/17/papal-visit-leaves-this-family-cold/.

251 **"During our first meeting in Rome, I sensed something very beautiful":** Pope Francis, "Address to the Second Meeting of World Popular Movements," July 9, 2015, w2.vatican.va/content/francesco/en/speeches/2015/july/documents/papa-francesco _20150709_bolivia-movimenti-popolari.html.

256 **"Faith opens a 'window' to the presence and working of the Spirit":** Pope Francis, "Closing Mass of the Eighth World Meeting of Families," September 27, 2015, w2.vatican.va/content/francesco/en/homilies/2015/documents/papa-francesco _20150927_usa-omelia-famiglie.html.

About the Author

MARK K. SHRIVER is president of Save the Children Action Network in Washington, D.C. Shriver also created the Choice Program and is a former Maryland state legislator. His *New York Times* and *Washington Post* bestselling memoir, *A Good Man: Rediscovering My Father, Sargent Shriver*, was published in June 2012 by Henry Holt and received a 2013 Christopher Award. Shriver lives with his wife, Jeanne, and their three children, Molly, Tommy, and Emma, in Maryland.

@Mark_Shriver

About the Type

The text of this book was set in Janson, a typeface designed about 1690 by Nicholas Kis (1650–1702), a Hungarian living in Amsterdam, and for many years mistakenly attributed to the Dutch printer Anton Janson. In 1919, the matrices became the property of the Stempel Foundry in Frankfurt. It is an old-style book face of excellent clarity and sharpness. Janson serifs are concave and splayed; the contrast between thick and thin strokes is marked.